BEYOND
PEACE

Also by Richard Nixon

Six Crises (1962)
RN: The Memoirs of Richard Nixon (1978)
The Real War (1980)
Leaders (1982)
Real Peace: A Strategy for the West (1983)
No More Vietnams (1985)
1999: Victory Without War (1988)
In the Arena: A Memoir of Victory, Defeat, and Renewal (1990)
Seize the Moment: America's Challenge in a One-Superpower World (1992)

Richard Nixon

BEYOND PEACE

Random House New York

All rights reserved under International and Pan-American Copyright Conventions.
Published in the United States by Random House, Inc., New York, and simultaneously
in Canada by Random House of Canada Limited, Toronto.

Library of Congress Cataloging-in-Publication Data
Nixon, Richard (Richard Milhous)
Beyond peace / Richard Nixon. — 1st ed.
p. cm.
ISBN 0-679-43323-6
ISBN 0-679-43366-X (lim. ed.)
1. United States—Foreign relations—1993– 2. World
politics—1985–1995. I. Title.
E885.N59 1994
327.73—dc20   94-10184

Manufactured in the United States of America on acid-free paper
24689753
First Edition
Book design by Bernard Klein

For Patricia Ryan Nixon
Ambassador of Goodwill

Contents

III
America Beyond Peace   171

Strong Government, but Limited Government
Equal Opportunity, Not Equal Outcomes
Hardheaded Idealism and Enlightened Realism
The Media: Freedom Without Constraint
The Myths of Government
Health Care "Reform": More Steroids for Big Government
Old-fashioned Learning for a New Era
Welfare: Sickfare for America's Cities
Crime and Race in America
The Corruptions of Popular Culture and Drugs
God and Family: Rediscovering the True Heart of America
Individual Mission, National Mission

I

Our Challenge
Beyond Peace

When I met with Mao Tse-tung for the last time in Beijing on February 27, 1976, I was shocked at how his physical condition had deteriorated since our first meeting in 1972. He was a shell of the man he had been. He was still sharp mentally, but a massive stroke had robbed him of his ability to put his thoughts into words. The charismatic communist leader who had moved a nation and changed the world with his revolutionary exhortations could no longer even ask for a glass of water.

As we sat together in his book-cluttered office in the Forbidden City, I was reminded of President Eisenhower's intense frustration after suffering a stroke in 1957. A few days after he had returned to the White House from the hospital, he described to me the ordeal that simple speech had become. He complained that when he wanted to say "ceiling," it would come out "floor." When he wanted to say "window," he would say "door." He smiled without much warmth and said that he was afraid that fighting for words sent up his blood pressure. I tried to relieve the tension by pointing out that his problem was that his brain worked faster than his mouth—the opposite of the problem most politicians have.

Fortunately, Eisenhower recovered completely. Mao never would. As we spoke in Beijing he was six months from death, and a succession crisis was already raging around him. But I was addressing a man who was still the revered leader of nearly a billion people, and who had played an indispensable role in bringing about the new relationship between our countries that had begun four years before.

During our conversation, I said that we must continue to cooperate in seeking peace, not only between our two countries but among all the nations of the world. It was painful to watch as he tried to respond. His face flushed as he grunted out half-words. His translator, an attractive young woman dressed in a drab, shapeless Mao suit—one of the worst punishments ever inflicted upon Chinese women by the old-guard communists—tried to put his grunts into English.

Mao knew enough English to realize that she had not understood him. He shook his head angrily, grabbed her notebook, and wrote out the words in Chinese. She read them aloud in English: "Is peace your only goal?"

I had not expected the question and paused briefly. "We should seek peace with justice," I answered.

My reply was adequate within the context of the Cold War. Today that is too limited a goal for the United States. Our goal then was to end the struggle between East and West in a way that would avoid a nuclear war and also ensure that freedom and justice would prevail over tyranny. Today, the communists have lost the Cold War. Marxism-Leninism has been utterly discredited as a political doctrine. The Berlin Wall, the ultimate Cold War symbol of political injustice, has been demolished, and pieces of it can be seen in midwestern town squares and the museums of presidential libraries. The threat of nuclear war between the United States and Russia no longer hangs over us. In a very real way, peace with justice has been achieved. Yet it is clear that the defeat of communism in the Soviet Union and Eastern Europe in the twentieth century was just the first step toward the triumph of freedom throughout the world in the twenty-first century. This will be assured only if the United States—in its policies at home and abroad—renews its commitment to its founding principles.

We live in a new world—a world we helped create. For

forty-five years, America and its allies fought one of the longest struggles in human history. The Cold War touched every region of the world and made most of it hostage to a vast conflict of political ideas and economic systems. For the United States, Korea and Vietnam were battles in that war. Our major goal for nearly five decades—first the containment and then the defeat of Soviet communist aggression—has now been achieved.

In the past five years, we have witnessed four of the greatest events of the twentieth century: the liberation of one hundred million people in Eastern Europe from Soviet-imposed communism in 1989; the defeat of Iraqi aggression in the Persian Gulf War in the spring of 1991; the collapse of communism in the Soviet Union in December 1991; and the failure of socialism and a mass movement toward capitalism in nations as different as Sweden, India, France, and even communist China.

We have achieved a goal we would not have dreamed possible five years ago: free-market capitalism, not socialism or communism, is the wave of the future.

These spectacular developments represent some of the greatest triumphs for freedom in history. Yet at a time when we should be celebrating victory, many observers are wallowing in pessimism, as if we had suffered defeat. Instead of pressing toward the mountaintop and beholding a new vision of peace and freedom for the future, they are wandering in a valley of self-doubt about the past.

One sign of this defeatism is that the leaders in Western Europe, Canada, and Japan who played major roles in winning the Cold War have either been rejected by the voters or have some of the lowest approval ratings in history. All of the Group of Seven industrial countries—the nations wealthiest in goods—are experiencing massive public discontent with their governments, their social and economic problems, and their nations' roles in the world. At the Tokyo summit meeting of the industrialized democracies in July 1993, President Clinton's approval rating was at a record low compared with those of his predecessors in their first year in office, and yet his rating was the highest among the G-7 leaders. Ironically, the only leader at the summit with a higher approval rating was President Boris Yeltsin of Russia, whose political and economic problems dwarf the West's.

The United States and the other members of the G-7 have the richest economies on earth. Economic power, however, is not the same as strength of national character. Our country may be rich in goods, but we are poor in spirit. As we sink further into a false, almost hypnotic contentment because we are at peace abroad, and a myopic preoccupation with our domestic problems, the persuasive power of our principles and our ability to project a worthy example for the rest of the world inevitably weaken. We are justifiably concerned about our budget deficit. But our crisis of values at home, coupled with our lack of a coherent mission abroad, has created an even more deadly spiritual deficit. We seem to be experiencing what Arnold Toynbee, in his *Study of History* sixty years ago, called "the dark night of the soul."

This phenomenon results from the way the Cold War ended, and also from the kind of struggle it was. In generations to come Americans will not celebrate V-USSR Day to mark the anniversary of the day the red flag over the Kremlin came down, or even V-B Day to celebrate the day the Berlin Wall fell. No surrender documents were initialed in solemn ceremony. No monuments were erected to the Cold War's fallen heroes, and no reunions will be convened for its veterans. It was a war of values, words, nerves, and sometimes surrogates, but it never became a war of bullets, at least insofar as direct conflict between the United States and the Soviet Union was concerned. The world was brought to the brink of nuclear war more than once, but the fatal shots were never fired. Then, suddenly, the Cold War was pronounced over.

In World War II, we won victory by forcing our adversaries to their knees in unconditional surrender. This dramatic triumph produced a sense of exhilaration. The end of the Cold War produced only a sense of exhaustion and anticlimax. In its final stages, the communist regimes of the Soviet Union and Eastern Europe, having been pushed to the brink by the leadership of nine successive American Presidents and a mighty Western alliance, finally imploded. Since our victory gave the impression of being a victory by default, the West was deprived of the sense of satisfaction it deserved over a job well done.

There are those who now argue that communism was never a real threat and that our efforts in the Cold War were unnecessary, even wasteful, since the Soviet Union would have collapsed anyway as a result of its internal contradictions and its failure to fulfill the boast that it would overtake capitalism. By 1986, when I first met with Mikhail Gorbachev, twenty-seven years after my "kitchen debate" with Khrushchev, the question had become not when the Soviet Union would overtake us but whether it would survive at all without drastic economic reforms. Had we done nothing, the argument goes, the results of the Cold War would have been exactly the same.

It is true that communism would eventually have collapsed, because it was and remains a false faith. Talking about the Russian people, John Foster Dulles presciently observed forty years ago, "People who understand the intricacies of the atom will eventually see the fatal flaws in communism." As history demonstrates, evil ideas inevitably fail because they are fundamentally at odds with human nature, but until they fail, they can do enormous damage to humanity. Evil regimes have prevailed for long periods of time and have won significant victories. Ultimately, however, unless they expand, they will die. In the Cold War, the United States and the West blocked the expansion of the idea of communism. Our active resistance to communist aggression, and the weapons of economic power we brought to bear on the communist regimes, ensured that communism would be defeated years, perhaps decades, before it would have collapsed on its own.

Our efforts during the Cold War prevented communism from spreading into Western Europe and also blunted its expansion in what was then called the Third World, particularly in Afghanistan, the only Third World nation where the Red Army committed its forces. The much-maligned military buildup under President Reagan placed enormous strains on the Soviet system to compete, which it ultimately could not do. That program, as well as the efforts of all the Cold War Presidents from Truman to Bush, prevented Soviet communism from making further gains and thus hastened its collapse. In doing so we saved millions from misery and tyranny.

We and our allies can be proud of our role in the Cold War. But the defeat of communism was a double-edged sword. Surveying the carnage in the aftermath of the Battle of Waterloo in 1815, where fifty thousand men fell in one day, Wellington said that there was "only one thing worse than winning a battle, and that was losing it." Historically there is always a period of exhaustion after a military victory. Victory in the Cold War was not just military. It was a complex ideological, political, and economic triumph. Our exhaustion is therefore felt in all of these dimensions simultaneously.

Throughout the Cold War, we looked forward to a time when we might live in a peaceful world, with harmonious international relations, prosperous economies reaping the benefits of unlimited global trade, the expansion of freedom and human rights, and the opportunity to enjoy life. These promises of peace crystallized into an idealized vision of a post–Cold War future. The fact that it has not been realized has produced a pervasive, enervating sense of anticlimax. The reality of peace is that it is only the foundation upon which a more prosperous and just world can be built. This effort will require just as much determination, vision, and patience as the defeat of communism required.

Yet a potentially devastating fallout of our post–Cold War letdown is that the American people have grown tired of world leadership. They were reluctant to have it thrust upon them in the first place. At a dinner I gave for him shortly before I went to China in 1972, André Malraux observed that the United States is the first nation in history to become a world power without trying to become one. We are essentially isolationist and become involved in foreign conflicts not simply when our interests are at stake but when we also believe we are engaged in a great idealistic cause.

Following World War II, the United States abandoned its traditional peacetime isolationism to wage the Cold War against communism around the world. We did so because we believed we were engaged in an ideological conflict with profound moral consequences. Many now believe that it is time for others to carry the burden of leadership abroad and that we should turn our attention and resources to our problems at home. This was candidate Clinton's major theme and the primary reason President Bush, a foreign policy expert, lost the election of 1992.

Most Americans thought that our victory in the Cold War, with its peace dividend, would help us solve our domestic problems. The opposite has occurred. The end of the Cold War has exacerbated our problems at home. Foreign challenges unite us. Domestic challenges divide us. What we must realize is that domestic and foreign policies are like Siamese twins—one cannot survive without the other. The American people will not support a strong foreign policy unless we have a strong economy at home. Conversely, a weak economy, as we learned in the thirties, almost inevitably leads to a weak foreign policy—with potentially devastating consequences. It is no accident that fascists rose to power in a Europe stricken by a depression aggravated by our shortsighted trade policies. Periods of prolonged peace are generally periods of stagnation. No one would say that war is good for a country, but it is undeniable that the United States has been at its best when confronted with aggression or some other significant international challenge (our space effort after the shock of Sputnik is a case in point). Most of our greatest

Presidents were war Presidents. Our greatest bursts of increased productivity and scientific advancement have occurred during war. To meet the challenges we face in the post–Cold War era, we must marshal the same resources of energy, optimism, and common purpose that thrive during war and put them to work at home and abroad during an era when our enemy will be neither communism nor Nazism but our own self-defeating pessimism.

Charles de Gaulle once said, "France was never her true self unless she was engaged in a great enterprise." This is true of the United States as well. Great causes push us to heights, as a nation and as individuals, that would not otherwise be achieved. Without a great cause to galvanize America, the very unity of our nation will be at risk as we struggle to meet the challenges of the coming century.

If America is to remain a great nation, what we need today is a mission beyond peace.

In the first years of my Presidency, the Cold War was a dark backdrop to the rage of the Vietnam War. Conflict abroad and at home was the rule; concord was the exception. In the early pre-dawn hours of May 9, 1970, at the height of the massive demonstrations against our involvement in Vietnam, I went to the Lincoln Memorial and visited with a group of student protesters who had gathered there. Most of them were privileged young people who had not had to serve in Vietnam. They told me they thought the war was wrong. I stressed that tens of thousands of young men of their generation were fighting in Vietnam so that they and their children would never have to fight in a war again. In the shadow of a monument to a President who had fought the bloodiest war in American history for the abstract, almost spiritual concept of national union, I tried to lift their sights above their confusion and bitterness over a war they thought was wrong but that was being fought for the sake of safeguarding their country's security and most fundamental principles.

After returning to the White House I dictated my recollections of the conversation:

> What are those elements of spirit that really matter? I knew that young people today were searching, as I was searching forty years ago, for an answer. I just wanted to be sure that all of them realized that ending the war, and cleaning up the streets and the air and the water, was not going to solve spiritual hunger—which all of us have and which, of course, has been the great mystery of life from the beginning of time.

The yearning for a better world felt by many of the more idealistic demonstrators found its most immediate expression in denunciations of the United States and its policies at home and abroad. They wanted equality, justice, and truth. Perhaps because they had not seen as much of the world as I had, they did not understand how scarce these qualities were in the rest of the world and how plentiful in their own country. All they knew was that they felt angry, hopeless, and spiritually empty. They believed that ending the war in Vietnam would end the pervasive climate of discord at home. When U.S. military involvement in Vietnam did end three years later, so did the demonstrations. But peace was not enough to fill the spiritual vacuum. Nor is peace enough at the end of the Cold War. Peace is a great goal, but it is not a panacea.

Neither is material wealth. Proponents of Marxism-Leninism believed that if the state provided all the necessities of life, people's greatest aspirations would be fulfilled—and yet communism produced the world's most drab, dispirited societies. The color of communism was not red but gray. Proponents of the Great Society programs of the 1960s thought the beneficent hand of government could salve the spirits of the poor by helping satisfy their material needs—and yet America's inner cities today are plagued with crime, drug addiction, and hopelessness. Those who are better off work their whole lives to assemble vast wealth, only to find that they are no happier, no more spiritually enriched, than before. Surveys show that many prosperous, aging members of the baby-boom generation are driving their Volvos and BMWs back to church, searching for answers in the same doctrines they once ridiculed their parents for honoring. These examples and countless others show that individual fulfillment cannot be found in sheer materialism, whether communist, socialist, or capitalist. Just as nations need causes greater than themselves, so do individuals.

In his book *The Morality of Law,* Lon Fuller drew an eloquent distinction between the morality of duty and the morality of aspiration, a distinction that applies to nations as well as to individuals. In times of war a premium is placed on the morality of duty, the absolute necessity of doing what is required, of doing right in the limited sense of not doing what is wrong. The morality of duty, while indispensable, is not an adequate standard for a great people in the era beyond peace. The morality of aspiration calls for us to strive to accomplish not just the things we are required to do but all that we are capable of doing. It is this higher challenge we must embrace now that we have fulfilled our duty as a free people in helping to bring about the defeat of communism. Every individual, every community, every nation, must dedicate itself to the fullest realization of its potential. We must make peace more than simply the absence of war. We must make it the means to a greater end.

At the beginning of the Cold War, when real peace seemed more distant than ever, President Truman delivered before a joint session of Congress a powerful appeal for military and economic aid for Greece and Turkey to meet the communist threat to those countries. Two freshmen congressmen, John Kennedy and I, voted in favor of the aid. The vote was difficult politically for him because the liberal Democrats in his Massachusetts district opposed all military aid. It was difficult politically for me because the conservative Republicans in my California district opposed all foreign aid. We voted for it because we were motivated by a great cause that transcended partisan politics: the defeat of communism. In voting as we did, we helped to launch the bipartisan effort that deterred Soviet aggression in Western Europe for four decades and united the nation in a great cause.

As a nation we responded magnificently to the threat of war then. Can we not now respond to the promise of peace? War brings out the best and the worst in men. Peace should bring out only the best.

Shortly after World War I, Winston Churchill eloquently described the same dilemma we seem to face today:

> Why should war be the only purpose capable of uniting us in comradeship? Why should war be the only cause large enough to call forth really great and fine sacrifice? Look at the wonderful, superb things people will do to carry on a war and win a victory. Look at what they will give up. Look at what toil they achieve— what risks, what suffering, what marvelous ingenuity, what heroic and splendid qualities they display. All for war. Nothing is too good for war. Why cannot we have some of it for peace? Why is war to have all the splendors, all the nobleness, all the courage and loyalty? Why should peace have nothing but the squabbles and selfishness and the pettiness of daily life? All the arts and science that we use at war are standing by us now ready to help us in peace. Only one thing do we require—a common principle of action, a plain objective that everyone can understand and work for.

In the years since World War II, Americans rose successfully to the moral challenge laid down by Churchill. While the Cold War fueled an intense military competition and erupted into hot wars in Korea and Vietnam, as well as dozens of smaller engagements from the Bay of Pigs to Afghanistan, it never brought the superpowers into battle against one another. In at least two confrontations that might have led to global nuclear war—the Cuban missile crisis during the Kennedy administration and the Yom Kippur War during my administration—the

Soviets eventually blinked. For forty-five years, the West's toil, ingenuity, courage, and heroism were brought to bear, as Churchill would have had it, on keeping the peace rather than winning a war. Someday historians will look back on the defeat of communism in the Cold War and recognize it for what it was: one of the most magnificent achievements of free people in the history of civilization.

We no longer face the threat of aggression by a powerful foe. The fear of nuclear annihilation has been drastically reduced. No nation currently has the power to threaten us, our allies, or our friends without risking a devastating response by our forces. The way should be clear for the complete triumph of Western ideals of political and economic freedom. Yet all over the world, and especially in the post-Soviet states and the nations of Eastern Europe, these ideals are on trial. It is by no means certain that they will prevail. "One of the great lessons of history," British historian Paul Johnson has written, "is that no civilization can be taken for granted. Its permanency can never be assured. There is always a dark age waiting for you around the corner if you play your cards badly and you make sufficient mistakes." Whether the ideals of freedom survive and thrive in soil that has been laid waste by generations of misuse depends on how well the United States, the shining example of the power of peace and freedom, shows the way. How well we show the way, in turn, depends on how well we have learned four great lessons of the Cold War. These lessons require us to recognize the sheer power of our own example. They require that we act to renew the same qualities that made us strong. They require that we not turn away from the very principles that former communist nations now eagerly embrace as their own.

We will play our cards well if we remember these four principles:

• *Only free markets can fully unleash the creative energies of people to drive the engine of progress.* The Cold War taught us that communism does not work, socialism does not work, and state-dominated economies do not work. Communism failed its people both politically and economically, but it was its economic failure that ultimately destroyed it. People will put up with shortages of political freedom far longer than with shortages of food, shelter, and clothing.

When we met in 1959, Khrushchev predicted that my children would live under communism. I replied, "Mr. Khrushchev, your grandchildren will live in freedom." At that time, I was sure he was wrong. I was not sure I was right. When I visited an open-air market that year in Moscow, the people were ebullient, upbeat, and optimistic about the future under Khrushchev's reforms. They were not free politically, but Khrushchev was at least better than Stalin, and most of them believed Khrushchev's assertion that they would overtake the United States economically.

In 1991, the last year of Gorbachev's Presidency, Soviet communism, *glasnost,* and *perestroika,* I visited a state-run store near the Kremlin. The people, as they waited in line for butter and a few pieces of gristly beef, told me that the economy had never been worse. For the first time in years, it was hard to get even basic foodstuffs such as bread and potatoes. Gorbachev had enacted significant political reforms, but the people were sullen and deeply pessimistic about the future. They were poor both in goods and in spirit. Just after dawn one morning, during a walk through Red Square, I came across a line in which thousands of people were waiting outside the GUM department store. They told me they had heard a rumor that food would go on sale later in the morning. As I looked into their angry, tired faces, I saw a rage at the prevailing system that had been absent in 1959, when Moscow was less free but more prosperous. I realized then that the people had lost faith in Gorbachev and that his attempts to reform communism were probably doomed. It was further proof that no politician, communist, noncommunist, or indifferent, can afford to forget that the greatest expectation people have of their leaders is that they create the conditions for economic growth and prosperity.

In our "kitchen debate," Khrushchev asserted that although the Soviet Union was trailing the United States in economic production at that time, it was beginning to overtake us, and in five years would be waving goodbye to us and urging us to catch up by emulating its system. During a famous United Nations session Khrushchev once shocked the world by rudely banging his shoe on his desk to protest the remarks of a speaker. Today, Khrushchev's famous shoe is on the other foot. Soviet communism is history. Even the remaining communist superpower, China, while still communist politically, is increasingly capitalist economically. A corollary to this development is that socialism is being rejected in the noncommunist world. The rejection of communism and socialism, however, does not mean the victory of capitalism.

Because of the inevitable pain of aborting a command economy and delivering a free-market economy, urgent voices are being raised in Moscow and elsewhere to slow the pace of reform. More startling, many Americans seem willing to promote and accept a larger role for government in American life, even as the dead hand of absolute government is being cast off in the former Soviet Union and Eastern Europe. We have too much government today, and the government we have does not do its job well enough. It chokes initiative, depletes investment pools, and hobbles business—as it did under communism to a more extreme degree. It is not that capitalism is perfect. One of Winston Churchill's most quoted statements is that "democracy is the worst form of government, except for all the others." It is also true that free-market capitalism is the worst kind of economic policy, except for all the others. The most important lesson of the Cold War is that too much government is the enemy of progress and prosperity.

The very fact that an economy is free makes it unpredictable and potentially unstable. But it is worth the price. In the long term, a free-market economy always outproduces a government-command economy. We must always remember that America is a great nation today not because of what government did for people but because of what people did for themselves and for one another. Government should reflect and draw upon their noblest aspirations, inspiring and sometimes goading them to the heights they are destined to achieve. Instead, since the 1960s government has become a one-trillion-dollar-a-year, grossly overweight, bullying nanny, punishing us when we say or think bad things and rewarding us with incentives and programs when we are good or are deemed especially worthy.

• *The United States must play a leading role on the world stage.* On dozens of occasions during the Cold War, the United States proved that it was the only nation in the free world that would consistently extend its power far beyond its borders to blunt Soviet aggression. It provided the indispensable glue that held the European alliance together, and it took up similar challenges of leadership in Asia. Time and again it has acted in its own interests and those of the West in the Mideast and the Persian Gulf. Millions of young Americans have fought selflessly and courageously to defend foreign soil. Had we not been willing to invest billions of dollars in these engagements and risk the lives of our servicemen and -women, the Cold War might be over—but the Soviet Union might well have won. No nation or empire in history has defended its interests and its allies more dependably, and more responsibly. That mistakes and poor judgments were occasionally made serves only to spotlight the overall consistency and profound effectiveness of U.S. policy.

By being strong, resolute, benevolent, and creative for forty-five years, the United States wrote the book on how to be a superpower. It is typical, in view of our capacity for being almost relentlessly critical of ourselves, that some so-called experts now want to burn that book. Because they subscribe either to the old isolationism of the right or to the new isolationism of

the left, they say that the era of vigorous American internationalism is over and that it is time for us to concentrate on our
domestic problems. They are correct in part. It is time to solve
our domestic problems—but not just for our own sake. We must
solve them so that the United States can address its international
responsibilities from a more commanding base. As the richest
and most powerful nation on earth, we must use our strength to
consolidate and extend those principles and qualities that make
us great wherever and whenever our interests permit us to do so.
Only then can we be true to ourselves. Only then can we find
strength in a renewed sense of purpose.

• *The United States cannot be strong in the world unless it
is strong at home.* I vividly remember Harry Truman's State of
the Union address in 1949. Fresh from his dramatic upset victory over Tom Dewey, he strode cockily down the aisle of the
House chamber, relishing his new reputation as the victorious
underdog. I recall little about the content of the speech except
the beginning. He said, "The State of the Union is good." It
brought down the house. Today, no President could honestly
begin a State of the Union address in the same way.

Two hundred years ago the United States was militarily
weak and economically poor, but to millions of people in other
nations America was the hope of the world because of the timeless values we stood for. Today America must be a worthy example for others to follow, but our example is tarnished with
every deepening domestic problem. Poor-quality secondary education, rampant crime and violence, growing racial divisions,
pervasive poverty, the drug epidemic, the degenerative culture of
moronic entertainment, a decline in the notions of civic duty and
responsibility, and the spread of a spiritual emptiness have all
disconnected and alienated Americans from their country, their
religions, and one another.

Many Americans have come to assume they are entitled to
lives of ease, even luxury, and that the defeat of the Soviet Union

means we will sit indefinitely at the pinnacle of the world. Those who were once called disciplined are now said to have closed minds. What was once called self-restrained is now called neurotic. What was once called modesty is now called prudishness. What was once called irresponsibility is now called "letting it all hang out." What used to be called self-indulgence is now called self-fulfillment. Traditional restraints on individual behavior are being removed or eased; and yet it remains the predominant view that the problems of crime, drugs, and pervasive poverty are the fault of "society." Rather than blaming ourselves, we blame society first. Unless we accomplish the renewal of America, the defeat of communism will be followed not by the victory of freedom but by a slow, steady decline into chaos in the world and an irrelevant role for our country.

America was created to protect the rights of the individual. Today, America accomplishes that mission, but we have forgotten that a well-ordered society also requires the individual to act in the interests of the whole, and that every right carries a corresponding responsibility. In a land of plenty, we have learned to take. To renew America in the era beyond peace, we must once again learn how to give. Above all we must prevent the debacle that the brilliant economist Joseph Schumpeter predicted sixty years ago in reflecting on the perils of prosperity. "Capitalism is being killed by its achievements," he wrote. "Its very success undermines the social institutions which protect it."

• *America is great because it acknowledges a power greater than itself.* It must never be forgotten that the people of the Soviet Union and Eastern Europe rejected communism not just because of its economic and political failures but because it tried to substitute materialism for enduring spiritual values. Communism preyed upon the bodies of its subjects through physical deprivations and attacked their souls as well. It could not produce materially, and it could not satisfy spiritually. Since the hammer and sickle over the Kremlin came down, the Russian people have flooded into the marketplace and the voting booth, and also into the churches.

On my first trip abroad as Vice President in 1953, I was profoundly impressed by Rajagopalachari, a close friend of Gandhi's, who was then the Chief Minister of Madras. I can see him now sitting on a straw mat, wearing just a dhoti and sandals. While many leaders in newly independent nations in the developing world thought that because of its successes in the Soviet Union and China, communism might be the wave of the future, he strongly disagreed. "Communism will never succeed in the long run," he said, "because it is based on a fundamental error. Self-interest is the motivating force for most human action. But by denying man the possibility of belief in God, the communists forfeit the possibility of any altruistic self-interest." He proved to be right.

The Soviet Union began by banishing God. The United States began as a community of people who wanted to worship God as they chose. Many factors contributed to the outcome of the Cold War. One crucial but underrated factor was that a system that attempted to blunt, deny, and even punish the spiritual aspirations of its people could not survive because it was fundamentally at odds with human nature. Man does not live by bread alone. Those in the United States whose desire to create a strictly secular society is as strong as Lenin's was should study this Cold War lesson closely. Communism was defeated by an alliance spearheaded by "one nation under God."

Poll after poll shows that most Americans believe in God and that church attendance is up. When Pope John Paul II visited the United States in 1993, hundreds of thousands of young American pilgrims journeyed to Denver to hear him. Many secularist intellectuals seem to find these developments unsettling, as though they proved that America is taking a step backward rather than forward. They are wrong. Our hunger for something to believe in is a profoundly positive development that members of the leadership class should celebrate, not fear.

It is important to observe the separation of church and state mandated by the Constitution. But in framing this provision, its authors could not have imagined a society in which religion did not play a dominant role. We should not use the requirement that religion be kept out of politics as an excuse to try to drive it out of our lives. With the end of the Cold War, we must ask ourselves what we stand for in addition to national strength and prosperity. Democracy and capitalism are just techniques unless they are employed by those who seek a higher purpose for themselves and their society. The communists denied there was a God, but they at least offered their people something to believe in—and for generations, millions did. We know that communism was a false faith, but the answer to a false faith is not no faith at all. We were against the false faith of communism during the Cold War. What faith shall we now champion in its place?

For forty-five years our mission was to be the strongest and the best so that we could defeat an enemy without war. Today, our enemy is within us. A century and a half ago, Alexis de Tocqueville warned that the universal obsession with materialism, the lack of enduring social bonds, and the shallowness of religious and philosophical thought in America had given rise to a "new despotism"—of mediocrity, of selfishness, of directionlessness. Such a new despotism threatens America today unless it rediscovers a new sense of common purpose—a mission it cannot accomplish unless its leaders overcome their own bickering, fractionalism, and pandering. Its leadership crisis is by no means limited to the incumbent administration, nor to government in general. A wide variety of political, cultural, and religious leaders proffer remedies for our spiritual crisis and lack of direction that are even worse than the disease.

The religious right gained enormous media attention during the 1988 and 1992 presidential campaigns. Their vehement stand against abortion, their intolerance of any family arrangement they consider nontraditional, and their demands for religious purity attracted fanatical support. While the religious right deserves credit for addressing the decline of values, too often their extreme tactics and exclusionary agenda put off those who might otherwise be open to their crusade for enhancing the spiritual life of our country. Meanwhile, as former Ambassador Henry Grunwald has observed, the religious left, as represented by many mainline churches, has increasingly turned away from saving souls to saving society. Those who join the religious right may be dispatched to lie down in the entrance of an abortion clinic, while those on the religious left can help you arrange a demonstration against U.S. policy in Latin America. Neither has much to offer the individual who is searching for answers to more fundamental, deeply spiritual questions.

The debate over economic policy is equally sterile. Those on the economic right argue that if free-market capitalism was allowed to function unimpeded by government, society's problems would evaporate, as gains from no-holds-barred free enterprise corrected them through sheer abundance. Such thinking ignores the human needs that only government can meet. People require protection in standards of health and safety, in the assurance of clean air and water, safe roads and skies. Capitalism without compassion is not enough. Rampant private enterprise, totally unrestrained by enlightened but limited government, would have a heart full of capital and an empty soul.

At the other extreme is the economic left, which believes, as did the architects of the Great Society, that government, rather than individuals acting through private business and other non-governmental institutions, is the driving force for progress. They envision not just a government safety net for those truly in need but a suffocating security blanket that would create a psychology of dependency throughout society. Such a psychology is dangerously close to taking hold already, as young and old, rich and poor alike clamor for "entitlements." Turning to new government programs to address our domestic problems, especially those that have been exacerbated by the failed programs of the past, is like using gasoline to put out a fire. Government cannot create jobs for everyone, enforce equality, or legislate to remedy society's spiritual deficit. Many of those who ask more of government than history shows it can deliver are those who are most eager, even desperate, to create some new America to match their own dispositions and ideologies.

Those on the right and left pursue their extreme convictions too uncompromisingly. But the most disappointing group of political leaders are the mushy moderates. They compromise and temporize, bend and bow, bob and weave, and hem and haw until they stand for nothing. In an attempt to please all sides of the debate, they end up pleasing no one. They are like the onion in Ibsen's *Peer Gynt:* You peel away layer after layer until you reach the center and find that it is hollow. They extol the virtues of prudence in policy and view. But prudence is more than caution. Prudence means making the right decision, which can be either to take strong action or to refrain from action. Prudence means anticipating consequences. The mushy moderates hide behind a veneer of prudence to justify doing nothing instead of prudently doing the right thing.

The renewal of America at home is necessary for the renewal of our example abroad. When the people of the world look to America for leadership, we want them to see not just the strongest and richest country on earth but also a uniquely good country. The American people are industrious, generous, and devout; they have great character and spirit. They rise to any challenge they are given. We still have the power to move others. Do we have the power to move ourselves? Ultimately, a country that has lost faith in its ideals cannot expect its ideals to appeal to others.

In a televised speech to the Soviet people in Moscow in 1959—the first time a major American official had ever addressed the Soviet people on television—I stated that our goal should be an "open world, a world of open cities, open minds and open hearts." In contrast to the beginning of the twentieth century, the beginning of the twenty-first century offers the first realistic chance for developing policies that could lead to a peaceful world, a prosperous world, a free world, and an open world.

The communications revolution, having helped win the Cold War by breaking down the ideological wall between East and West, has made dictatorships of all kinds obsolete, since to keep power they require total control over information, and that is now impossible. No dictator can survive in tranquillity for long with CNN being beamed into his country. There is an ever-growing flow of ideas among the world's cultures. This does not mean that we are destined to be a dull, homogeneous world. It does mean that future generations will have an opportunity to travel to all parts of the world, or at least see them on television. An open world will lessen the chance of war, increase the chance to move beyond peace, and ultimately enrich us all.

Building a more open world beyond peace means moving beyond transient pleasures, beyond superficial happiness, beyond the collection of emblems of earthly status, beyond the pursuit of power for its own sake, and beyond the contentment found in the attainment of peace. It means moving to a new plane of national mission. It is a call to a new glory—not the glory of war but the glory of peace. It is a call to take up not the arms of war but the tools of peace.

What, then, is the promise of peace? It means an even better life for all Americans—more and better jobs, improved education, less crime and drug abuse, a cleaner environment, and a government that better responds to people. More important, the promise of peace means a better spiritual life, in which hope is heard not just in empty echoes of rhetoric but in the voices and actions of every citizen, and faith guides the life of the nation.

The United States must lead. We must lead to open the eyes of those still blinded by despotism, to embolden those who remain oppressed, and to bring out from the dungeons of tyranny those who still live in darkness. The question remains whether the United States will meet its responsibilities of leadership beyond peace as it did to defeat the communists in the Cold War. History thrusts certain powers at certain times onto center stage. In this era, the spotlight shines on the United States. How long it stays on us—and how brightly it shines—will be determined by us alone.

We cannot lead solely by example or solely by power but must combine the best elements of both. Today we must find the moral equivalent of war to unify and inspire us. We do not seek a war at home or abroad, but we do need a mission that will evoke the same selfless response in individuals. When the people of the world look to us, they should see not just our money and our arsenal but also our vast capacity as a force for good.

Peace demands more, not less, from a people. Peace lacks the clarity of purpose and the cadence of war. War is scripted; peace is improvisation. As writer Sophie Kerr observed, "If peace . . . only had the music and pageantry of war, there'd be no more wars." Our conduct at home and abroad will determine how well we improvise beyond peace.

When Mao asked me if peace was America's only goal, he too had been searching for something beyond peace. His answers were the Great Leap Forward and the Cultural Revolution, ruthless attempts to create political and social utopia in China that resulted in misery, devastation, and death for millions. Progress cannot be commanded; renewal cannot be dictated. The inspiration for a true leap forward for America must come from within—from within the people making up the nation, and from within the soul of the nation itself. In moving beyond peace, we must recognize that while human nature prevents us from ever attaining perfection, the infinite potential of human beings compels us to embark on a search for the best practicable good. We stand at a great watershed in history, looking back on a century of war and dictatorship and looking forward to a century we can make one of peace and freedom. The future beyond peace is in our hands.

II

A New World
Beyond Peace

America Must Lead

Leaders of small countries at times have a clearer understanding of how the world works than do leaders of major countries, who are burdened with the day-to-day responsibilities of world leadership. During a conversation I had in 1967 with one such leader, Singapore's Lee Kwan Yew, he likened the world to a forest. "There are great trees, there are saplings, and there are creepers," he said. "The great trees are Russia, China, Western Europe, the United States, and Japan. Of the other nations, some are saplings that have the potential of becoming great trees, but the great majority are creepers, which, because of lack of resources or lack of leadership, will never be great trees."

Since he made that statement twenty-seven years ago at the height of the Cold War, a political forest fire has swept over the world. Although Russia, China, Japan, Western Europe, and the United States are still the only giant trees in the forest, the fire has dramatically changed them and the world around them. Communism has collapsed in the Soviet Union. One hundred million people in Eastern Europe have been liberated from communist domination. China is no longer an enemy of the United States and is using capitalist tools to achieve communist goals. Japan has become an economic superpower. Western Europe, no longer united by the threat from the East, is searching for a new rationale for NATO, a new relationship with the newly liberated nations of Eastern Europe and the former Soviet Union, and a new momentum toward economic unity. After bearing the burden of free-world leadership for forty-eight years, the American people, as indicated by the 1992 presidential election, want to devote their attention and their resources to their problems at home rather than those abroad.

Profound disagreement exists about the role the United States should play in the era beyond peace. A number of arguments against a continued American leadership role in the world have wide appeal:

• Because of the downfall of the Soviet Union, there is no need for American global leadership.

• Since the United States carried the major burden of the Cold War, other nations should lead now.

• Even assuming that we are the only ones who can lead, we should give priority to our pressing domestic problems.

• The United States, with huge budget deficits and trade imbalances, can no longer afford to lead.

• Because of our massive problems at home, the United States is not worthy to lead.

All of these statements are wrong.

Only the United States has the combination of military, economic, and political power a nation must have to take the lead in defending and extending freedom and in deterring and resisting aggression. Germany and Japan may have the economic clout but they lack the military muscle. China and Russia have the potential military might, but they lack the economic power. None has sufficient standing with all the world's great powers, none has the record of half a century of leadership. As the only great power without a history of imperialistic claims on neighboring countries, we also have something all these countries lack: the credibility to act as an honest broker.

The popular idea that the United Nations can play a larger role in resolving international conflicts is illusory. During the last forty-eight years, the U.N. has debated, passed resolutions on, and contemplated intervention in scores of conflicts in every part of the world. But it has acted militarily on only two occasions: when the Soviet Union boycotted the Security Council vote during the Korean War, and when President Bush enlisted the U.N. to support our efforts to defeat Iraqi aggression during the Persian Gulf War. As former U.S. Ambassador to the U.N. Jeane Kirkpatrick has observed, "Multilateral decision making is complicated and inconclusive. U.N. operations—in Bosnia or in Somalia or wherever—are characteristically ineffective."

Those who have led their peoples through the ultimate crisis of war understand better than anyone else that no leader can permit his country's interests to be held hostage to the whims of an international body. Winston Churchill was one such leader. I vividly remember my last meeting with him in 1958. I had gone to London to represent the United States at the dedication of the chapel at St. Paul's Cathedral honoring the American dead in World War II. I called on him at his home, where he was recovering from a stroke.

As I saw him slouching down in a big chair before a wood-burning fireplace with a shawl over his legs, I thought how lethargic he seemed, compared with the extraordinary energy he radiated when I first met him in Washington just five years earlier, after he had returned to power.

Marshall Tito and his wife had called on Churchill during the same period. She told me later that they too had noticed a striking change in him. He had been ordered to cut back on his smoking and drinking, and he looked on enviously as Tito smoked a huge Churchill cigar and drank Churchill's scotch as well as his own. Speaking to no one in particular, Churchill had said, "How do you stay so young? I know. It's power. Power keeps a man young."

I found that while Churchill had lost his power and some of his energy, he had lost none of his unique understanding of how the world worked. After a limp handshake, he ordered a glass of brandy. The effect when he drank it was like lighting a match to dry twigs. Our discussion ranged far and wide, from developments in the Soviet Union to a minidispute between Ghana and Guinea. When I asked him about the U.N., he said that he had supported it from the beginning and believed it had a significant role to play. But he added, "Under no circumstances can a major nation submit an issue affecting its vital interests to the U.N. or any other collective body for decision."

The concept of "assertive multilateralism" being advanced by some U.N. supporters can only be described as naïve diplomatic gobbledygook. A collective body cannot be effective unless it has leadership. As de Gaulle told André Malraux shortly before his death, "Parliaments can paralyze policy. They cannot initiate it." Even a collective body as closely knit as NATO was not able to be "assertive" in Bosnia. Can anyone seriously suggest that a collective body such as the U.N., one third of whose members have populations smaller than that of the state of Arkansas and half of which are not stable democracies, could be "assertive"?

This does not mean that the United Nations should be thrown on the scrap heap of history. It does mean that without leadership from the world's strongest nation, the U.N. will not act. We should enlist U.N. support for our policies but not put the U.N. in charge of them. The suggestion that the United States should put American troops under a U.N. command to give collective security a chance to work is completely unacceptable. To serve as President means accepting ultimate responsibility for the lives of troops put in harm's way. It would be not only unwise but immoral for him to deliver the lives of American soldiers into the hands of an international bureaucrat selected by the United Nations. As Senator Bob Dole has pointed out, the Secretary General of the United Nations was not elected by the American people.

The idea that the United States cannot afford to lead is fallacious. As Herb Stein has observed, "The United States is a very rich country. We cannot afford to do everything, but we can afford to do everything important." The United States is the world's top economic power, with the highest productivity per worker, the most advanced technological base, and one of the highest per capita GNPs in the world. It exports more goods, generates more scientific discoveries every year, and produces more Nobel Prize winners than any other country. Over $12.7 trillion in defense spending, $1.1 trillion in foreign aid, and more than one hundred thousand lives were the price the United States paid to ensure victory in the forty-five-year war against tyranny. We can well afford the infinitely smaller amount necessary to ensure that we do not lose the peace for which we sacrificed so much.

In the 1992 presidential campaign, a sign in the Clinton campaign office read, "It's the economy, stupid." That was good politics but poor statesmanship. There is a world of difference between campaigning and governing. We cannot have a strong domestic policy unless we have a strong foreign policy. We cannot be at peace in a world at war, and we cannot have a healthy economy in a sick world economy.

Since the end of World War II, the United States has been the world's most powerful symbol of political and economic freedom. The Cold War was not merely a conflict between two opposing armies. It was a conflict over two opposing ideologies. We triumphed because we were rich economically and strong militarily, but we were rich and strong precisely because of our dedication to the ideas of freedom. The values of political and economic freedom that have guided our country since the days of the American Revolution are the moral imperatives that impel us to play a leading role in the world.

Those who doubt our worthiness to lead should look at our record over the past forty-eight years. We have helped our enemies as well as our friends to recover from the devastation of World War II. We returned Okinawa to Japan and integrated both Japan and Germany into the community of Western nations. We have provided over $1 trillion in foreign aid to nations in the developing world. Since the end of the Cold War, we have returned Subic Naval Base to the Philippines; launched aid programs to Eastern Europe and the former Soviet Union; continued to protect South Korea and Japan; freed Kuwait and protected Saudi Arabia and other Gulf states from Iraqi aggression; safeguarded Israel's security; assisted anticommunist forces in Angola, Cambodia, and Afghanistan; supported peaceful democratic revolutions in the Philippines, in Latin America, and in South Korea; and been generous in our humanitarian aid to Somalia and other countries suffering man-made or natural disasters. Our record has not been perfect, but no other nation in history can match it. It is a record of benevolent leadership and of advancing not only our selfish interests but the values of political and economic freedom.

As we enter the twenty-first century, we must adopt a clearheaded policy based on practical idealism and enlightened realism. For the first time in fifty years, we have the power to set a course for the next century so that all, not just some, nations can experience the victory of freedom over tyranny in the world.

Over the past few years, foreign policy observers have made the following points in articles and commentaries:

• The democratic revolution in Russia and its political and free-market reforms are irreversible.
• European political and economic integration will eliminate the need for a continued U.S. role in NATO.
• The disappearance of the Soviet threat in the Far East means the end of geopolitical competition and conflict in East Asia.
• The U.S.-led victory in the Persian Gulf War ensured the stability of the Middle East and Western access to Middle Eastern oil.

All of these statements are false.

When the reactionary left's coup against Mikhail Gorbachev failed in August 1991, a half-century of superpower conflict ended. Yet Russia remains vulnerable to extreme nationalists and reactionaries intent on reversing free-market and democratic reforms. The European Community has stalled in its effort to achieve economic and political integration, and Europe is falling victim again to parochialism. Asia is threatened with conflict based on competing interests and traditional rivalries. The Persian Gulf remains a tinderbox that could catch fire at any moment.

We have not achieved perfect peace, which philosophers have been writing about for centuries and which Immanuel Kant described as "perpetual peace." This idea has always had enormous appeal. But it will never be achieved, except at diplomatic think tanks and in the grave. During my last meeting with Leonid Brezhnev in the Crimea in 1974, I jotted down this note on a pad of paper: "Peace is like a delicate plant. It has to be constantly tended and nurtured if it is to survive. If we neglect it, it will wither and die."

After the collapse of communism in the Cold War and the defeat of aggression in the Persian Gulf War, many observers concluded that we were witnessing the beginning of a new world order. They were wrong. The Cold War divided the world, but peace did not unite it. Instead of order, we find disorder in many areas of the world. The United States and the Soviet Union have kept the lid on potential small wars, but since World War II there have been one hundred and fifty of them. Eight million more people have been killed in those small wars than lost their lives in World War I. Most of those wars would have occurred had there been no superpower conflict. Since the end of the Cold War, the threat of small wars has substantially increased. Today, seventy-seven conflicts, based on tribal, national, ethnic, or religious hatreds, are being fought, and ruthless dictators such as Saddam Hussein, Kim Il Sung, and Muammar Qaddafi are poised to attack their neighbors.

During the Cold War, the leaders of the United States and the Soviet Union knew that they had the power to destroy each other and the rest of the world. This sharply reduced the possibility of global nuclear war. Pariah nations such as North Korea and Iraq, which are now trying to join the nuclear club, would not have these restraints. Consequently, the danger of a nuclear war is greater now than during the Cold War. Stopping nuclear proliferation therefore must be a top priority for all of the major nuclear powers—Russia, China, the United States, Great Britain, and France.

All of these issues—the former Soviet Union, the future of Europe, the rivalry in East Asia, the stability of the Persian Gulf, and avoiding nuclear anarchy—represent strategic priorities for the United States. None of them can be resolved without a commitment of American world leadership. We cannot react to every emergency call like an international 911 operator. But we *must* respond to those that affect our vital interests in the world.

The debacle in Somalia was a lesson in how not to conduct U.S. foreign policy. What began as a highly popular humanitarian relief program under President Bush became a highly controversial U.N. nation-building project under President Clinton. As the world's richest nation, we should always be generous in providing humanitarian aid to other nations. But we should not commit U.S. military forces to U.N. nation-building projects unless our vital interests are involved, a test that neither Somalia nor Haiti satisfied. When we do intervene militarily to protect our vital interests, we should follow President Bush's example in the Persian Gulf War, using the U.N., not being used by it.

The fallout from America's indecisive conduct in Somalia, Haiti, and Bosnia reaches far beyond those small nations. As *Washington Post* correspondent Stephen Rosenfeld has observed, "Would a country that reversed course after suffering one day's casualties in Mogadishu be likely to stand up to a nuclear-armed North Korea, Iraq, or Iran threatening their American-allied neighbors? Is it even faintly conceivable that the United States would extend and that Israel would accept an American nuclear guarantee as a substitute for Israel's own bomb?"

Above all, we should not allow our peripheral conflicts, such as those in Somalia and Haiti, to divert our attention from major conflicts where our interests *are* at stake.

The new buzzword in the American diplomatic community is *enlargement*. After containing communism for forty-five years, we are told that our goal now should be to enlarge free-market democracy. This begs the question whether what works for us will work for others with different backgrounds, but even given that limitation, the concept is acceptable only if it is conditioned on American self-interest. This is not opportunism. Kim Holmes puts it well: "The U.S. does not violate its own ideals by pursuing its own interests. We should support democracy abroad when it is in our interests to do so, which fortunately is more often than not."

But defending our interests is not enough by itself to mobilize American support for American foreign policy initiatives. After our rather belligerent exchanges in Moscow in 1959, Khrushchev was trying to appear reasonable as we sat together at a lavish state dinner in the Kremlin. He pointed down the table to one of his vice premiers and said, "Comrade Koslov is a hopeless communist." There is no question but that in foreign policy Americans are, at times, hopeless idealists, which is a source of great strength and a potential weakness.

No one would question that our vital interests were involved in World War I, World War II, and the Cold War. But American Presidents invariably clothed our interests in idealistic rhetoric. World War I was not simply a war to defend our interests against imperial Germany's aggression. It was a "war to end war" and to make the world safe for democracy. World War II was not just a war to defend U.S. interests against Nazi and Japanese aggression. It was a war to extend four great freedoms to all people. The Cold War was not just a war to defend our interests against aggressive communism. It was a war to defend and extend freedom and democracy in the world. No war more seriously involved our vital interests than the Persian Gulf War. But even then, the practical objective of defending our access to oil resources was coupled with the idealistic goal of preserving the independence of Kuwait and advancing the cause of democracy.

As realists, we do not want to become involved in foreign ventures unless our interests are threatened. As idealists, we insist that what is right for us must also be right for others. Bill Safire properly observed, "America will not defend with its lives what it cannot defend with its conscience."

Enlargement is a tricky word. In photography, a negative can be enlarged to a three-by-five snapshot or a wall-size mural. Based on the record so far, the present administration is aiming for wallet-size. Some officials clearly believe that the United States overextended itself during the Cold War, particularly in Vietnam, one of its major battles. They tend to resist American involvement, except in humanitarian activities that have overwhelming public support. They have yet to face up to the fact that it will at times be necessary to use American power and influence to defend and extend freedom in places thousands of miles away if we are to preserve it at home. It is a role that will require global vision and big plays from this President and every successive one in the era beyond peace.

In his Inaugural Address, John F. Kennedy vowed "to pay any price, bear any burden, meet any hardship, support any friend, oppose any foe, in order to assure the survival and the success of liberty." Even during the Cold War, such a policy was praiseworthy but unrealistic. Then, as now, world peace was threatened by several enemies of liberty. We cannot afford to fight them all at once. Since the Cold War, the choices about how and when to fight for peace and freedom have become even more complex.

We must begin by asking ourselves what kind of world we want, now that we have peace. Ideally, all nations should have free economic systems, free political systems, and an unfailing commitment to social justice and human rights. But the world is not a blank canvas on which we can paint our vision. We must take its myriad realities into account as we seek to realize our goals. The United States cannot become involved in every nation or region where our ideals have not been achieved. We favor extending peace and freedom—but extending peace without compromising our interests or principles, and extending freedom without risking peace. If peace is our only goal, then the victory of freedom may be imperiled. If freedom is our only goal, then peace will be imperiled. It is the burden of being the only superpower that there are things we do not wish to do that we must do, and it is the burden of being a responsible superpower that there are things we wish to do that we cannot do.

In a world without a dominant enemy, we must consider each situation on its merits. Will our involvement be consistent with our values? Will it serve our interests? Will it serve the interests of our friends? Will it serve the interests of those directly involved? During the Cold War, the answer to each of these questions, where our efforts to oppose communist expansionism and Soviet aggression were concerned, was yes. The answer to each question should also be yes regarding our efforts to help bring about the victory of freedom in the former Soviet Union. No other single factor will have a greater political impact on the world in the century to come than whether political and economic freedom take root and thrive in Russia and the other former communist nations. Today's generation of American leaders will be judged primarily by whether they did everything possible to bring about this outcome. If they fail, the cost that their successors will have to pay will be unimaginably high.

Russia and the Victory
of Freedom

Writing this spring in *The Washington Post,* one of the United States's most distinguished foreign affairs observers asserted, "Russia is no longer a world power and will not be for some time." If the United States falls into the trap of making this fatally flawed assumption the basis of its policy, prospects for peace and freedom in Russia, Europe, and elsewhere in the world will be gravely imperiled.

Those who suggest that its massive problems disqualify Russia from being treated as a great power ignore an unpleasant but undeniable fact. Russia is the only nation in the world with the capability of destroying the United States. For that reason alone, it remains our highest foreign policy priority. But the importance of Russia does not turn only on our immediate national security. Many millions of Russian people, who for three quarters of a century suffered under the most entrenched and brutal totalitarian dictatorship in history, depend on the survival and success of economic and political freedom.

The failure of freedom would also have a profoundly negative global impact. The reestablishment of a dictatorship and a command economy in Russia would give encouragement to every dictator and would-be dictator in the world. Since an authoritarian Russia would be far more likely to adopt an aggressive foreign policy than a democratic Russia, freedom's failure would threaten peace and stability in Europe and around the world. If Russia turns away from democracy and economic freedom and we have not done everything possible to prevent it, we will bear a large measure of responsibility for the ominous consequences.

As we develop policies toward Russia for the future, it is essential that we understand its past. The Bolshevik triumph in the Revolution of 1917 and in the civil war that followed shaped the course of events in the twentieth century and led to the rebirth of the Russian empire in a new, more deadly totalitarian form. The communist victory also contributed to the polarization of world politics, facilitating the Nazis' rise to power in Germany. Despite the brief alliance with the West during World War II, the Soviet Union became the principal threat to world peace. As a result, the United States had no choice but to make victory in the Cold War its number-one foreign policy priority.

Even before the Bolshevik Revolution, the requirements of building and maintaining the empire had a debilitating impact on Russia's political and economic development. Empire was incompatible with liberalization and democracy. The cost of maintaining a huge standing army was an obstacle to economic growth. The constant provoking of fear and hostility in neighboring countries proved incompatible with Russia's own security. In the process of empire building, Russia was both aggressor and victim. While enslaving others, the pre-communist Russian empire had isolated and enslaved itself.

When the communists came to power in 1917, the pattern of Russian imperialism and internal decline went from bad to worse. By the late 1970s, the Soviet empire was so overextended that even its own rulers began to recognize that the costs of expansionism threatened their ability to govern. By 1985, a significant part of the communist *nomenklatura* was ready to experiment with domestic reform and "new foreign policy thinking." Mikhail Gorbachev became their standard-bearer.

Gorbachev sought to reform the Soviet empire in order to save it. Contrary to the illusions of many of his admirers in the West, he wanted to save communism, not abandon it. This was an impossible task. His totalitarian empire, built and sustained by force and coercion, could not be fundamentally reformed. The crucial flaw in Gorbachev's thinking was his failure to comprehend the law of history that dictatorial regimes collapse precisely when they begin to relax controls and create expectations they cannot fulfill.

It was inevitable that, liberated from strict totalitarian controls, the peoples of the Soviet Union would seek to remove from power the communist authorities in Moscow who continued to determine their national destinies. Yeltsin's unique contribution to Russia and the world was his understanding of this historical fact and his courageous determination to give his people a chance to enjoy political and economic freedom by putting an end, simultaneously, to communism and the empire. As Isaiah Berlin has observed, "Never before has there been an empire that caved without war, revolution, or invasion."

Often the demise of old adversaries leads to the emergence of new, sometimes more dangerous challenges rather than to peace and harmony among nations. After the defeat of the German and Austro-Hungarian empires in World War I, Woodrow Wilson and many other idealistic Americans hoped we would have an era of peace under the League of Nations. Instead, the United States was confronted with communism in Russia, fascism in Germany and Italy, militarism in Japan, and ultimately a new global war.

Our justifiable satisfaction with the end of the Cold War must not obscure the urgent need to address the extremely difficult and contradictory transition in the post-Soviet region. Until this transition culminates in irreversible political and economic freedom and nonaggressive foreign policies, there is the danger that the remnants of the shattered Soviet empire will strike back at the world, with devastating consequences.

Will Boris Yeltsin be able to continue to provide the leadership Russia needs to achieve the goals of the second Russian revolution—political and economic freedom at home and a nonaggressive foreign policy abroad? History is made by the acts of individuals, and history has placed enormous problems and extraordinary opportunities on President Yeltsin's agenda.

No one questions his courage. We all remember his standing on a tank, facing down a group of card-carrying communist killers who were supporting the coup attempt in August 1991. Most would agree that he is a strong leader. He did not hesitate to use the necessary military force to put down the reactionary mob that rampaged through Moscow in October 1993. In the process he taught a lesson to those who resort to arms rather than votes in a democracy.

Some observers make the fatuous argument that Yeltsin demonstrated a disregard for law by not following the provisions of the Soviet-era Russian constitution and by dissolving the Gorbachev-era Congress of People's Deputies. To his credit, despite the fundamental flaws of the Soviet-era constitution, he did not disregard it lightly. Only after a great deal of hesitation did he come to the conclusion that the Congress of People's Deputies and the Parliament had become intractable roadblocks not only to reform but also to responsible government.

Other leaders might have handled the difficult relationship with the Congress of People's Deputies in a less confrontational manner. I myself urged that he do so when we met in Moscow in February 1993. But he turned out to be right. Within certain reasonable limits, leaders should do what is natural for them. Each must find his or her own way to deal with challenges. Winston Churchill, Charles de Gaulle, and Ronald Reagan were all effective in serving their nations. Yet they had different styles and used different methods to accomplish their objectives. The product of a unique period in Russian history, Yeltsin cannot be judged as if he were the president of a stable democracy with an established constitutional order. If he acted like one, he would probably fail.

We should learn from history. This is the second experiment with a Russian transition to democracy. In 1917, the Provisional Government under Kerensky tried to adhere to strict democratic standards. It failed to develop close ties with the military and continued to fulfill its obligations to the allies to pursue the war with Germany, despite Russia's desperate situation. The outcome was the Bolshevik takeover and more than seven decades of communist dictatorship. The United States does not need another Kerensky at Russia's helm at this moment of trial. It is shortsighted of Yeltsin's Western critics to attack him for precisely the kind of conduct that makes him an effective leader under these extraordinary circumstances. And it is hypocritical of them to be less patient with him and his fellow reformers after barely a year of dramatic progress than they were with Gorbachev after six years of timid incrementalism and broken promises.

Now that a new constitution has been adopted and a new Parliament democratically elected, the charges against Yeltsin have become moot. In view of the massive problems he confronts, Russia is fortunate that he has not been more authoritarian in trying to implement his reforms.

To evaluate Yeltsin, it is useful to compare him with Gorbachev. Gorbachev should be remembered as a great leader in Russian history. His political reforms made Yeltsin possible. Yeltsin, on the other hand, holds Gorbachev's place in history in his hands as he tries to implement the economic reforms Gorbachev was unwilling and unable to carry through.

Both Gorbachev and Yeltsin had history working against them. Generally, good revolutionary leaders are not good nation builders. Revolutionary leaders must destroy the old institutions. Nation builders must create new ones. Two leaders as different as George Washington in the United States and Jawaharlal Nehru in India were able to be both good revolutionary leaders and nation builders. Gorbachev failed that test. Now Yeltsin must demonstrate that he can succeed where Gorbachev failed.

Both began their careers as peasants. Gorbachev became a man of the world. Yeltsin remained a man of the people. This has proved to be his major source of strength in the crises he has confronted as Russia's President. When I saw him in 1992, I told him that as he traveled around the world, it was far better for him to be seen tipping glasses with a peasant than with a President. His early popularity was due to the fact that he attacked the obscene perks of the communist *nomenklatura*. He must be careful not to indulge in some of the same luxuries that he once criticized.

I have often described Gorbachev as being an excellent politician. Yeltsin is a better one. Both exude charisma. But Gorbachev seems more contrived; Yeltsin seems more genuine. Gorbachev is more sophisticated; Yeltsin is more down-to-earth. Gorbachev is better in drawing rooms; Yeltsin is better in family rooms. Gorbachev seems to speak more from the head than the heart; Yeltsin seems to be talking more from the heart than from the head.

When confronted with a crisis, Gorbachev frequently appeared at a loss and resorted to pathetic half-measures; Yeltsin, on the contrary, draws strength from crisis. His authority has come not from established political structures but from a special chemistry with the people.

The difference between Gorbachev and Yeltsin that matters most is that they stand for different values. Czech President Václav Havel told me, "Gorbachev is still a captive of communism. Yeltsin has liberated himself."

Unlike Gorbachev, Yeltsin both preaches and practices democracy. He is the only elected Russian head of state in a thousand years. Gorbachev refused to risk his power in a free election. Unlike Gorbachev, Yeltsin has repudiated both socialism and communism. Most important, Yeltsin has adopted a nonaggressive foreign policy and has made massive cuts in Russia's nuclear and other weapons.

American commentators from both ends of the political spectrum deplored Yeltsin's recent actions. While liberals were outraged that he dissolved the Congress and used force, conservatives fear the new Russian foreign policy assertiveness, which they view as a sign of neoimperialism. While both groups of critics are right in part, both miss the point.

Yeltsin is a tough and sometimes ruthless Russian patriot. Otherwise he would never have been able to come to power and withstand the numerous challenges to his rule. Gorbachev started reforms without understanding their likely consequences and then backed down when the dangers became apparent, exposing himself—as one former senior Soviet official described him to me—as a "brutal wimp." It should be remembered that Gorbachev had appointed the reactionaries who led the attempted coup against him in 1991. In contrast, Yeltsin acts preemptively and decisively. This is the key to the continuing support he has among the Russian people, despite all the pain associated with his country's transition to democratic capitalism.

Pushkin wrote in the nineteenth century that rebellions in Russia tend to be "bloody and senseless." It is a political miracle that the unprecedented transition from dictatorship to democracy and from a command economy to a free-market economy is being accomplished relatively peacefully. The remarkable aspect of the October 1993 rebellion by hard-line reactionaries is that so few lives were lost, owing in great part to the fact that after some hesitation the armed forces stood by the democratic government.

Many observers have expressed concern about Yeltsin's personal weaknesses. Some say he has a drinking problem. Heavy drinking has been a characteristic of most Russian leaders throughout history, and of some American leaders as well. After Grant's victory at Vicksburg in 1863, as Lincoln was considering appointing him commander of all Union forces, one of his advisers urged him not to do so because Grant drank. Lincoln reportedly responded, "Get me the name of his brand of whiskey so that I can give some to my other generals." Yeltsin's personal habits matter only if they affect his conduct in office.

Yeltsin sometimes becomes depressed after winning a battle against those who oppose him. This is not an uncommon characteristic of leaders. What matters most is that Yeltsin so far has met the test when the stakes were highest. He himself has admitted in a television interview that he is at his best when the going gets rough but does not always follow through once the crisis is over.

Yeltsin is the most pro-American Russian leader in history. He is at times too pro-American for his own good at home. Any of his potential successors would have a hard time following an equally moderate foreign policy. It is vitally important that we do not put Yeltsin's administration or that of any democratic successor in the position of appearing to go in lockstep with the United States on foreign policy. This would do irreparable damage to the chance that political and economic freedom will survive in Russia.

It is also important that we never put our chips on just one man, even one as powerful and able as Yeltsin. Our concern should be not the man but rather what he stands for. We stuck too long with Gorbachev. As long as Yeltsin has a foreign policy that serves the interests of peace and a domestic policy that serves the interests of the Russian people, he deserves our support.

In spite of the growing drumbeats of his opponents, he remains the most popular politician in Russia and remains the best guarantor of Russian democracy and stability until his term expires in 1996. No one currently on the scene has the stature to fill his shoes. The United States should treat him with respect and continue to work with him closely. It is a pity that his frequent absences from Moscow, his illnesses, and his increasingly erratic behavior have deprived him of much of the mystique he acquired from his historic role in the destruction of Soviet communism.

But his critics are far too quick to write him off. He has on several occasions demonstrated great recuperative powers. It is in our interests and those of the Russian people that he bring his term to a successful conclusion. Eagerly bandied rumors of impending coups and mysterious, debilitating presidential illnesses may make fascinating theater and newspaper copy, but they are enormously damaging to Russia's prestige and its ability to establish a stable society. Many Russian leaders I met during my tenth visit to Moscow in the spring of 1994 complained that foreign investment had dropped dramatically over the past year because of investors' understandable fears of political instability. With the elections of December 1993, when voters created a new Parliament and sanctioned a new constitution, Russia opened a new chapter in its political development. The best thing that can happen for the next generation of Russians is for that chapter to come to a close in 1996 with a peaceful, productive ending to Boris Yeltsin's term as President and a vigorous campaign to choose his successor—peacefully, openly, and democratically.

Yeltsin in the meantime should be supported but not idolized. Western officials have sometimes gone too far in taking an uncritical view of Russia's actions. By saying that nothing in Yeltsin's domestic conduct or Russia's conduct vis-à-vis other post-Soviet states gives the West cause for concern, Western officials have ignored some aspects of Moscow's recent behavior that cannot help but worry the West, even as it continues to support Yeltsin. By idealizing Yeltsin's government, the West runs the risk of personalizing its Russian policy and creating a potential trap for itself. If he fails to live up to our overly optimistic expectations, the West's Russian policy—while basically sound—may lose public support.

We should avoid giving Yeltsin the false impression that as long as he maintains fundamental commitments to economic reform and to a peaceful relationship with the West, other things do not matter. I was disturbed to hear from Russian officials that the United States had told them in advance that it would be all right to take "resolute" steps against the Parliament as long as they accelerated economic reforms. Encouraging departures from democracy in a country with such an autocratic tradition as Russia's is like trying to put out a fire with combustible materials. The American public can stomach only so much restriction of freedom. This is a fact of U.S. political life, and to let Yeltsin believe otherwise is a disservice both to him and to the U.S.-Russian relationship.

While supporting Yeltsin, we should remember that there are other democrats in Russia—many of whom have disagreements with him about the constitutional division of labor between the executive and legislative branches, the type and pace of economic reforms, and the tactics of Russian foreign policy.

I have met with numerous Russian democratic politicians who have differed with Yeltsin. All of them—although stressing Russia's specific national security interests—demonstrated strong interest in continuing a strategic partnership with the United States. Nothing can be gained and a great deal can be lost by recklessly alienating these political elements. It would be a mistake to play favorites in Russian politics by supporting the most radical reformers at the expense of everyone else. Such tactical errors would put at risk the broad-based constituency needed in Russia to build a new relationship with the United States.

Russia now has a democratic government. As is the case in our relations with other democratic governments, we should negotiate exclusively with the elected leaders, but we should keep channels of communication open to members of the loyal opposition. Under no circumstances should we take sides in political campaigns in which both candidates share our values and are supportive of a friendly U.S.-Russia relationship.

In the wake of the 1993 elections, Boris Yeltsin is still a political heavyweight, but he is no longer a superman. In 1994, for the first time in ten visits to Moscow in thirty-five years, I was able to meet with all the leading opposition leaders. When Russia was a dictatorship as part of the Soviet Union, a good relationship with the man at the top was all that was necessary. That is no longer the case. The Boris-Bill relationship in our case and the Boris-Helmut relationship for the Germans are no longer enough—not only because other leaders have come to the fore, but because of the decline in Yeltsin's authority that has resulted from his recent behavior.

If we do not develop good working relationships with the new generation of Russian leaders, we will be caught flat-footed by unexpected shifts in the political landscape, as we were by the strong showing of Vladimir Zhirinovsky's Liberal Democratic Party in December's parliamentary elections. Our Moscow-based diplomats, who once composed entire cables based on observing who was standing next to Brezhnev on top of Lenin's Tomb during the Soviet Union's annual May Day parade, must now learn to appreciate all the subtle gradations of political thought in the new Russia. As Russia's economy grows and matures, our political and economic officers must overcome their bureaucratic aversion to the nuts and bolts of business and private investment. They also need a more sophisticated grasp of monetary and fiscal policy. Reading tea leaves and reporting barroom gossip about who was up and who was down once passed for diplomacy in communist Moscow, but it will not wash in free Moscow, any more than it does in postings such as Paris, Bonn, or Tokyo.

On March 14, 1994, I had the privilege of being the first American in history to address a formal meeting of an elected Russian Parliament when I appeared before an expanded hearing of the Committee on Foreign Relations of the State Duma, the lower house of the new Russian Parliament. The questions, posed by representatives of parties from Zhirinovsky's Liberal Democrats to the Women of Russia, were wide-ranging and blunt. There were no softballs. As I fielded the deputies' pointed queries about U.S. "meddling" in Russian internal affairs, the intentions of the United States and NATO in Eastern Europe, and many other issues, I realized that there was no more dramatic illustration of Russia's emergence as a democratic state than this new forum for debate and decision making. After the December elections, many in the West expressed disappointment that the Duma was not more reflective of Yeltsin's wishes. In fact, the Duma is reflective of Russia—its diversity, its disunity, and its potential for greatness. The highest priority for President Yeltsin and his successors will be marshaling the political and creative energy of their vast nation by building sturdy governing coalitions in Parliament. Even more important, the Duma is the breeding ground for future Presidents. Every leading candidate in the 1996 elections, with the exception of Alexander Rutskoi, is a Duma deputy.

Russians will have a wide variety of choice. The second-most-popular politician in the country after Yeltsin is Gregory Yavlinski, author of Gorbachev's never-implemented Five Hundred Days reform plan. He is charismatic and intelligent, and he gets excellent press in the United States because he speaks English and takes a strong line in favor of free enterprise. Sergei Shahrai, Minister of Nationalities, was one of the most thoughtful leaders I met in the new group of those in their late thirties and early forties. His keen insights about the need to find new ways to cope with simmering tensions among Russia's scores of nationalities and ethnic groups are particularly impressive. Economics Minister Alexander Shokhin is now the government's key reformer. If he meets and masters the numerous challenges now before him, he is a certain contender for the Presidency. Viktor Chernomyrdin, the fifty-five-year-old Prime Minister, is generally acknowledged to be the front-runner to succeed Yeltsin when he completes his term. One Western leader with whom I have discussed Russian politics summed up Chernomyrdin's strengths and weaknesses perfectly: "He is dry, nonvisionary, like an accountant," he said. "But he is a great pragmatist. We could have worse than that. Also, he keeps his promises."

Many in the West were shocked when former Vice President Alexander Rutskoi and others charged in the armed uprising against the Yeltsin government last October were released from prison by the State Duma's grant of amnesty to them and to those who had tried to overthrow Gorbachev in August 1991. Outrage was understandable. Lives were lost during Rutskoi's October uprising, and Yeltsin went to great lengths in his attempt to prevent the amnesty. For all this, Rutskoi's almost certain reentry into public life will have a positive political impact.

In March 1994, I called on General Rutskoi, whom I had met twice before, in his apartment in Moscow. He is a ramrod-straight war hero who looks at the world in a pointedly direct way. He had been out of prison for only ten days and was still wearing the beard he had grown during his five months there. Our talk had an eerie quality because of a simultaneous and totally incomprehensible conversation between two large parrots in separate cages in the middle of Rutskoi's sitting room. He apologized for the noise, saying that the birds had had more room in his dacha, but that the Yeltsin government had taken the dacha away. The birds were not speaking English, and I knew enough Russian to know they weren't speaking Russian. He said that he had acquired them during a tour in Kuala Lumpur, and that they spoke only Malaysian.

Rutskoi said that he intended to run for President in 1996 but added ruefully that while he was in prison Zhirinovsky had "appropriated a lot of my political base." As we discussed his impressions of the domestic scene, including the shocking rise in both organized crime and street crime in Russia, he said somewhat ominously, "I am able to bring law and order. I know how to do it." He predicted that Russia's transition to true democracy would take a minimum of ten years.

Rutskoi, Zhirinovsky, and others with comparable views appeal to those who miss what they remember as the Soviet Union's proud imperial past and who are also convinced that Russia's enormous problems require a strong, authoritarian hand at the helm. One reason Zhirinovsky's showing in the December parliamentary elections was so dramatic was that the substantial pro-reform vote was split among several parties. In the next election the reformers' goal must be to overcome their differences and at the same time encourage divisions among the anti-reform candidates. It will help reform enormously if Rutskoi and Zhirinovsky end up competing for the same votes.

While I was opposed to the amnesty when it was first granted, my talks in Moscow convinced me that it was necessary. It was needed to transform Rutskoi's status from jailed hero to everyday politician and to help Yeltsin and the government deal with their political and policy challenges. For weeks in Moscow, as the economy continued to deteriorate, all anyone talked about was whether Rutskoi and his fellow prisoners should be granted amnesty. As Sergei Shahrai told me, the prisoners' release resulted in a limited but crucial period of entente between President Yeltsin and the State Duma—a window during which Russia could move forward if both sides used the time well.

Zhirinovsky, leader of the ultranationalist Liberal Democratic Party, has a charismatic personality and is endowed with physical dynamism. Winston Churchill called Parnell "a volcano under an ice cap." In Zhirinovsky's case there is no ice cap. He is a ruthless demagogue whose outrageous views bubble out of him almost without restraint. But he is canny enough to know that he is striking chords with those Russians who bemoan the loss of their empire and resent foreigners' incessant lecturing. When I questioned him in March 1994 about some of his most ludicrous statements—that California would one day become part of Mexico, that Miami would be a black republic, that Paris would be an Arab city—he began his answers by referring to polls that showed how popular his positions were. He hotly denied he was anti-Semitic. His numerous statements to the contrary are a matter of public record. But those who say he is a Russian Hitler miss the mark. For Hitler, anti-Semitism was a faith. For Zhirinovsky, it is a tactic—a cynical attempt to exploit popular biases and resentments.

I share the view of Ukrainian President Leonid Kravchuk and of virtually all the other Russian leaders I met that Zhirinovsky will not be elected President of Russia. He lacks both the presence and the conviction to lead a great nation. One of his top deputies told us that Zhirinovsky had intentionally adopted the extravagant posture of a holy fool, or *yurodiviye*—an opposition figure who, because everyone knows he is not up to the job, is not punished for his outrageous views. The Russian people have a soft spot for holy fools, but they have never become Russian leaders, as Zhirinovsky will discover when he enters the presidential sweepstakes.

The important thing about Zhirinovsky is that his success at the polls has created a bloc of support upon which some other, more palatable leader could well build a credible platform for seizing political power. One of Russia's leading reformers told me, "Thank God we have Zhirinovsky as we have him now. It would be much worse if we had someone stronger as the beneficiary of this situation." Those who spend so much time demonizing him would do well to work to ensure that a more formidable devil does not rise in his place. The most effective way to relegate extremist political figures to a permanent place on the sidelines in Russia, as anywhere else, is to attack the root causes of their popularity. This means focusing our attention on bringing about the victory of economic stability and political pluralism in the new Russia. If Russia is strong, Zhirinovsky and his ilk will be speaking to an empty hall. If Russia is weak, no amount of internal or international condemnation will stop his movement from bringing Russia to the brink of chaos.

As far as the ultranationalists and communists are concerned, we should be careful where and how we indicate our profound disagreement with their philosophy and actions. Public criticism by U.S. officials delivered on Russian soil can play into the hands of xenophobic demagogues, helping them to consolidate their political base and generate an anti-American backlash. Most Americans would not appreciate it if visiting foreign leaders attacked an American politician who had won millions of votes, even if they found his views abhorrent.

In developing a policy toward the new Russia, we must begin by recognizing that the Russians did not lose the Cold War. The communists did. The United States and our allies deserve credit for holding the line against Soviet expansionism in Europe and turning back Soviet probes in the Third World. But the knockout blow to Soviet communism was delivered by democratic forces in Moscow who defeated the reactionary coup in August 1991 and then buried the Soviet Union the following December.

We should therefore treat the Russians not as defeated enemies but as allies who joined with us in defeating Soviet communism in its heartland—Russia. As Al Haig has observed, "The American arms buildup and tough diplomacy contributed to the Soviet disaster. But that disaster was fundamentally made in Moscow. A militant multinational empire equipped by an archaic ideology gradually choked on its own contradictions, inefficiencies, and corruptions."

There are neither easy answers nor readily available road maps for navigating the massive changes in post-Soviet political territory. The Soviet empire left a terrible heritage of economic inefficiency and excessive centralization. Its populations lack entrepreneurial skills, capital, and the work ethic. More dangerous, these nations are riddled with ethnic grievances, dominated by a suspicion of compromise, and bereft of any real democratic traditions. Their antagonisms will be played out across artificial borders established by communist masters in order to divide and conquer.

What kinds of foreign policies do we want to encourage in Russia and its newly independent neighbors, and what kinds of Western policies should be adopted to encourage democratic and free-market reforms in those nations?

Throughout my career as a congressman, senator, Vice President, private citizen, President, and former President, I was rightly described as an unapologetic Cold Warrior and enemy of communism. Some consider it ironic that having been a lifelong critic of Moscow's inhumane, expansionist policies under communism, I now visit Moscow annually as a proponent of massive Western private and public investment and support. I have not changed. My position has changed because the democratic revolution in Russia has created a unique historical opportunity to bring Russia into the community of Western nations and to lead Moscow away from its authoritarian and imperial past. We now have a vital interest in promoting a stable and nonaggressive Russia and in consolidating the independence of the non-Russian republics of the former Soviet Union.

Some observers have argued that it makes no sense to help build up Russia because Moscow might someday reemerge as a strategic antagonist, this time of the right instead of the left. Any strong nation can become a potential adversary as a result of a change in leadership or some other unanticipated development. But basing our policy on such a contingency would require an element of cynicism that would violate American foreign policy traditions. We did not act this way toward Germany and Japan after World War II, and we should not act this way toward Russia after the Cold War. Throughout the Cold War we spoke out against communism not only because of the threat its proponents posed to us but also because of the plight of the millions who lived under it. It would be the height of hypocrisy for any Western statesman who spoke movingly of the plight of the Soviet people living under the communist yoke to withhold the hand of friendship from the Russian people now that communism has been defeated.

Russia has the potential to become a great power again. It has a rich civilization, a proud history, a deep tradition in the arts, enormous natural resources, and a strong people capable of great suffering and sacrifice, as they demonstrated so vividly during World War II. There are some who say that it would be in our interest for Russia to disintegrate and to become weak.

This is not one of our options. Russia will inevitably be strong again. The only question is whether a strong Russia will be a friend or an adversary of the West. We must do everything in our power to ensure the former rather than the latter.

The twentieth century was Russia's lost century culturally as well as politically. The nineteenth century was the golden age of Russian music, art, and literature. Czarist rule was dictatorial and repressive, but it at least permitted some artistic expression. Communist rule sought total control of mind, body, and spirit, stifling the creativity that is the soul of any people. Great works are generated by individual inspiration, not by consensus. The democratic revolution in Russia holds out the hope that it will once again find its creative voice and share its great talents with the world.

Our interest in a strong Russia does not mean that our support for the Russian government should be unequivocal. We would criticize what we considered irresponsible behavior by England, France, or Japan, and we should not hesitate to criticize the Russians should they take actions we believe are inconsistent with our interests and those of peace in the world. But we should not withhold support from Russia now because of the possibility that it might take on a hostile character in the future. Practically speaking, our influence at such a time will be greater if our economic and political relations with Russia are strong. Morally speaking, we owe the Russian people our support now. Personally speaking, I am glad that I lived to see the Russian tricolor flying over the Kremlin, to shake the hand of a pro-Western leader within its walls, and to say to my fellow Americans, from the unique perspective of the quintessential living Cold Warrior, that it is time for us to match our rhetoric with our money in supporting our new friends in the democratic Russian republic.

No practicing American politician or diplomat has ever dealt with a nation like the new Russia. It is not a defeated enemy like Japan or West Germany that we are nursing back to health. It is not an ally like France or England, with which we have obvious historical and strategic interests in common. It is not a strategic adversary like the old Soviet Union. It is a powerful, independent nation with which we have some interests in common and some interests, prospectively, in conflict. Those used to the easy answers of the Cold War will have to find a new measure of maturity and subtlety if they are to develop constructive policies toward post–Cold War Russia, a fundamentally friendly great power that may at times pursue its interests in an aggressive manner that we will find objectionable.

In terms of military strength, including nuclear weapons, Russia is still one of the most powerful nations in the world. If economic and political reforms succeed, within a generation it could once again achieve the status of superpower. As Russia grows in power and influence, the United States should be candid when our views do not coincide. But the inevitable clashes in our views must be seen as differences between friends and not between potential enemies.

The most dangerous mistake we could make would be to ignore our differences or attempt to drown them in champagne and vodka toasts at feel-good summit meetings. Rather than papering over differences with diplomatic gobbledygook, we must find ways to disagree without damaging one of the world's most important strategic relationships.

The second most dangerous mistake would be to neglect our responsibility for assisting Russia in its transition to freedom, or arrogantly to scold or punish it for every foreign or domestic policy transgression, as though it were an international problem child. I saw Helmut Kohl in Bonn after visiting Moscow in early 1994, and he had an apt summation of the importance of treating Russia as a great power. "My mother was a wise, simple, pious woman," he said. "She told us several adages that apply to politics as well as to private life. One was that you always meet everyone twice in your lifetime. The first time, always have in mind the impression you will make the second time. We are going to meet these Russians again in a few years, I'm convinced of that."

The recent flap over the indictment of a highly placed Russian mole in the CIA was a glaring example of how unprepared many Americans are to think of Russia as a great power with its own interests and prerogatives. Many observers were quick to condemn Yeltsin, even though the mole was first recruited under Gorbachev. But the demands that we should not send aid to a country that spies on us were disingenuous at best. How many of these same critics called for a cutoff of our massive aid to Israel in the wake of the Pollard spy case, where Israeli intelligence was spying on the United States? As that incident and others show, most nations reserve the right to gather intelligence about both friends and foes. Although the Cold War had been over for more than three years, the CIA budget in 1993 was an estimated $30 billion. What did we spend it on—finding out whether they were growing coffee instead of cocoa in Ghana?

Twenty-seven years ago, two years before I took office as President, Charles de Gaulle told me that the United States should reestablish relations with China before its power impelled us to do so. A generation later, China's explosive growth and burgeoning economic, diplomatic, and military power represent a total vindication of de Gaulle's assessment. A similar sense of anticipation must govern our relations with Russia. Its seemingly overwhelming problems will not last forever. Its human and natural resources, and thus its capacity to recover and ultimately to excel, are virtually unlimited. The United States and the West should develop a collaborative, businesslike relationship with Russia today so that when we meet these Russians again, we will do so as friends, if not necessarily as partners, rather than as potential adversaries.

What the United States wants most from Russia is a nonaggressive foreign policy. While being sensitive to Russia's legitimate interests, the administration, in discussions with the Yeltsin government, should not hesitate to raise questions about aspects of Russia's international conduct that affect our interests. Our support for Russia's reformers does not justify failing to present security concerns to Moscow forthrightly and early on, while there is still a possibility of having an impact without causing a conflict.

Any attempt to reestablish the Russian empire by force, coercion, or destabilization of its neighbors would be contrary to U.S. interests. To avoid any possible misunderstanding, the American government should make this clear to the Russian leadership at the outset. In addition, the other newly independent states need to be reassured that America's desire for partnership with Russia does not imply neglect of their security interests.

While the collapse of the Soviet empire may be seen as a historically progressive development, the disintegration of the Russian Federation would be a different matter. It is hard to imagine an amicable divorce between the central government in Moscow and the Russian republics and regions. Twice before in Russian history—in the seventeenth century during the so-called Time of Troubles, and at the beginning of the twentieth century during the rule of the Provisional Government of 1917—separatist trends split Russia apart. The separation triggered bloody civil wars and the emergence of governments in Moscow that came to power through the barrel of the gun, reunited Russia with an iron fist, and soon became a menace to Russia's neighbors.

It is impossible to overstate the dangers of a civil war in a nation with thousands of nuclear weapons, dozens of nuclear power stations, and numerous depots with chemical and perhaps biological weapons. The consequences of such a conflict would inevitably extend far beyond Russia's own borders.

Stability does not mean the re-creation of a unitary state. Russia is too big, too complex, too diverse a country to be run from the Kremlin in an efficient yet democratic way. The most stable arrangement for Russia is a genuine federation as set forth in the new Russian constitution, under which the republics and regions have considerable control over their own affairs and a meaningful voice in the central government.

The Russian armed forces do not now represent a serious threat to the United States. Russia lacks any serious nonnuclear force projection capability. Its conventional forces are grossly understaffed and underpaid. Military manpower has fallen below the 1.5 million authorized by the former Supreme Soviet and continues to shrink. Draft dodging is a chronic problem: In the spring of 1993, 60 percent of all eligible males avoided the draft. The military does not have the necessary funds for even minimally adequate training, and its logistical base is deteriorating rapidly. Major offensive operations outside the former Soviet region are completely beyond the capability of the Russian military for the foreseeable future. The strategic nuclear forces, in the absence of any serious conflict, are not a significant threat to the United States. Today, with Russia's GNP roughly a third of the former Soviet Union's, it will be difficult to rebuild the military machine from scratch.

At the same time, the West must take note of warning signs on the horizon. Russian military thinking is becoming more nationalistic and more assertive in defense of Russia's interests in the other former Soviet states bordering on Russia, and more supportive of the use of military force as an instrument of foreign policy.

Russian policy toward other post-Soviet nations represents the greatest dilemma for the United States. A new attempt by Moscow to rebuild its empire would be a tragedy for Russia and its neighbors alike. In view of the Russian-Soviet historical legacy, it is understandable that Russia's neighbors are sensitive to any signs of new assertiveness on Moscow's part. It took Germany and Japan several decades to rehabilitate themselves after World War II, and even today some European and Asian nations are nervous about Berlin's and Tokyo's more assertive conduct.

Perceptions and fears of aggression have real consequences

in that they affect international security. The United States cannot be indifferent to the fears of Russia's neighbors, particularly because in many instances those fears are based on new, disturbing elements in Russia's own behavior. There is considerable evidence that Russian security thinking during the two years since the collapse of the Soviet Union has moved in a more aggressive direction. Force has become a more acceptable instrument in Russian foreign policy, and the "divide and rule" technique is frequently relied upon by the Kremlin in such places as Georgia and Azerbaijan.

That Russian policy has become more assertive, even heavy-handed, is not in dispute. Yeltsin and his pro-Western Foreign Minister, Andrei Kozyrev, talk proudly about the newly muscular defense of Russian interests in the "near abroad"— the Russians' term for the other former Soviet republics. Ukrainian President Kravchuk and former Latvian President Anatoly Gorbunous, now Speaker of the Parliament, are ex-communists and not anti-Russian firebrands. But they personally expressed concern to me last year about the Russian tendency to push their countries around.

Still, I do not think a new imperialism looms. I have spoken with many Russian politicians of different persuasions, including President Yeltsin, who were nostalgic for at least some aspects of the former Soviet empire. But with the exception of the supernationalistic fringe, all the Russians with whom I have spoken seem to understand that the past can no longer be recreated. Russia's Defense Minister, General Pavel Grachev, has told me that he was adamantly opposed to any Russian military intervention in former Soviet republics. Others confirmed that the understaffed and poorly supplied Russian armed forces were not enthusiastic about a greater role outside their country's borders.

Similarly, both Yegor Gaidar, then the Russian First Deputy Prime Minister, and Oleg Lobov, Secretary of the Russian Federation Security Council, made a strong case to me that

Russia does not want to accept economic responsibility for other newly independent states. Russian monetary and economic policies during the past year have actually been pushing other former Soviet republics out of the ruble zone—hardly a policy one would undertake if planning to re-create the Soviet Union.

All this does not mean that the United States should not be concerned about heavy-handed Russian actions in the "near abroad." We should be realistic about our limited leverage in Russia's backyard and should avoid creating the impression that the United States wants to proceed with a new encirclement of Russia. It would be contrary to our interests to give Moscow the impression that we are prepared to help only as long as Russia remains on its knees. Russia is a great country that deserves to be treated with appropriate respect. U.S. leverage depends upon the perception in Moscow that America is a friendly nation that wishes it well and takes it seriously as a major power. At the same time, Moscow has to be told unequivocally that there is a line beyond which unscrupulous conduct in the "near abroad" will be incompatible with good relations with the United States. In this context, it should be explained in particular that Ukraine and the Baltic States occupy a special place in the American heart and—because of their location in the center of Europe—U.S. strategic thinking. The Russian government is entitled to be made aware that encroachments in that region would seriously damage U.S.-Russian relations.

It is not premature to indicate to Russia's leaders at the highest level, quietly, but with complete clarity, that Russia's conduct is coming dangerously close to the point at which no American administration would be able to ignore it. While appreciating Yeltsin's need not to surrender the patriotic high ground to reactionaries, we cannot allow his need to outmaneuver political opponents to become a permanent excuse for an aggressive foreign policy.

It is likely that Russia's leaders, even those who advocate a more nationalist policy, will be practical about the consequences of any steps that could be construed in the West as aggression against their neighbors. They will bear in mind the fragility of the political coalitions supporting aid to Russia in the West's recession-strapped capitals. They also will certainly not forget that the Cold War was waged not only against communism but on behalf of the people who were suffering under it inside and outside Russia, particularly in Ukraine, Latvia, Estonia, and Lithuania. Having seen these and other republics finally win their independence, Americans would not tolerate seeing them subjugated again.

Similar sensitivity must govern our policies toward the other post-Soviet states. Of these, the one requiring the most subtlety and finesse is Ukraine. The United States must become much more active in reducing tensions and rivalries between Ukraine and Russia, encouraging political and economic reforms in both, and always taking care to be perceived as neither anti-Russian nor anti-Ukrainian unless either adopts policies that threaten our interests.

Russia and Ukraine have a number of complex issues to settle, ranging from Ukraine's need for Russian energy supplies to the status of Crimea. What matters to the United States is not so much the particular outcome of their disputes as that they are settled amicably. Over time, our involvement in this relationship will be as important in ensuring regional peace as was our role in bringing about improved relations between Israel and the Arab states. Two diametrically opposite possibilities loom along the Russian-Ukrainian border. They could develop a flourishing partnership such as the one between the United States and Canada, or they could find themselves behaving like India and Pakistan, two superarmed scorpions trapped in a bottle. Ukraine's history of domination by Moscow would seem to make the unhappier prospect the more likely one. United States policy should be designed to ensure that both sides realize that the happier prospect is in their interests.

In implementing such a policy, we have a possible ally in Ukraine's President. Leonid Kravchuk is a former hard-line communist who has shown a remarkable knack for ending up on the winning side in Ukraine's internal political warfare. When I first met him in Kiev in 1991, before Ukraine had won its independence from Moscow, I asked him, over a gourmet dinner in the state guest house, whether he thought Gorbachev would win a popular election if one were held the next day in the Soviet Union. He answered quickly. *"Nyet."* Then I asked if he thought he himself would win an election if it were held the next day in Ukraine. This time he paused for a moment. After a shrug and a resigned smile, he again said *"Nyet."*

He was half right. Today, Gorbachev is a fixture on the international lecture circuit, while Kravchuk is the elected leader of an independent nation of fifty million people that is destined to be a major European power.

After she first met Gorbachev in 1985, Margaret Thatcher shook up some of her anticommunist supporters when she said, "I can do business with Mr. Gorbachev." I would say categorically that we can do business with Kravchuk if we recognize him for what he is—a cold, shrewd, tough-minded political operator who was always more a Ukrainian than a communist. (Holding on to power will take all of this resourceful survivor's remaining nine political lives.) Once the breadbasket of the Soviet Union, Ukraine is now one of Europe's worst basket cases. Its economy makes Russia's look like Singapore's. Its currency is virtually worthless. Industrial production has all but collapsed. It is torn by ethnic, religious, and political divisions. Unlike Russia, it has made hardly any progress toward free-market reforms.

As we cultivate better relations with Kiev, we should stress that economic reforms must go forward if the Western investment it so desperately needs is to materialize. Meanwhile the West should open its market to Ukraine and other nations of Eastern Europe and the former Soviet Union. When I saw him again in 1994, Kravchuk told me that his country had become an economic orphan. "The Russians cannot buy from us because they have no money," he said, "while the Europeans limit our imports with quotas." Economic revitalization is as much in our interests as in Ukraine's. If Russia were to revert to authoritarianism, a strong Ukraine would be a vital deterrent to aggression. A prescription for disaster in Europe would be a weak, vulnerable Ukraine joining forces with a newly imperialist Russia. Also, Ukraine is far more likely to follow through on its disarmament commitments if our relations with it remain strong. We should move forward on the full range of cooperative policies, including military-to-military contacts, economic assistance, and wide-ranging educational exchanges. Once Ukraine adopts real economic reforms, every assistance program open to Russia should be open to Ukraine.

Moscow may question our efforts to build up Ukraine. Its concerns will be understandable. We can ease them by finding ways to be pro-Ukraine that do not appear anti-Russian and by stressing that our policy is based on the manifestly correct view that our interests and those of Moscow and Kiev will benefit from both nations' being strong, open, and free.

While I have always been anticommunist, I have never been anti-Russian. As a friend of the Russian people, I understand that it is not easy for many Russians to accept that the country they considered their own no longer exists. I understand why they are concerned about the twenty-five million Russians who, when the Soviet Union collapsed, suddenly became foreigners in their own lands, where they are not always treated with kindness. I also understand why Russians do not wish indefinitely to supply energy and other raw materials at below-market prices to the other newly independent nations, who, after all, decided voluntarily to go their own way. Nostalgia is not a crime, as long as people do not act on it.

As a realist, I am aware that Russia is a big and powerful nation with armed forces stationed in many post-Soviet states.

Many of these states are in turmoil—turmoil that Moscow did not invent—and it is well within Moscow's national security interest to be concerned. I am also aware that when Yeltsin announced Russia's interest in performing a special peacekeeping mission in the "near abroad," he did not threaten to do it unilaterally, but instead asked for a U.N. mandate.

Advancing political and economic freedom in this tumultuous setting will not be easy. In fact, it may be impossible. But our vital interests require that we do everything we can to assist those who support these goals. James Billington, the Librarian of Congress, has graphically described the situation: "The failed coup in 1991 brought an unexpected simultaneous end to the largest empire—the Soviet Union; the most influential religion—communism; and the most powerful political machine—the Communist party of the Soviet Union." He added that what we are seeing is "not a traditional evolutionary or even revolutionary change, but convulsive physiological actions of a large disturbed society occurring in the entrails—the bowels more than in the brains—extending a new vulgarity, banality, and corruption, yet providing its young democratic reformers, who are reviled as 'shitocrats,' with the capability in which a new civil society is rapidly growing from the bottom up rather than from the top down." He accurately noted that the profoundly significant difference between this revolution and the Bolshevik Revolution is that, in contrast to 1917, it gives more power to the people rather than to an elite class—a "vanguard" at the top.

Yeltsin and his reformers face mind-boggling problems. Russia's $820 billion economy has shrunk over 10 percent for the third straight year. In 1993 inflation was at an annual rate of 900 percent, while decreases in oil production could transform a country with the world's eighth-largest oil reserves into a net energy importer by 1995. There is incredible corruption. A report prepared for Yeltsin last year showed that almost all private enterprises and commercial banks in major cities must pay a tribute of up to 20 percent to organized crime. And while the murder rate in Moscow is still lower than that in Washington, D.C., street crime is up 26 percent, and crimes committed with firearms are up 250 percent. The once-proud armed forces are in disarray, lacking housing, adequate pay, and a mission.

Many believe that Russia may be too huge and too complex to be ruled by a democratic government. We are not talking about Poland or Czechoslovakia, where shock therapy has worked remarkably well. Russia covers eleven time zones and includes thirty-one republics, all of which have declared their sovereignty and some their independence from Moscow. There are 132 different nationalities. After seventy-five years of communist brainwashing, compared with forty-five years in Eastern Europe, there is no Russian free-market managerial class.

Yeltsin and his newly elected Parliament must revitalize an agricultural system that lacks the infrastructure to bring food to the marketplace before it rots, salvage a Russian ruble that makes Monopoly money look strong by comparison, convert a huge military-industrial complex to civilian purposes without triggering massive unemployment that could lead to revolution, and find adequate housing for hundreds of thousands of Soviet soldiers returning from Eastern Europe and from the other former Soviet states. Their task is immense—perhaps the greatest peacetime enterprise ever undertaken by one people. It is the work not of a year or a decade but of a generation at least, and the United States must remain intricately involved in the process if Russia is to have any chance of succeeding.

It is not surprising that many observers believe Russia is beyond hope. But they overlook what Yeltsin has already achieved in his short time in power. Anxious to find the bumper-sticker message of the December parliamentary elections, too many commentators decided that it was "Reform is dead." The real message is far more subtle: Reform is different. In Moscow, too, there are many who are very proper in their embrace of classic free-market principles but go on to say naïvely that Yeltsin has failed because he has not applied them in Russia. In effect, the critics are asking Yeltsin not only to jump from *A* to *Z* in a matter of months but from *A* in Russian to *Z* in a language few people in Russia even know how to speak. A little tongue-biting is in order for leaders in the United States and other nations in the recession-ravaged West: We have plenty of trouble applying principles of free enterprise in our own countries. We do not have to deal with legislatures as fractious and fractured as the State Duma, nor with a nation that has no tradition whatsoever of economic freedom. And yet in every conversation I had in 1994 with Russian leaders, running the gamut from radical free-market reformers to doctrinaire communists, not one favored taking Russia back to a total command economy. Even the blustery, hard-nosed leader of the communists in the State Duma, Gennady Zyuganov, knows that the past is gone forever, much as he might wish it were otherwise. "No," he told me, "we cannot cross the same river twice."

One of the ablest leaders I met during my most recent visit was Russia's forty-year-old Minister of the Economy, Alexander Shokhin, whom I had first met in 1993 when he was a junior minister. He is a rare bird among economists: He is an optimist. During our ninety-minute meeting he expressed hope about declining inflation rates tempered with concern about falling production. He bristled when I asked whether the departure from the government of radical reformers such as Yegor Gaidar and Boris Fyodorov meant an end to real economic reform in Russia. "We can have [the West's favored] reformers in government and still have difficulty, while reforms can go forward without these people," he said. "Perhaps you now have a more pragmatic team," I offered. He smiled wearily. It was long past dinnertime, and he had come directly from a marathon meeting with the Prime Minister and others in the government who were trying to cut the budget enough to satisfy the International Monetary Fund's strict requirements. "The team spends so much time convincing others that they are for reform," he said, "that there is not much time for being pragmatic."

The government of Prime Minister Viktor Chernomyrdin is not pursuing reforms as quickly as its most vocal critics in the West would like, but its efforts are not totally stalled. Privatization is being stepped up, as are efforts to cut spending and boost revenue. Those now guiding the reforms are more aware of the limitations imposed by Russia's sprawling, nascent democracy. Purists may see a larger state role in electrical power, transportation, and other key industries than they would wish. But rather than criticizing the Russian reforms for their shortcomings, international supporters of the historic transition to freedom in Russia should praise the government for accomplishing as much as it has. Muscovites love to argue about politics. Everyone from Duma deputies to hotel clerks has an idea of the road that Russia *should* follow. So do Western diplomats and journalists, who supply endless advice based on their intimate grasp of undergraduate microeconomics and their kindergarten grasp of Russian politics. Finding the one road that Russia *will* follow will take tough, principled, pragmatic political leadership. That leadership will be distinctly Russian and will therefore not correspond to Western ideals. As a result, it will be more likely to succeed.

The best news from Moscow in the spring of 1994 is that no politician with any chance of attaining the Presidency wants to go back down the communist road. As Russians know better than almost anyone else in the world, the road to communism and a command economy is a dead end. After seventy-five years of godless communism, communism is dead in Russia. God is alive.

It is time to emphasize more of the other positives. All of Russia's troops will have left Eastern Europe by the end of 1994. Russia signed a historic arms-reduction treaty with the United States to vastly reduce its nuclear arsenal. Yeltsin has drastically slashed the military budget. He has held the freest elections in Russian history. Russia is a very rich country, not a nuclear-armed Bangladesh. It is rich in natural resources. As Bruce Lincoln has pointed out, Siberia has a sixth of the world's gold, a fifth of its platinum, a third of its iron, and a quarter of its timber. It is rich in human resources. Ninety percent of Russians are literate. Ninety-five percent of the workforce have the equivalent of a high school education. Russia has outstanding scientists and engineers. The first man in space was a Russian, not an American. Private enterprise is expanding far faster than anyone predicted, with over 30 percent of the Russian workforce now employed in the private sector. Over $1.6 billion in foreign capital has been invested in Russia since 1992.

The decline of the Russian economy began long before Yeltsin was elected President. The economy was terminally sick when Gorbachev came to power. He tried to treat a malignant growth with aspirin, beginning with political reforms rather than economic reforms—exactly the opposite of what the Chinese are doing and what the South Koreans, Taiwanese, and Chileans did.

The United States cannot afford to remain a bystander in the historic drama unfolding in the post-Soviet region. The great need is for a hardheaded evaluation of developments in the post-Soviet region and their relationship to crucial U.S. security and economic interests. The promotion of human rights and political freedom should be an important American objective. But the pursuit of freedom in the explosive Russian environment, with its unique traditions and circumstances, cannot be based on ideal Western notions that may have little to do with local circumstances.

We should not expect Russia to adopt American-style democracy. Serge Schmemann reported in *The New York Times* that the Russians are really looking for a third way—a blend of the Soviet welfare state with the prosperity of capitalism and some "dollops" of Christianity. "Communism was a grand failure, but it is hard to overstate how deeply it inserted itself into the hearts and minds of the nation," he wrote. "Russia is locked in a fateful race between the collapse of its inherited structure and the growth of new ones; between nostalgia for the enforced security of its past and the promise of freedom only vaguely understood."

Sergei Stankevich, a democratic member of the State Duma and a leading Russian political thinker, stresses that Russia was socially oriented long before communism and will therefore have a larger welfare system, closer to those of Germany and France, than the United States has. He pointed out that there are three models of capitalism—the American, the European, and the Asian. Each works because it conforms to its society's principles and values. Russia will have to select elements from all models to get a successful, fully developed free market.

The United States has a vital interest in Russia's becoming a democratic nation, and not just because Americans are freedom-loving people. Although the historical record does not always support the conventional wisdom that democracies never fight one another, a democratic system of checks and balances makes it more difficult to launch aggressive wars. American public opinion would be better prepared to support an enduring strategic relationship between the United States and Russia if Russia was seen as a nation committed to freedom and human rights.

In advocating democracy in Russia, we must be realistic and patient. If we demand that the Russians become instant Jeffersonian democrats, we may end up with people in power who are not democrats at all. Russia has to find its own path to freedom. "A shock-therapy-style economic reform at home and a foreign policy that responds to all of Washington's preferences abroad," Dimitri Simes has warned, "cannot in all probability be supported by a democratically elected Russian Parliament."

The impressive showing by Zhirinovsky's party, as well as by the communists and their allies in the Agrarian Party, suggests widespread disaffection with the policies of the current Russian government. Forty-three percent of those who voted in the December 1993 parliamentary elections selected these parties, while only about 15 percent supported Russia's Choice, the bloc most identified with radical economic reform. These results should not be overdramatized. For weeks after the Russian election last December, every bizarre utterance Zhirinovsky made was front-page news in the West, as though the 23 percent of the vote his party received represented a majority rather than a fringe. To put his showing in perspective, in 1968 in the United States, George Wallace received 14 percent of the presidential vote, and in 1992 Ross Perot received nearly 20 percent of the vote. And yet Wallace was never perceived to be anything more than a regional-protest candidate, and Perot's influence probably peaked in the election among Americans who refused to vote for Bill Clinton and yet wanted to vent their frustration about President Bush's handling of the economy.

Zhirinovsky's showing in Russia should be viewed in a similar context. Polls indicated that many voted for his party as a protest against Boris Yeltsin and the economy. To others, he represents Russia's lost empire, just as Wallace was to many southerners the pride of the Old South. When I saw him in 1994, he told me that his most effective issue has been his promise to crack down on the so-called Russian mafia. Zhirinovsky has even less chance to be elected President of Russia than Ross Perot has to be elected President of the United States. For us to rethink our entire Russia policy as a result of his party's limited success would be a major mistake. Centrist elements in Russian politics received a larger share of the vote in 1993 than Bill Clinton did in 1992. In view of the progress the Russian people have already made toward a free political system and a free economy, we should accentuate the positive rather than dwell obsessively on the negative in the unfolding Russian saga.

Still, the magnitude of the protest vote must be taken into account by Yeltsin if he is to succeed in governing democratically. And we should be sympathetic to his efforts to find the right balance between the requirements of economic reform and of politics. Confronted with fierce resistance from communist and nationalist reactionaries, the young and fragile Russian democracy must be able to defend itself. Temporary detours from perfect constitutional norms may be necessary, and some emergency limits on political expression may be inevitable. The United States supported some temporary restrictions on political activities in post-Nazi Germany. It is shortsighted and hypocritical when liberal American commentators go ballistic every time the Yeltsin government, under extreme circumstances, makes even minimal departures from Western-style democratic procedures.

The military only reluctantly supported Yeltsin against the now-defunct Parliament. They did not want to become involved in politics or to spill Russian blood. Yeltsin is keenly aware that their loyalty cannot be taken for granted. As a result, he has gone a long way to cultivate the military. He doubled officers' pay in September 1993, promised more money for military housing, and also began to pay greater tribute to "patriotic" values. If Yeltsin gets involved in a confrontation with the new Parliament, his reliance on the military may become too great for comfort. Then the generals could become arbiters of power in Russia and demand a considerable price for their support.

Instead of developing a long-term policy with specific goals, the United States and the West have reacted crisis by crisis. Almost half a year elapsed after Yeltsin launched his economic reforms before the West announced a major aid program, and most of that aid has yet to be delivered. Ignoring the problems in Russia may have been convenient because of short-term domestic political considerations, but it was disastrous for our long-term security interests. President Clinton has justifiably been criticized for his administration's snafus in Bosnia, Somalia, and Haiti. But he deserves credit from his critics as well as his supporters for recognizing the importance of the success of political and economic reform in Russia, for mobilizing Western support for economic aid, and for being the first major Western leader to speak up in support of Yeltsin during his conflict with the reactionary majority of the old Congress of People's Deputies.

Our aid should be targeted to Russia's emerging private business sector, not dying state-owned enterprises or government boondoggles. We should particularly channel more funds into loans to new small businesses, which will not only hire unemployed workers but also begin the essential accumulation of domestic capital. These principles too often have been honored only in the breach. Our efforts so far have been scattershot, uncoordinated, and ineffective. In 1994, not a single Russian leader had a positive word to say about the U.S. aid program. A recent Senate report said millions had been squandered. After World War II, the West created what became the Organization for Economic Development to oversee and coordinate the Marshall Plan. A similar organization should be created for Russia and the other former Soviet states. These mechanisms will assure the people of the West that their resources are not being wasted.

Aid from the United States and other Western governments has been supplemented by loans and grants from multilateral international organizations. Unfortunately, the International Monetary Fund has imposed draconian conditions on its loans. They are virtually impossible to meet. The approval in March 1994 of a $1.5 billion loan package was a classic example of too little, too late. Too often, IMF policies are based on normal conditions in a normal country. Russia's case must be considered on a separate basis because the penalties of economic failure there are infinitely higher than elsewhere. There has to be a unique Russian solution to the unique Russian problem. The IMF must act like an international lending organization, not an international loan shark. It must be more willing to loosen its conditionality to fit Russia's situation. If it does not do so, the United States should provide aid to Russia and other former Soviet states unilaterally rather than through international organizations, for which, as it is, we pick up over one third of the tab.

Encouraging Russia to implement economic reforms is one thing. Insisting on immediate adherence to the strict Western model is another matter altogether. Russia may have to pursue less ambitious but more realistic reforms to develop its economy over the long run. We should not ask the Russians to destroy their economy in order to save it. Throughout history they have shown an extraordinary capacity for suffering. But even Russians cannot bear their hardships much longer, as the ultranationalists' and communists' strong showing in the recent elections warns us.

The administration is undoubtedly concerned that slowing down Russian reforms will only prolong Russia's agony. But ultimately the Russians themselves will determine the success or failure of their economic changes. The West may have better economists, but the Russians are better experts on the political situation in their own country and the best judges of how far and how fast reform can proceed without triggering a social explosion. The administration and the West in general would be wise to resist the temptation to try to save the Russians in spite of themselves.

We should also judge Russian reforms by their substantive content rather than according to the political interests of the Western favorites within the Russian government. The new corps of young, Westernized economists, with their good English and well-tailored suits, are easier for U.S. officials and international bankers to relate to than the more traditional industrial managers from the Russian provinces. But our experience in both postwar Germany and Japan indicates that the members of the old structures at least know how to make the trains run on time. Left to their own devices, they would take the train of reform in the wrong direction. Yet without them the train can easily be derailed and in the process discredit both the reforms and their Western supporters.

Russia's economy is straining under the burden of loans recklessly made to Gorbachev's communist regime by Western banks, governments, and international organizations. The entire $84 billion debt should be rescheduled over a period of at least fifteen years, as Yeltsin has requested. Most important, Russia must not be forced to use aid to repay loans. Western banks that made the mistake of loaning billions to communist governments of the former Soviet Union should not be bailed out with Western aid to the democratic government of Russia. Without total debt rescheduling, no amount of aid will get Russia's economic development off the starting line.

Our allies in Europe and Japan should increase market access for Russian exports, as well as economic aid to Russia. This is particularly true for those allies who benefited from our aid after World War II. They can repay that debt by helping the Russians recover from the Cold War the same way that we helped them recover from World War II.

We should also put much more emphasis on developing broader cultural and educational exchange programs with Russia, as James Billington has strongly urged. Universities and colleges in the United States should expand exchange programs with sister institutions in Russia to facilitate the exchange of students, teachers, and ideas. More American and Russian businessmen, farmers, and members of other professions should visit each other's country so that Russian reformers can see firsthand how a free-market economy works. As President Clinton told me before I left for Moscow in March 1994, there should also be more exchanges and communication between Congress and the Russian Parliament.

Far more important than all the government foreign aid is the need to increase investments in Russia from the private sector in the West. China has the fastest-growing economy in the world today. Over half of its GNP is produced by the private sector. This has been accomplished primarily with private investment rather than government foreign aid. It would be the highest irony if, as a result of China's success and Russia's failure, a communist government could provide better investment opportunities for private enterprise than a democratic government.

Our primary goal should be to increase the American private sector's role in Russia's emerging private sector. All of the Western economies, including Japan's, are either in recession, going into recession, or, like the United States, just beginning to come out of recession. As a result, government aid programs are severely limited by budgetary constraints. Private-sector investments are limited only by opportunity. Archer Daniels Midland's Chairman Dwayne Andreas has estimated that if the Yeltsin government adopted all necessary market reforms, Western companies within five years would invest over $700 billion in Russia's private sector. This is in striking contrast to the $60 billion that is the highest estimate of aid that is likely to be provided by Western governments to Russia.

Another major advantage of private investment over government aid is that private enterprise brings the management expertise, training, and new technology needed for the transition from a communist to a free-market economy. More than anything else, Russia needs contact with the West's private sector. Communist bureaucrats cannot run a free-market economy. Nor can government bureaucrats from the West tell them how to run their economy. Bureaucrats have done enough damage to Western economies; in Russia, their advice could be fatal. American foreign service officers are among the best in the world on political issues. Like some politicians, however, many of them know very little about economics, and much of what they think they know is wrong.

If private investments are to be made in Russia, the Russian government must establish a legal framework to support a free-market economy. If a communist government in China can do this, a democratic government in Russia can do so too. It must guarantee the rights of ownership for private property, control the money supply to attract foreign investors, encourage privatization and private entrepreneurs, and decollectivize agriculture. The Russian government should curb subsidies to inefficient state enterprises, free prices on goods and services, build a stable market to eliminate black-market bartering, and develop reasonable tax policies to raise revenues while encouraging the private sector.

It will take time to achieve these goals. Seventy years of communist brainwashing in Russia cannot be eradicated in one year, or five, or even ten. But Yeltsin and his new Parliament must commit themselves irrevocably to those goals if they are to succeed in attracting the private investment from abroad they so desperately need.

President Clinton has some able political experts advising him on Russia. But as Hank Greenberg, chairman of the American International Group, has pointed out, what the President now needs is a topflight businessman reporting directly to him, with responsibility for coordinating private investment from the United States and government aid programs. He should enlist the brightest and the best from the American business community and induce them to go to Russia and the other former Soviet states to give advice and guidance to private businesses. The Peace Corps and the foreign service can play important roles. But Russia's greatest need is advice—not on politics or on government policy but on how to manage a private enterprise.

We should abandon the well-intentioned efforts to enlist economists and political scientists from the United States to instruct the Russians as to how to run a democracy and a free-market economy. We have enough trouble running our own economy to be qualified to tell others how to run theirs. Only experienced business leaders can fill the managerial void in the Russian private sector.

It was hard enough for a Republican administration in this era of giant government to stress private-sector solutions to an economy's problems. It will be even more difficult for a Democratic administration, many of whose members were reared on 1960s liberalism. The President's "New Democrats" have learned to talk a good line on free enterprise and public-private partnerships. It remains to be seen whether this is a matter of conviction or just of rhetoric. The fact remains that Western business can do vastly more than government to make Russia and the other post-Soviet republics prosperous and stable. In the era beyond peace, the smart politicians will let Western capital help build a new Russia and will put their speechwriters and pollsters to work figuring out how to make sure the politicians get the credit.

Because Russia has taken the lead in reform among the newly independent states, we must make Russia the focal point of Western aid in the short term. With the exception of the Baltics, none of the other former Soviet states has matched its commitment to tough economic reforms, and none can match its influence in the entire region. Until they adopt the reforms needed to transform their countries, aid to Russia should be the centerpiece of our policy.

In the long run, however, Russia's chances for success will increase as other former Soviet republics succeed. In light of their historic ties and economic interdependence, neither Russia nor the other former Soviet states can succeed on their own. Only by adopting a "one for all, all for one" approach to reform can these countries overcome the massive obstacles before them. Russia and the other newly independent states have a choice between a future of conflict or a future of progress. The United States and the West should help them make the right choice.

We should make clear to Russia and the other post-Soviet states that Western assistance will be fruitless if they engage in counterproductive economic warfare among themselves. Any amount of aid we could provide would be insignificant compared with the costs they will inflict on one another if they sever all their economic ties and try to go it alone.

In our relations with Russia, Ukraine, and the other newly independent states, we must keep one point foremost in mind. There is no time to lose. General MacArthur once said that the history of failure in war could be summarized in two words: "Too late." The same two words summarize the history of failure to win the peace after victory in war. In the wake of the collapse of communism, the United States and the West have failed to seize the moment.

As I write these words on March 30, 1994, the overwhelming conventional wisdom in the U.S. foreign policy establishment is that the prospects for the survival and success of economic reforms in Russia are bleak. The reformers are assumed by all the so-called experts to be in retreat after their election losses. Anti-reformers—most of them ex-communist bureaucrats—are ominously gaining strength. It is tempting, in view of the political and economic disarray, to throw in the towel. But this is the time for the West to become a more active participant in Russia's success, not a passive observer of its failure.

We should not be surprised by the difficulty Yeltsin and his colleagues are experiencing. This is an unprecedented transition—the transformation of the world's strongest dictatorship into a democracy and the world's largest command economy into a free market. All of the Western nations, including the United States, know that the development and management of a free-market economy take time and ingenuity; building one from scratch is an almost insurmountable task. It cannot be done overnight or without help. I am convinced that the Russian people will not turn back to communism. But if they have no choice, they will turn to some kind of political dictatorship, which will at least promise the safety-net guarantees that were supposed to have been delivered by the communist regime.

Before writing off the Russians, we should recognize that they are a great people. It was the Russians who defeated Napoleon, and as President Eisenhower once told me, it was the Russians who, after incredible suffering and sacrifice, played the indispensable and primary role in defeating Hitler. Their powers of resilience are legendary, and are usually underestimated by those in the West who have not experienced such ordeals. We should also recognize that in addition to Yeltsin there are a number of other extremely capable pro-reform leaders. They have lost an election, but they can come back, and they deserve our support as they try to do so.

The gamble for political and economic freedom in Russia is being played for enormously high stakes and against great odds. The reformers may fail, but let it not be said that they failed because we did not provide for them, our allies in defeating communism in the Cold War, as generously as we did to help our enemies, Germany and Japan, recover from World War II. The situation is desperately precarious. The reformers can still prevail, but we must do more to help them pull off the greatest transition from tyranny to freedom in history. We must help them beat the odds.

For seventy-five years, the Soviet Union tried to export the ideas of communism to the rest of the world, using propaganda, subversion, and naked aggression. Now democratic Russia can offer the rest of the world an example of a great people enjoying economic and political freedom. The profound unanswered question will be whether democratic capitalism in Russia can compete with communist capitalism in China. If it fails to do so, and if Russia turns to reactionary leaders, the hard-line leaders in China and other dictators in the world will be heartened. If it succeeds, political and economic freedom will be the wave of the future in the twenty-first century.

America and Europe:
New Missions for Old Friends

For half a century, Europe dominated United States foreign policy. During World War II, we helped save it from Nazi Germany. During the Cold War, defending it against Soviet aggression was the primary mission of our armed forces. Yet today it has receded to the back pages of American newspapers, is seldom the lead story on television news programs, and receives little attention from the foreign policy establishment. Even the agony in the former Yugoslavia is covered as though it were an obscure disaster in a faraway place where we have only a humanitarian interest.

Yet Europe is just as important to the United States as ever. We cannot afford to neglect a region with 345 million people and a GNP of $7 trillion, compared with the United States' $6.2 trillion. Its political stability, its economic health, our access to its markets, and the character of its relations with the rest of the world are all vital American interests. Cooperation between Europe and America is indispensable if we are to preserve peace and promote economic progress for ourselves and the rest of the world. Disunity would cause us to risk squandering all the gains we fought for together in war and peace.

America's new isolationists—the "bring the boys home" crowd—take the view that the only thing that held the West together was fear of the Soviet Union. With the overwhelming Soviet threat gone, they argue, the very idea of "the West" has no meaning as a unifying factor; instead we are now told that the overwhelming danger we face is that the French will flood our markets with subsidized Bordeaux and drive producers of California Chardonnay into bankruptcy.

The isolationist view ignores the huge economic stake we have in a stable, secure Europe. It ignores the implicit commitment we have made to participate indefinitely in Europe's security arrangements, for the sake not only of deterring aggression but also of preserving our common heritage. And it ignores the progress we have made, since the heyday of the isolationists between the world wars, in stitching the United States into the fabric of transatlantic political and economic life. The major argument of the isolationists between World War I and World War II was that the United States should not risk being drawn into Europe's wars. Our active membership in NATO today is the best way we can reduce the danger of war in Europe and also play a powerful role in preserving peace in other parts of the world.

The new spirit of political correctness notwithstanding, Europe and the United States belong to the same civilization. Our traditions and values are uniquely close. This does not make European countries better than others or more deserving of American support when our views collide. But it does mean that when great issues are at stake, even the most adamantly independent European leaders will back the United States, as Charles de Gaulle did during the Cuban missile crisis. This almost hereditary sense of unity is a valuable resource that no American President should neglect.

It is particularly important that the unique relationship between the United States and Great Britain be sustained. The ties of common heritage and language are the most obvious, but ultimately they may not be the most enduring. Nor are the ties based on the memory of Americans fighting and dying in both world wars to protect British soil, or American and British soldiers fighting side by side in the Persian Gulf. In the era beyond peace, the more significant link may well be the two societies' virtually simultaneous experiments with bloated government. In the first generation after World War II, both nations built massive welfare states. During the late 1970s and 1980s, both turned to more conservative, pro–free enterprise policies and experienced astonishing economic growth as a result. During the 1990s, the political fortunes of conservative leaders have faded as a result of the worldwide economic downturn. If England and the United States make the right choices in the months and years ahead and pick leaders who stress individual and private enterprise rather than government interference, it will be because they learned not only from their own experiences but from each other's.

America's new isolationists draw much of their strength from a proposition that is especially attractive during economic hard times: that we could use what we are spending to keep our forces in Europe to solve our urgent domestic problems. The Europeans have reason to worry that Americans are becoming too inward-looking. But at the same time, the Europeans themselves have become more inward-looking since the end of the Cold War. Their problems at home are as pervasive and distracting as ours.

For forty-five years, Europeans dreamed of a time when the ugly wall that divided Europe would be torn down and when, relieved of the threat of war from the East, they could turn their attention homeward. In retrospect, the Cold War was the longest period of peace and economic progress Europe has ever enjoyed. Now Europeans have found that the peace of war has been replaced by the wars of peace. Bitter, long-suppressed ethnic hatreds have exploded in the Balkans. The journey toward a new Europe with a new, common economic and foreign policy has been derailed.

The hopes for European economic unity have been dimmed in part because of the absence of history's greatest unifying force—a common enemy. World War II and the Cold War produced strong popular leaders such as Churchill, de Gaulle,

Adenauer, and De Gasperi. Europe's peacetime leaders, able men plagued by nagging domestic problems, find that their popularity is lower than that of Boris Yeltsin, whose economic and political problems are infinitely greater than theirs. A deep recession, during which unemployment has increased to over 10 percent, has created a new wave of pessimism, with the ghosts of racism and protectionism haunting the continent.

The elation over the liberation of one hundred million people in Eastern Europe in 1989 from communist repression has turned to disillusionment as Europe's leaders tally up the cost of repairing the damage of a brutal communist economic system that promised progress and produced poverty.

At the beginning of the Cold War, Europe faced the twin threats of the military aggression by Stalin's armies and the ideological appeal of communist propaganda in Europe's war-devastated economies. The United States played a decisive role in meeting those threats. We joined our allies in deterring the military threat through NATO and the ideological threat through the Marshall Plan. With the end of the Cold War, communism has been discredited and Russia is a friend, not an enemy. But we are finding that the challenges beyond peace are greater than those we faced during the Cold War.

Logically, the Atlantic alliance, created to deter the Soviet threat, could have been expected to disappear once the threat was gone. Yet there are no serious discussions about dissolving NATO. Uncertainties in Central and Eastern Europe, war in the Balkans, and instability in Russia make NATO's existence a source of comfort in Western Europe.

Key elements of a potential Russian threat are still present—large conventional forces, strategic nuclear capability, and a tradition of using force. While no one now feels threatened by the democratic government of Russia, the situation there is still unpredictable. We need NATO as insurance against a renewed threat from the East in the event that extreme Russian nationalists come to power.

The large-scale dispersal of arms to eager buyers in the Middle East, the Persian Gulf, and elsewhere creates a time bomb with direct implications for Europe and America. Europeans are deeply concerned about refugees from Eastern Europe and economic migration from North Africa. Both have triggered xenophobic reactions in Europe. Violence in the Balkans is a threat to Western interests.

Advocates of a Europe free of U.S. forces have argued that organizations such as the Western European Union and the Conference on Security and Cooperation should replace NATO as a security arrangement in Europe, and that NATO should be buried alongside other relics of the Cold War. Events have totally discredited this concept. Belgian Foreign Minister Mark Eyshen had it right during the Persian Gulf War: "The European Community was an economic giant, a political dwarf, and a military worm." America took the lead then, and individual European countries, notably Britain and France, responded by committing their armed forces. But traditional rivalries, parochial interests, and the collective indecisiveness of the major European powers have frustrated an effective response to the violent and tragic breakup of the the former Yugoslavia. Europe can unite behind a common purpose only if the United States continues to play a leading role.

The key is an expanded NATO rather than a weakened one, with a strong U.S. presence and a new mission. For the United States, NATO is our principal institutional link to Europe, and one we must not break.

Secretary General Manfred Worner has observed that more than any other international institution, NATO has already changed significantly to meet new challenges. It has a new strategy and force posture, it has started to strengthen its European pillar, and it has established relations with its former adversaries through the North Atlantic Cooperation Council. Its member nations have started to participate in crisis management well beyond NATO borders. We are indeed witnessing the birth of a new NATO, but the birth pains are excruciating. The NATO summit in Brussels in early 1994 demonstrated that the Europeans want American leadership, but it also showed that there is no clarity on either side of the Atlantic about the strategic role of post–Cold War NATO. The alliance is still deeply uncertain about what threatens Europe, about the Europeans' wider interests, and about how to organize itself for the future. These paramount issues must be addressed before the alliance can undertake highly ambitious new initiatives outside its traditional area.

The alliance's response to the resurgence of the nationalisms that repeatedly bloodied Europe over the past century has been dangerously inadequate. The Soviet nuclear legacy and associated risks of proliferation have yet to be brought under effective control. Conflicts among the new states of the old USSR—some with nuclear weapons—are possible. A call for the rapid use of NATO forces could prove a political and logistical nightmare. Diplomacy, U.N. resolutions, and economic sanctions would simply give a rogue state the time it needed to succeed in the deployment of a credible threat.

The Conference on Security and Cooperation in Europe agreed that the frontiers of Eastern Europe and the successor states of the USSR should be changed only by peaceful means. During the Cold War this well-intentioned provision had about as much credibility as a U.N. General Assembly resolution condemning aggression. Today, an opportunity exists to replace that unenforceable agreement with something more solid. The NATO allies, including the United States, are reluctant to offer security guarantees that they would have difficulty honoring, however, so nothing has come of the good intentions.

None of these strategic challenges will be met unless the French and the Americans can overcome thirty years of proud and sometimes bitter rivalry over primacy in Europe. The "French question" involves the deeper issue of whether France can achieve its current goal of security and independence through closer European union while at the same time the United States is retained as a full participant in guaranteeing European and international security. This will require political imagination and leadership in Washington as well as in Paris. The bureaucracies in Foggy Bottom and the Quay d'Orsay, deeply suspicious of each other, will have to be firmly guided to new attitudes and a new strategy.

All Europeans, including the French, understand that neither conflicts to the east nor instabilities in the south can be addressed by the alliance unless the United States is an active member. Europe fears the United States may drift away. It is troubled by the Clinton administration's decision to give much greater weight to Asia as the most likely source of growth in the international economy in the coming years. Over half the growth in the world economy between 1990 and 2000 will occur in Asia and only about one sixth in Europe, but to pull the rug out from under NATO for this reason, or allow it to be pulled out, would be a strategic blunder of historic proportions.

Great Britain's Lord Ismay, NATO's first Secretary General, reportedly said that NATO had been created to keep the Russians out, the Americans in, and the Germans down. But NATO turned out to be precisely the vehicle by which Germany rose—because others needed a German role in the defense of Europe as much as the Germans needed their support. The immense American NATO military deployment in turn permitted Germany to return to power without threatening other states. For the first time in its history, Germany had a powerful and positive role in a global alliance system.

We must strengthen the U.S.-German partnership. Today the top three economic powers—the United States, Japan, and Germany—account for over 40 percent of the world's GNP. Once Germany overcomes the economic problems caused by reunification, it should be ready to use its massive economic muscle in Eastern Europe and in the former Soviet Union to serve the interests of the West as a whole. To quell fears of German power, we should make sure that Berlin enters the game as an integral member of the Western team, not a passive player kept on the sidelines.

With U.S. political leadership, NATO should agree quickly on a new strategic agenda. We should support the democratic government in Russia economically and politically. We should support economic development in the other former Soviet states and in the nations of Eastern Europe. We should create better controls on the transfer of lethal technology, develop defensive systems against theater ballistic missiles, and draft contingency plans for nonnuclear surgical excision of potential nuclear threats.

We should cooperate in addressing urgent international problems that were overshadowed by the Cold War. Common global and regional problems that transcend national boundaries, and outstrip national capabilities, now occupy center stage. One example is the explosion of international refugees, from 2.5 million in 1970 to 19.7 million today, not counting the 24 million who have been forced from their homes in their own countries.

So far, foot-dragging on the new international challenges is the rule. As has been the case in the Bosnia tragedy, multilateralism has often functioned as an escape hatch from individual responsibility.

NATO needs a much smaller conventional and nuclear force than we had in the Cold War, but it must be enough to deter any aggressor and reassure European countries that it can handle any challenge. This requires a minimum of one corps of U.S. ground troops to demonstrate our commitment to the stability of the continent. The level of U.S. military forces in Europe is likely to be less than a third of the former 325,000, and they will be configured for rapid deployment to areas well outside

NATO boundaries—even well outside Europe. There should be no further cuts in our NATO forces below this level. Our commitment to Europe must be based on solid military capabilities, not empty political rhetoric.

NATO should also take full advantage of the military-technical revolution by deploying global, space-based command; high-tech control and communications; stealth technology; rapid mobility; and precision-guided munitions. It must not weaken or dismantle its existing infrastructure, command and communications capabilities, and other assets. They are indispensable for operations outside of the European theater. It should attempt to coordinate changes in members' force structures so that our remaining forces are complementary and so that they can operate as a unified rapid-response force. This would not only lead to greater cooperation but also enable our forces to respond to crises more effectively.

Historically, American leadership within the Atlantic alliance was as important for transatlantic cohesion as was the Soviet threat. In the future, American leadership will continue to be important, but its form and style will be completely different. In the past, the American role in NATO was more dominant than it is now or will be in the future. During the Cold War we built up positions of strength against the central threat and reacted to outbreaks on the periphery. Our allies—those to whom we provided security against the Soviet threat—had to go along with us. That will not work now. Neither will isolation. What will work today is a new strategy of patient, long-term confidence-building, supported by regional coalitions such as NATO.

It is clearly in the U.S. interest to support the emergence of a real European pillar in the alliance in the form of the Western European Union. The United States should accept European influence over—though not a veto of—the use of U.S. forces based in Europe, including deployments from Europe to other regions. We should also be ready to support European initiatives when shared interests are at stake. At the same time, we should not block European action if we do not believe our interests are at risk.

American leadership is indispensable. No other nation has our power or strategic position. Above all, we have the ability to rally others to a good cause—the most eloquent proof of leadership. As the past two years and three acute crises have shown—the Persian Gulf War, Yugoslavia, and Somalia—things happen only when America leads, and things don't happen when America fails to lead. We must use this power and prestige to head off future crises and to build regional security structures for the long haul.

In his speech before a joint session of Congress after he was dismissed from his command in Korea by President Truman, General MacArthur profoundly moved his audience when he concluded with these words: "Old soldiers never die. They just fade away." Although NATO will not die, its central role in world events will fade away unless it rethinks its mission, strategy, and tactics from the bottom up. Conceived to counter a threat from across the Elbe River, in its post–Cold War maturity NATO must ring the world. "NATO must go out of area," Senator Richard Lugar has warned, "or out of business." Those who yearn for an international body to serve as a framework for key elements of American strategic planning need look no further than NATO, whose credibility, dependability, and formidability far outstrip the United Nations'. No nation acting alone, the United States included, has the resources or even the credibility to act as the world's policeman. Acting together, with the prestige that comes from being history's most successful peacetime alliance, the NATO nations can be a force for stability and security without peer in the world.

In adopting such a global mission, each NATO member must recognize that in the absence of the Soviet threat it must be more internationalist, not less. The Persian Gulf is a prime example of a region where the NATO nations have a common interest. Except for Britain, Europe is far more dependent on

Gulf oil than is the United States. Threats loom on other fronts as well. To Europe's south, the African population is estimated to triple by 2020, which will further strain the continent's tenuous stability. The Middle East, the Persian Gulf, Central Asia, and the Indian subcontinent all have volatile mixes of poverty, explosive demographics, and political instability. Incomes in Western Europe are forty times what they are to the south. The regions on Europe's periphery also contain all the major nuclear proliferators, except North Korea and South Asia.

None of these new threats is easy to define. Nor are they susceptible to the deterrence strategies NATO pursued during the Cold War. Deterring aggression by old Bolsheviks was one thing; Saddam Hussein in Iraq, radical fundamentalists in Iran, or passionate ethnic warlords in the Caucasus pose new threats requiring new thinking, especially when such rogue forces are armed with nuclear weapons. These threats may not be deterrable, but U.S.-European cooperation in nonproliferation, antimissile defense, and contingency plans for conventional preemption should be at the top of the agenda for both Europeans and Americans.

In out-of-area operations, NATO should capitalize on the vast experience and expertise of its major European members. France has an unparalleled understanding of how to operate in Africa, where it played a critical role in managing regional conflicts and blunting the thrusts of Soviet clients. Cuban forces in Angola would have conquered mineral-rich areas of Zaire, and Libya would have created a significant new sphere of influence, had it not been for French intervention. If ethnic and tribal conflicts spread across Africa in the future, only France will have the political instruments and skill to try to control the violence.

Britain also has capabilities and expertise that NATO would be foolish not to employ in out-of-area problems. Though smaller than during its imperial era, Britain's armed forces still have a significant global reach. Its counterterrorist forces are the best in the world and a key asset for the new kinds of challenges the West will face. As we seek to stabilize the Persian Gulf region, Britain's intimate knowledge of the intricacies of its politics will be vitally important.

It would be politically impossible in many circumstances for the United States to act unilaterally. In the Persian Gulf War, the fact that not only the United States but also Britain and France were sending major combat forces to Saudi Arabia was essential to building the worldwide coalition that defeated Iraq's war machine. The forces of our allies were important militarily. They were indispensable politically.

The capabilities of the United States, France, Britain, Italy, and other European allies are complementary. The United States has unique capabilities in intelligence, space communications, logistics, and high technology that can tremendously enhance the abilities of its allies to project military power and political influence to deal with out-of-area issues. But the United States alone would be significantly limited if it could not use forward bases in Europe or bases controlled by our European allies outside of Europe. NATO's capabilities as an alliance can be vastly greater than the sum of its parts.

With the collapse of communism in the Soviet Union, Eastern Europe has become an orphan—no longer supported by Russia to the east and not yet accepted by the West. President Lech Walesa expressed his disillusionment in highly emotional terms when I met with him in Warsaw in February 1993. "Poland gave the West a great gift—military and political victory in the Cold War," he said. "The West will not take this gift, and you can't force anyone to take a present they don't want."

The idea among some foreign policy observers that Eastern Europe should serve as a buffer between East and West has no support whatever among the leaders of either Eastern or Western Europe. When I mentioned the concept to President François Mitterrand last year, he was incredulous. "Where did such an odd idea come from?" he said. "Eastern Europe has always been part of Europe, except for the period Europe was divided by the Cold War."

We should unequivocally and actively support the goal of full integration of the new democracies in Poland, the Czech Republic, Slovakia, and Hungary into NATO. Concern that their joining NATO would be perceived as anti-Russia are unfounded. As President Václav Havel has observed, "Democratic forces in Russia understand that NATO is not Russia's enemy but its partner. The expansion of NATO would not be a hostile move but would bring closer to Russia a region of democracy and prosperity."

The success of the Russian reactionaries in the December 12 elections may be a blessing in disguise, to the extent that they advance the prospects of the Central European nations for full NATO membership. The United States can reasonably tell the Russian leadership that placing Poland, the Czech Republic, Slovakia, and Hungary in a category separate from that of Soviet successor states, should be interpreted not as a hostile gesture but as a minimal precaution in the event that neoimperialists come to power in Moscow.

The United States and our NATO allies are faced with two major security challenges in Europe. The first is to maintain the close strategic partnership between the United States and Europe; the second is to prevent the resurgence of Russian imperialism. The Partnership for Peace adopted at the NATO summit in January 1994 addresses the second of these challenges. Its formula for a gradual enhancement of ties between NATO and Russia is satisfactory; less so is the formula for security ties between NATO and the other Warsaw Pact countries. Its advocates' excessive sensitivity about provoking nationalist elements in Russia caused them to neglect the legitimate security concerns of the former Warsaw Pact nations.

Unfortunately, the Partnership for Peace does not adequately address the first challenge—the need to maintain strong security links between the United States and Europe. NATO, the principal strand connecting the two sides of the Atlantic, is in search of a new mission. There is a serious danger that proceeding at full speed with the Partnership for Peace with Russia before determining NATO's new character may irreparably damage the cohesion of the alliance. Like arms control in the 1970s, which was intended to serve national security interests but eventually became almost an end in itself, the Partnership for Peace has the potential to become NATO's principal preoccupation for years to come. This process could well make NATO too amorphous to be effective in addressing the numerous challenges of the post–Cold War world.

It would be fundamentally unsound to put everyone and everything from the Atlantic to the Pacific—countries with completely different histories, traditions, levels of economic development, commitments to democracy, and security requirements—under the Partnership for Peace umbrella. One United Nations is enough.

Central European nations that were an integral part of Western civilization for centuries, whose occupation by Adolf Hitler led to World War II, whose brutal subjugation by Stalin triggered the Cold War, and that in 1989 were the first nations to overthrow their communist governments are entitled to expect treatment different from that given to Soviet successor states. These proud nations should not now be consigned to a diplomatic "halfway house" and compelled to prove they are worthy to be accepted as members of the European alliance, whose values they share.

Told by administration officials that the Partnership for Peace is the only game in town, the Central Europeans have decided to join. Their reluctant acceptance, however, should not blind us to the need to find a formula that would make those nations feel both secure and proud to be a part of the New Europe.

Full NATO membership for these countries should be announced as a definite goal. The timetable for full membership should depend on a number of factors, including the nature of the threat from Russia and the utility of NATO security guarantees in facing that threat. The West has to find the appropriate balance between taking reasonable precautions against the return of Russian imperialism and making that return a self-fulfilling prophecy as a result of hasty, provocative actions while relatively democratic and nonaggressive forces are still in control in Moscow.

Moscow will inevitably and understandably complain about any arrangements that move NATO closer to its borders, especially if they include measures to make it easier for Central European nations to join. Some Russians may resent any suggestion that NATO retains even a small element of its founding mission as an anti-Moscow alliance. Such concerns deserve to be addressed and should not be permitted to disrupt our relations with Moscow or our commitment to its former satellites. The Russian government should be assured that no nonindigenous forces will be stationed in any Central European nation unless it faces the threat of aggression. It should also be offered the same security benefits NATO's new members will receive under the Partnership for Peace plan.

The administration should develop a formula that would protect NATO's cohesion, be fair to Poland, Hungary, the Czech Republic, and Slovakia, and address Russia's legitimate security concerns. It would recognize that the first priority must be the establishment of NATO's new role. Only after that is done can the decision be made on full implementation of the Partnership for Peace, which entails so much potential for changing the very nature of the alliance. Such a formula should accept that Poland, the Czech Republic, Slovakia, and Hungary are in a special category and are entitled to full-scale NATO membership, but it should simultaneously make it clear that their inclusion in NATO will take place in the context of the evolving European economic and security environment. NATO should also make certain that every nation, including Russia, understands that the pace of Central Europe's integration into NATO may be accelerated if the Russian threat once again becomes a reality. This understanding would encourage more responsible conduct on Moscow's part.

Those who oppose admission to NATO of the nations of Eastern Europe for fear of Russian nationalism are indulging in excesses of caution that threaten to increase rather than lessen instability in Europe. During the Cold War, critics of the U.S. policy of containment frequently asserted that we had to prove to Soviet leaders that we were for peace. The Soviet leaders knew we were for peace then, just as most Russians know we are for peace today. NATO was never a threat to an aggressive Soviet Union during the Cold War. It is ludicrous to suggest that an expanded NATO that includes democratic Central European nations would be a threat to a peaceful democratic Russia. Zbigniew Brzezinski is forceful on the point. "That the expansion of the zone of democratic Europe's security would bring the West closer to Russia is no cause for an apology," he wrote. "It is with a stable and secure Europe that an eventually truly democratic Russia should wish to link itself."

Regardless of what NATO does, Russian demagogues will exploit for political gain the Russian people's economic distress and frustration over the loss of the Soviet empire. Our policy should be aimed not at the margins of Russian political life but at the mainstream, and the Russian mainstream knows that NATO, whether supplemented by the nations of Eastern Europe or not, represents no threat to Russia. "No reasonable observer," as Henry Kissinger has written, "can imagine that Poland, the Czech Republic, Hungary, or Slovakia could ever mount a military threat against Russia either singly or in combination." Still, careful steps must be taken to ensure that efforts to strengthen and expand NATO are not misconstrued by some Russian leaders as threats to their nation's security. We can increase Russia's comfort level by consulting closely with its military every step of the way, and also by stressing to the Kremlin leaders that the principal reason for expanding NATO is to improve conditions for the development of democracy and free enterprise in Russia, which does not want instability along its borders any more than we do.

It is also essential that the United States continue to play a leadership role in NATO, since an alliance led by the United States is bound to be far less alarming to the Russians than one in which Germany played a more decisive role.

Some who argue against admission to NATO of the nations of Eastern Europe do so not because they fear such a move would further provoke nationalism in Russia but because they believe these nations do not yet come up to our standards politically or economically. This attitude, although typical of some analysts' perfectionist approach to foreign policy, is dangerously flawed. There should be no question about the sincerity of the leaders of nations such as Hungary, Poland, Slovakia, and the Czech Republic when they say that they want to transform their countries into free-market democracies. They suffered too long under statist tyranny to return to it voluntarily. Once they are brought under the protection of NATO's umbrella, and thereby freed of the necessity of providing entirely for their own security, their economies and democracies will develop much more quickly—just as those in West Germany and Japan did when the United States and its allies assumed responsibility for their security after World War II.

Soviet successor nations are in a different category. The administration should be supported in its policy of offering Russia, Ukraine, and other newly independent states a variety of forms of security cooperation, ranging from joint maneuvers to access to NATO military schools. But there is no need to connect this cooperation to NATO membership, any more than there was in the case of American-Japanese security arrangements.

The last thing the United States should do is to allow the Partnership for Peace to create the impression in Tokyo, or for that matter in Beijing, of a U.S.-Russian condominium. Russia is too big and too important a power to be added to the NATO alliance without a fundamental reassessment of security in Japan, China, and other nations as well. This is obviously not what the architects of the Partnership for Peace have in mind. But statesmanship is about anticipating the unintentional consequences of well-intended actions.

Eastern European nations should also be integrated into the European Economic Community. As British Prime Minister John Major has observed, "If we fail to bring the democratic nations of Eastern and Central Europe into our community, we risk re-creating divisions between the haves and the have-nots." A new economic wall would divide Europe between the rich and the poor.

The West Germans have learned that the cost of bringing East Germany up to the economic standards of West Germany is incredibly high. The cost of bringing the rest of Eastern Europe up to the standards of Western Europe will be even higher. Arnaud de Borchgrave reports that the European Reconstruction and Development Bank has estimated that it will take thirty-five years for Eastern European incomes to reach a level one half that of Western incomes. It will be a long, expensive trip, but the price we would pay for not lending a hand would be infinitely higher.

Free trade is essential for the long-term growth of the nations of Eastern Europe. Senator Sam Nunn stressed the essential point: "Today's Iron Curtain of Western European trade barriers is a greater threat to Eastern Europe's democratic and free-market reforms than a distant, weak, and demoralized Russian army." The United States and our European allies must knock down our trade barriers and provide these countries with access to our markets. During the Cold War, Eastern European trade was almost exclusively with the Soviet Union. That market has drastically declined. Trade with Western Europe should take up the slack. But only 1.4 percent of Western European trade in 1992 was with Eastern Europe. To give Eastern Europe a chance to stand on its own feet, the United States and our European allies should not just prop up the region with the financial crutch of aid but should open our markets to Eastern European nations so that they can eventually walk on their own.

Eastern Europe needs the antidote of Western investment to overcome the poisonous effects of forty-eight years of communism. There have already been some major success stories. Czechoslovakia had the highest per capita income in Europe before World War II. After the bloody Prague Spring of 1968, it had the most repressive communist government in Eastern Europe. Its free-market economic policies since 1989 have attracted such American companies as Westinghouse and General Electric. Czech exports to Western Europe and the United States rose 20 percent last year. With this year's estimated growth rate at 6 percent, the Czech Republic's GNP will have increased by 60 percent from 1991 to 1994.

Poland also has recovered remarkably well. It has liberalized prices, opened its borders to free trade, privatized state-run industry, cut deficit spending, and encouraged entrepreneurship. Unfortunately, the pain caused by free-market policies created a backlash that led to the victory of former communist forces in parliamentary elections. Poland has gone too far with its free-market reforms to turn back, but if the West does not continue to provide aid and to open up its markets, Poland, the Czech Republic, Slovakia, and other Eastern European countries may turn away from the path to political and economic freedom.

History has left a tragic legacy of conflict on the European continent. The scars of centuries of war mark the entire region. The Cold War at least established a cold peace in Europe. Our challenge is to see that the end of the Cold War does not open the door for future hot wars that would inevitably draw not only Eastern Europe but also Western Europe into their flame.

U.S. foreign policy in the past has often been criticized for tilting too much toward Europe at the expense of Asia. Today it is not surprising that the administration tilts toward Asia, in view of the fact that, except for a temporary slowdown in Japan, Asian nations have by far the highest economic growth rates in the world. But we must not allow our fascination with Asia to blind us to the enormous potential economic power of Europe.

Our goal should be a rich united Europe competing equally with a rich America and an Asia rapidly becoming rich. This will serve us all. Economic competition is not a zero-sum game. No rich nation gains in the long run because its competitors are poor. Now that we have succeeded in tearing down the ugly wall that divided free Europe from communist Europe, our goal beyond peace should be a united Europe in a world that is not divided into blocs by economic walls. We seek a world in which economic progress for one serves all.

Our occasional differences with our friends in Europe must never obscure our timeless common interests. We have been allies in war and should remain allies in peace. We are all democracies committed to respect for human rights. Some dabbled in socialism, but we are all now committed to free-market economic policies. Despite our current disputes over details, we are all trading nations committed to the principles of free trade.

We share an uncommon cultural heritage. Sixty years ago, Arnold Toynbee, in his *Study of History,* perceptively predicted Europe's future: "Tomorrow we Europeans must look forward to seeing our little European world encircled by a dozen giants of the American calibre," he wrote. "Whatever the process may have been, they have all been brought to life by being brought within the ambit of that Western civilization of which Europe has been the fountainhead."

Many Americans and Europeans will remember President Kennedy's eloquent declaration in Berlin in 1961: "I am a Berliner." Americans, with our rich multiracial and multiethnic background, would not now say, "We are Europeans." But there is no question that, in view of our history, our closest cultural ties are with Europeans. In seeking new friends in Asia, we should not forget our old friends in Europe.

Asia and the
New American Century

In 1905, a twenty-five-year-old army first lieutenant named Douglas MacArthur embarked with his parents on a nine-month tour of Asia. Reflecting sixty years later upon the wonders he had seen, MacArthur wrote in his memoirs, "It was crystal clear to me that the future and, indeed, the very existence of America, were irrevocably entwined with Asia and its island outposts."

Today, almost a century after he first visited Japan, China, Singapore, and five other Asian nations, MacArthur would be amazed at how slow his fellow Americans have been to grasp that the United States is destined to be a major Asian-Pacific power—not only in war, where MacArthur himself led so magnificently, but in peace. Some have said that if the twentieth century was the American century, the twenty-first will be the Asian century. The twenty-first can be a second American century—but only if we understand that we must be as intimately involved politically, economically, diplomatically, and culturally in the Asian-Pacific region as we have been in Europe.

The United States has repeatedly been the dominant factor in Western Europe's equation of freedom, by ensuring victory in both world wars and spearheading the NATO alliance. In the era beyond peace, the United States must play a comparable role in Asia.

The debate in the United States between Europe-firsters and Asia-firsters made little sense during the Cold War, and it makes no sense now. Both must come first. A U.S. role in Europe will remain indispensable. And yet those who doubt the importance of Asia to the United States or the necessity of our commitment to its future are oblivious to history. Over the last fifty years, the United States endured hundreds of thousands of casualties in the Pacific theater in World War II and in the Korean and Vietnam wars. Although the Cold War is over, rising tensions exist throughout the region that, if ignored, could involve the United States in future conflicts.

While the three major East Asian powers—Russia, China, and Japan—are not natural enemies, they are not natural friends. Since our diplomatic opening to China in 1972, the United States has had better relations with these three powers than they have had with one another. While we may be trusted by only some Asian nations, we are respected by all. As the only major Pacific power that is not viewed as a potential aggressor by these three major countries, we can play a unique role, for the benefit of all, in maintaining peace and stability.

Asia is by far the most dynamic economic region of the world. In coming decades, it is where the major action will be. The average growth rate in Asia in 1992 was 6.6 percent, compared with 1 percent in Western Europe and 2.1 percent in the United States. It has been estimated that at the end of the decade East Asia will account for 30 percent of the world's GNP and that a billion Asians, virtually equal to the entire population of North America and Europe, will be living in middle-class households, creating a massive new market for trade with the West. Asia's explosive growth will triple the number of its consumers who have incomes equal to the Western average.

Our trade with Asia is already 50 percent greater than our trade with Europe. Motorola Corporation projects that in four years half of its pocket pagers will be beeping in China, while Carrier believes that in six years half of its air conditioners will be cooling Asian living rooms. These are just two American companies with thousands of workers whose families will have a stake in a stable, prosperous Asia. Exports to Asia on this scale—compounded by all the industries that produce goods and services Asians will want—will dwarf the trade deficits that move American politicians and pundits to such rhetorical excesses.

The West should welcome Asia's exciting economic growth. As *The Economist* has observed, "Asia's successes have come through hard work, optimism, openness, a passion to learn, a willingness to change and a conviction that there are no free rides. These methods are not a threat to the West. They are what made the West in the first place."

Unfortunately this astounding economic growth has not been accompanied by political stability. The nations of East Asia trust each other only slightly more than we trusted the Soviet Union during the Cold War. If left unchecked, these animosities could boil over, leading to regional arms races and even war. They make continued U.S. leadership vital. With no formal security alliance like NATO, Russia, China, and Japan will engage in a delicate balancing act that will determine the Pacific Rim's future. The United States is the only great power that possesses sufficient political and economic leverage with all three powers and their many neighbors to channel their relations in constructive directions.

China needs ties with the United States to guarantee that Japan will not return to an assertive foreign policy and to prevent Japanese economic domination of the region. Japan needs a U.S. military presence as a protective shield against Russia, China, and a future united Korea. Russia needs the United States to maintain a military presence adequate to check the growing political and military influence of China and Japan in the region. South Korea needs the United States to prevent North Korean aggression and to help stabilize the process of Korean unification.

Everyone knows that with the end of the Cold War a new Russia has emerged on the world scene. What we must also recognizc is that a new Japan and a new China have also taken the stage.

THE UNITED STATES AND JAPAN: IN LOCKSTEP INTO THE NEXT CENTURY

Japan is our greatest potential friend and greatest potential rival in Asia. In the Cold War we shared a common interest in deterring Soviet advances in East Asia. This alliance laid the foundation for Japan's incredible economic recovery and growth over the past five decades. With the Soviet threat gone, our economic competition and differing political interests will place heavy strains on our alliance.

Both countries still benefit from this relationship. Because of the burden of its atrocities and inhumane occupation policies during World War II, Japan must rely on close ties with the United States to allay the fears of its neighbors, particularly as it adopts a more outward-looking foreign and defense policy. The United States needs access to bases in Japan to maintain the forward presence we require to protect our interests in East Asia and to facilitate Japanese-American security cooperation. A nonnuclear Japan needs a U.S. military commitment not only to defend its home islands but also to promote stability in Asia and thereby keep regional military spending at reasonable levels.

Our economies are profoundly interdependent. Japan's economic prosperity could not survive without the U.S. market. As American exports to Japan increase, the reverse will also be true. In the case of automobiles, the interdependence is so great that half the parts of some Japanese models are made in the United States and half in Japan, with final assembly plants situated in both countries. With respect to many models, it makes no sense to talk about "Japanese" or "American" cars—they are actually "Japanese-American" cars. These close connections could be severed only at great cost to the United States and Japan.

During my first visit to Japan in 1953, Prime Minister Shigeru Yoshida, who, with MacArthur, was the architect of Japan's economic miracle, emphasized that his country, still recovering from the devastation of World War II, should put top priority on the development of a strong free-market economy. Because of its economic weakness then and its defeat in World War II, he believed Japan should have a "low posture" foreign policy, similar to those of medium-size European nations.

During the Cold War, Japan reaped enormous economic benefits by relying on the American security umbrella and keeping its defense spending low. The trauma of World War II eradicated Japan's thirst for political leadership in the world for two generations. Yoshida's carefully groomed successors followed his lead. In the 1970s, Japan emerged as a geostrategically stunted economic superpower. Permitting the United States to provide the bulk of its security needs neatly fitted Japan's psychological profile and did wonders for its economic portfolio as well. Rarely has a nation turned a necessity into such a profitable virtue.

The end of the Cold War changed the Japanese people's outlook on the world. Today, Japan is a nation of new people. Over 68 percent of its population were born since World War II. It is also a nation of new leaders. For the first time in forty years the Liberal Democratic Party is not in power. Only five of the twenty-one members of the Hosokawa cabinet were alive when Japan started its reckless imperial expansion in the early 1930s. And it is a nation of new policies. At home, it is moving toward reforms that will give ordinary Japanese more control over their nation's political system. In foreign policy, it is charting a gradual but steady course toward a more assertive position on the world stage.

While it is crucial that Japan and the United States sustain their bilateral partnership, recent tensions have weakened the strong bonds between us. Some Japan-bashers in America argue that we should no longer foot the bill for Japan's defense. Some America-bashers in Japan argue that America is a corrupt society that should not serve as an economic or political model. They believe Japan should break its ties with America and go it alone. Security concerns once hid these tensions. Now, with these restraints lifted, political and economic differences are transcending security issues. When nations become friends primarily because they have a common enemy, they tend to quarrel with each other when they no longer have an enemy to unite them.

The Yoshida policy that served Japan so well during the Cold War is now obsolete. Japan's economy, which was one thirteenth the size of America's economy in 1953, has grown to half the size of our economy today. Lee Kwan Yew foresaw Japan's changing role in 1967 when he told me, "The Japanese inevitably will again play a major role in the world. They are a great people. They cannot and should not be satisfied with a world role that limits them to making better transistor radios and sewing machines, and teaching other Asians how to grow rice." Japan, then a middleweight economic power, is now the top contender in the heavyweight economic championship. The time has come for it to play a foreign policy role commensurate with its economic power.

There is wide disagreement about what that role should be. Some suggest that with the disappearance of a nuclear-armed and aggressive Soviet Union, the U.S. security guarantee has lost its value to Japan. Others say that with the rise of pacifism in Japan, its neighbors no longer fear its presence in the region. Both of these arguments are flawed. As Japan's leaders look at their neighbors in East Asia, they see a Russia that is no longer communist but still a nuclear superpower, a nuclear-armed China rapidly becoming a military and economic giant, and a belligerent North Korean regime frantically trying to acquire nuclear weapons. As Japan's neighbors look eastward, they see a resurgent Japan that they believe might someday view the rest of Asia as its prey.

For Japan to rearm or to acquire nuclear weapons is politically unacceptable at home and abroad. The lingering concern in Europe about a potential military threat from Germany is infinitesimal compared with the fear in Asia that Japan might again become a major military power. North and South Korea, the Philippines, China, Taiwan, Malaysia, and Indonesia have one thing in common: All have been enemies of Japan in the past and fear that they could become enemies of Japan in the future. If Japan decided to increase its military forces above the level necessary to defend its home islands, all the countries that suffered under Japanese occupation before and during World War II would increase their defense spending. Such an arms race would make the U.S.-Soviet competition pale by comparison.

Japan's own people are also deeply ambivalent about remilitarization. Japan is the only nation that has suffered the devastation of nuclear weapons. Even those too young to remember World War II would strongly oppose Japan's acquiring them. Many Japanese believe that the same factors of territorial aggrandizement and regional dominance that characterized the Japanese culture in the 1930s could resurface in Japan and drive the country to reassert its power in Asia. They also recognize that any gain made in repairing relations with neighboring countries would vanish overnight if Japan adopted a more aggressive foreign policy.

Still, Japan is no longer a military pygmy. It has assumed 50 percent of the costs of stationing U.S. forces on its soil, developed a 240,000-man Self-Defense Force to protect its territory, and built a powerful navy to keep its sea lanes safe from hostile threats. While Japan spends only 1 percent of its GNP on defense, it spends almost the same amount in absolute terms as many of our Western European allies because its economy is so much larger.

Political candidates in the United States have found that a

surefire cheer line is to say that Japan is rich enough now to provide for its own defense and that we should "bring the boys home." Apart from its obvious demagoguery, this statement is dangerously wrong. If the United States withdrew its troops from forward bases in the Pacific Rim, Tokyo would face two unappealing choices. It could arm itself with nuclear weapons, which would trigger volcanic regional instability. It could ally itself with either Russia or China, which would tilt the balance of power in Asia and destroy prospects for regional cooperation. Without the U.S. security shield, Tokyo would be forced to take action that would benefit no one and disturb everyone.

If the United States did not play a role, the Pacific triangle of Japan, China, and Russia would be as unstable as a three-legged stool. The cost to the United States of continuing to play a balancing role in Asia is infinitely less than the price we would pay if we withdrew now and had to return later to stabilize the relationships among these three great, potentially aggressive powers. While it is important to maintain American forces in Europe, it is indispensable to maintain the present level of American forces in Asia.

It is politically unfeasible for Japan to increase its defense budget, but Japan's leaders should substantially increase their foreign aid budget so that its total national security burden—the combination of defense spending and foreign aid—is similar to our own as a percentage of GNP. Japan's $11 billion foreign aid budget is equal to that of the United States, but its spending for defense plus foreign aid equals only 1.5 percent of its GNP, compared with the 4.5 percent of GNP the United States spends for defense and foreign aid. In expanding its foreign aid budget, Japan should take decisive steps to counter the widely held impression that its economic assistance programs are designed not to aid others but to aid Japan.

Japan's perception problem was described graphically to me in 1985 by a Southeast Asian statesman who, while not anti-Japanese, was concerned about the impact of Japanese foreign aid in his country. "The trouble with the Japanese when they provide foreign aid is that they act like semiconductors," he said. "They take everything in and give nothing in return."

Japan should use aid and investment to promote not just its narrow economic interests but also its broader national security interest in peace, economic progress, and political stability throughout Asia. While no aid program can be justified unless it serves the interests of the donor nation, it will not be effective unless it also serves the interests of the nation receiving aid.

In increasing and redirecting its foreign aid programs, Japan should become the major contributor of aid to Russia, the other former Soviet states, and the nations of Eastern Europe. Any immediate economic return would be small, but such aid would represent a long-term investment in peace and the region's economic progress. All free nations have a huge stake in the survival of a nonaggressive, democratic government in Russia and in stable governments in the other newly independent former Soviet states. Yet while South Korea has pledged $3 billion and has delivered $1.5 billion in bilateral aid to Russia, Japan has pledged $3 billion and delivered only $1 billion, even though its GNP is twelve times South Korea's.

Russia's refusal to return Japan's four northern islands, which were seized by Stalin at the end of World War II, is the main obstacle to Japan's increasing aid to Russia. Following the example of the United States, which returned Okinawa to the Japanese during my administration in 1972, Russia should return these islands to Japan without conditions. For Japan to link aid to Russia to the return of the islands would be politically and strategically stupid. Should Yeltsin's government be overthrown by hard-line Russian nationalists, the Japanese would never get the islands back. With the Yeltsin government still in power, Japan should simultaneously negotiate the return of the islands and develop a broad-based economic assistance plan for Russia and for other Soviet republics. Japan has started to move in this direction, but not vigorously enough in view of the crisis in Russia.

Middle East stability is another vital Japanese interest. Japan should be the major contributor of aid to Arab states as they seek peace with Israel after forty-five years of war. The United States could get along without Persian Gulf oil. Japan could not. Yet during the Persian Gulf War, Japan barely managed to contribute noncombat naval forces and medical personnel. Japan will not win a seat at the table among leading world powers unless it finds ways to use its economic power for political effect. Supporting the Arab-Israeli peace process financially as well as diplomatically is an ideal opportunity. Another is more generous participation in international peacekeeping operations in Asia and elsewhere. Like the Germans, the Japanese have refused to provide military personnel for U.N. peacekeeping operations on the grounds that their constitution limits the use of their armed forces to the defense of the home islands. This line sounds increasingly like a self-serving rationalization. No one should expect the wealthy Japanese to supply foreign aid and peacekeeping support on demand, like cash at an automatic teller machine. No one should expect them to do other than act according to their interests, as great nations must do. But if they want to be taken seriously in the world and to share fully in the fruits of global stability, they must use their vast power to promote the interests of other countries as well as their own.

We should continue to support Japan's application for a Security Council seat if it demonstrates a willingness to share the risks and burdens of membership. Over time, membership in the world's most exclusive diplomatic club will impel Japan to take a more responsible internationalist perspective across the board—broadening its foreign aid program, contributing both financial support and manpower to peacekeeping efforts, and, perhaps most important, taking more energetic steps to reduce the subtle institutional and cultural barriers to foreign investments and imports.

By far the most neuralgic issues in U.S.-Japanese relations are economic. Mobilizing domestic support in both countries behind strong U.S.-Japanese security ties will be impossible unless we are able to reduce trade tensions. Complaints about Japanese trade practices have led some in the United States to the exaggerated view that Japan is turning America into its economic colony. This is not true. Japanese firms own only 23.1 percent of all foreign-owned businesses in the United States, compared with 22.6 percent owned by the British, 14.6 percent by the Dutch, and 7.0 percent by the Germans. Too often the popular culture and perceptions about politics and public policy lag far behind reality. One of 1993's popular movies, *Rising Sun,* stressed Japanese technological excellence and economic rapaciousness, while at the same time analysts were hailing the dramatic increase in the quality of Detroit's new models and documenting the decline in the sales of Japanese cars in the United States. Moreover, the movie opened just as Japan's recession, after four years of falling corporate profits, hit new depths and several of its larger companies announced plans to abandon the concept of guaranteed lifetime employment. It is, of course, the height of naïveté to expect Hollywood's distorting prism to depict America accurately. Unfortunately, movies, television, and popular music have an enormous impact on our nation's perception of itself and its position in the world.

None of this is to deny that we have an economic problem in our relationships with Japan. It lies not in the seizing of our assets by the Japanese but in the current account imbalance. Our trade deficit with Japan has grown from $10 billion in 1980 to $51 billion in 1992. Exchange-rate fluctuations, countercyclical economic trends, large budget deficits, and differing savings and growth rates are among the real causes of this imbalance. Unfortunately, politicians on both sides of the Pacific exploit U.S.-Japanese trade problems to score political points on the home front. Just as America cannot blame its deficit problems on Japan, the Japanese cannot blame global economic downturns on America's fiscal policies.

Our economic relationship will grow only if we both make concessions on certain issues. We must accept responsibility for the part of the trade deficit that results from uncompetitive American goods and the effects of our budget deficit. We should not place tariffs on Japanese goods, but we should work with our European allies at trade talks and G-7 economic meetings to convince Japan that it must open its markets to our goods. We should retaliate against the Japanese only if they do nothing to address unfair trade practices that clearly penalize American firms.

Japan should start on its own to lower its trade barriers and reduce its tariffs. Measures such as reforming its monopolistic and anticompetitive pricing system would help to improve Pacific trade competition. The willingness of the Japanese government to make concessions in its rice markets represents a good symbolic start, but the future of U.S.-Japanese relations depends on far more cooperation to prevent unfair trade practices from blowing up into a full-scale trade war.

While the trade deficit does not have the economic impact in the United States that Japan's critics claim, the political impact is undeniable. As long as Japan's markets are not as open as ours, relations between the United States and Japan will suffer, especially in economic hard times. To many, it appears that Japan is refusing to play by the rules. In fact, it is playing by its own rules. They are not necessarily wrong, but they are a powerful disincentive to the development of a stable working relationship between our two countries.

Many politicians and commentators have made virtual careers out of warning Americans against the rising peril of Japan. Their efforts have been constructive to the extent that they have helped awaken us to the vital importance of competing more vigorously. But they are counterproductive when they begin to breed fear and hostility. The late John Connally, who early in his career served as an aide to FDR, once told me of a fascinating meeting that he and several other young Democrats had with the President during World War II. Roosevelt hugely enjoyed giving political advice to his young protégés. As the meeting ended he tilted back his chair, gestured expansively with his cigarette holder, and said, "Boys, always remember—to be a success in politics, it helps to have an enemy."

It is no secret that nations also are often at their best when fighting an enemy. Politicians can sometimes win elections by running against an imaginary enemy, but responsible nations cannot indulge in such a luxury. In the era beyond peace, the United States does not need a new adversary on the scale of the former Soviet Union in order to stay strong. It needs only to understand that the maintenance of prosperity, peace, and freedom at home and their extension abroad are causes as noble and as worth uniting behind as were the efforts to win World War II and the Cold War.

Japan-bashing in the United States and U.S.-bashing in Japan are totally irresponsible. There have never been two great nations more different and yet more alike. We are both democracies. We both have free-market economic policies. We are both trading nations with a stake in free trade. Neither of us has designs on the territory of the other. Yet culturally we are light-years apart. I know from experience that the Japanese can be infuriating in economic and diplomatic negotiations. I am sure that we are probably just as infuriating to them. But we must keep a proper sense of perspective, as historian Walter McDougall has insisted:

> It would benefit Tokyo and Washington to recognize that their common security concerns are vastly more important than their commercial spat. To walk into the twenty-first century in any posture other than lockstep would be madness. Japan and America, pooling their complementary strengths, can assist Korean unification, the development of China and Siberia and provide the foundation for a multilateral regime with minimum danger to themselves or threat to others. But a Japan and U.S. at odds and underarmed would again, in the second Pacific century, bow their necks to the cruel yoke of geopolitics.

Such advice should be heeded by those—liberals, a few isolationist conservatives, and Ross Perot—who have advocated that the United States raise the banner of protectionism. A policy of economic, political, and strategic isolation was tragically wrong in the 1930s. It is wrong now as well. The United States is inextricably bound to a world trading system. Exports currently account for 11 percent of our GNP, and that figure is bound to rise significantly with the implementation of NAFTA and GATT. Rather than hunkering down in the foxhole of protectionism, we should relish the opportunity to achieve excellence by competing with others.

"Managed trade" is the code term in the United States for a solution of our economic problems with Japan. While popular in some quarters, it would be a disaster for the United States. In such a contest, Japan, where government and business act as one, would have an enormous advantage over the United States, where government is often antagonistic toward business. Setting targets for Japan is only thinly disguised protectionism.

We should under no circumstances adopt a national industrial policy under which unqualified bureaucrats would dictate business decisions better left to private markets. Nor should we subsidize American industries to even the score with Japan or other industrial powers. Governments cannot predict economic winners or have the imagination to identify the boundless possibilities of the future. Only private entrepreneurs can. The answer to our trade deficit is for American business to make better products, for which only free trade and free markets provide adequate incentives.

The debate about the highly technical issues involved in NAFTA and GATT has obscured the simple but very profound stake the United States has in aggressively supporting a policy of free trade.

Free trade is an investment in peace. While nations that trade with each other have often fought with each other, trade is a powerful incentive to avoid war. Trade is also an investment in jobs. Exports were behind half the new jobs created in the 1980s. Under GATT and NAFTA, they will create over two million more by 2004.

Free trade is also an investment in progress. Americans are a competitive people. We want to be the best. We can be best only if we compete with the best. When we build walls of protectionism around us, we doom ourselves to mediocrity.

Contrary to alarmist cries from Japan-bashers, U.S. exports to Japan are increasing at a higher rate than those to the rest of the world. Since 1987, our exports have increased at a rate of 13.9 percent annually, while those to Japan alone have increased at an average rate of 15.1 percent. Since almost all the new U.S. jobs created in the same period came from export growth, it is imperative that these rates be sustained and increased. Because of the link between new exports and new jobs, we must continue to resist protectionist pressures, despite the siren calls of the trade demagogues. It is estimated that over the next few years 25 percent of the growth in Western economies will come from increased demand in Japan and the rest of Asia. To take protectionist measures now would be the height of irresponsibility.

More significant than the Japan trade deficit is the Japan attention deficit. As Japan begins to pay more attention to the world, U.S. policymakers must lead in paying more serious attention to Japan. There are too few Japan experts in the upper echelons of the State Department or in the media. Since the end of the Cold War, much of the drama has gone out of summit meetings between the leaders of the United States and Russia, and yet they receive far more coverage than visits to Washington by Japanese Prime Ministers, which are usually played only slightly more prominently in the newspapers than the annual delivery of the official national turkey to the White House on the day before Thanksgiving. Until recently, Presidents have appeared to spend no more time worrying about Japan than about Mexico—and the neglect of Latin America by successive administrations has itself been appalling. We must waste no time now in getting our priorities in line with economic realities. For example, the Asia-Pacific Economic Cooperation group, which includes Australia, Brunei, Canada, China, Hong Kong, Indonesia, Japan, Malaysia, New Zealand, the Philippines, Singapore, South Korea, Thailand, and the United States, is pathetically underfunded. A high U.S. profile in the APEC process is essential if our interests are to be protected. Yet we contribute only $382,000 a year, compared with $50 million spent on the Europe-based Organization for Economic Cooperation and Development, and $70 million for the Latin America–based Organization of America States.

When I first met Harold Macmillan in Washington forty years ago, he said, "Alliances are held together by fear, not love." Until the end of the Cold War, the U.S. strategic relationship with Japan was strong, but it was based on fear. With the fear gone, we cannot expect that we will love each other. In fact, there are times we may not like each other. We must build a new relationship, based not on the fragile foundation of fear but on the solid foundation of mutual economic and security interests.

To do business together economically, politically, and diplomatically in the era beyond peace, both the United States and Japan must change. The United States must bring its budget deficit under control, learn to put a premium on excellence, and reverse the flow of power and money toward the federal government in Washington. Japan must play a major role on the world stage, empower its consumers by opening its markets, and reform its political system to give more authority to its elected leaders instead of to the insulated bureaucrats who have ruled Japan for decades. Political and electoral reforms adopted in January 1994 provide the first real chance of fundamental change since the United States imposed a constitution on Japan in the wake of World War II.

Bureaucrats are still infinitely more powerful in Japan than in the United States, where voters would not tolerate a political system that gave elected officials so little real power. But the bell may finally be tolling for them, in spite of the skeptics who say that they will emerge from this latest round of reform even more powerful than before. For years, when anyone complained about the unresponsiveness of Japan's bureaucratic political system, the standard answer was *"Shikata ga nai"*—"It cannot be helped." But beginning with the July 1993 elections, when the Liberal Democratic Party lost its majority in the Diet for the first time since 1955, there has been a glimmer of Japanese *glasnost*. A new group of reform leaders is working to wrench control from the bureaucrats. Change will not come quickly, but it will come. If it is possible for the Berlin Wall to come down and the communists to be driven from the Kremlin, it is also possible that Japanese voters may someday have the same ability to change the course of events as voters in the other industrialized democracies have. It will be tragic if the resignation of Premier Morihiro Hosokawa, who personified the reform movement, prevents the Japanese from achieving what they deserve: a larger say in their own destiny.

Japan is neither the all-powerful Wicked Witch of the East nor an economic Wizard of Oz who relies on special effects to cloak his all-too-human weaknesses. It is coming to the end of a damaging recession, its second major downturn since World War II. Its economy actually shrank during the last half of 1992. Most of its leading corporations faced the possibility of earnings slumps or even losses. As a result of these and other developments, the conventional wisdom was that Japan, portrayed during the 1980s as the world's up-and-coming bully heavyweight, was on the ropes in the 1990s.

As usual, the conventional wisdom was wrong. At the depths of its recession, Japan's unemployment rate was 3 percent—high for Japan, but less than half that of the United States. Its budget is balanced. Its domestic savings rate is 31 percent, compared with 15 percent in the United States. By late 1993, Japan's growth rate was over 2 percent a year. Like the United States, Japan will come out of its recession leaner and stronger than before—a worthy competitor and, if we adopt correct policies, a valuable friend. Approaching our problems with Japan rationally, without fear, distrust, or awe, will contribute substantially to maintaining constructive relations with this vital ally.

Speaking to the Japanese-American Society in Tokyo in 1953, I said that cooperation between the United States and Japan was essential to peace in the Pacific. The statement is even more true today. The Japanese people, among the world's most ingenious and industrious, are destined to be a major world power. They will make enormously valuable contributions to regional stability and the world economy. Peaceful competition and cooperation between the world's two economic superpowers is essential if the twenty-first century in Asia is to be one of peace, prosperity, and expanding political freedom.

CHINA: "THE BIGGEST OF THEM ALL"

During one of our meetings in San Clemente twenty-one years ago at the second U.S.-Soviet summit, Leonid Brezhnev expressed concern about the growing threat of China. I assumed this was a ploy to induce the United States to choose sides in the Sino-Soviet conflict. When I said that it would be at least twenty-five years before China became a significant economic and military power, he held up both hands with fingers outstretched in what I thought was a sign of surrender.

The translator finally interpreted his gesture. "Ten years," he said. Brezhnev was closer to being right than I was.

China has become the fastest-growing economic powerhouse in this decade and could become the world's strongest economic superpower in the next century. Over the last forty-five years it has moved from a backward agrarian society to a rapidly developing economic giant. Today its growth rate is 14 percent, the highest in the world among major nations. It has surpassed Germany as the third-largest economy in the world, behind the United States and Japan. Forty percent of China's GNP is in trade, a percentage higher than that of Japan, the United States, or India. Thirty percent of its exports go to the United States. As a measure of confidence in China's future, foreign investment in China increased by 171 percent from January to September in 1993.

While most industries are money losers owned and subsidized by the state, over half of China's GNP is now produced by profitable private enterprise. Per capita income has tripled in the last ten years. The world's largest communist society could become the world's richest capitalist economy in the next century.

Napoleon, who never visited China, saw this coming. Almost two centuries ago, he said, "China—there lies a sleeping giant. Let him sleep, because when he awakes he will move the world." The giant is awake and is beginning to move the world.

During my first visit in 1972, most of the Chinese on the streets of Beijing were walking. In 1982, the majority were riding bicycles. On my last visit in 1993, huge traffic jams congested the streets of Beijing, Huangzhou, Guangzhou, and Shanghai.

In 1972, we left behind a satellite TV-broadcasting unit that we had brought with us for the use of the American press. It turned out to be a Trojan horse for Western influence in China. At that time, there were about three hundred thousand television sets in China. In 1993, a billion Chinese saw television on 146 million television sets, most of them manufactured in China. The communications revolution has made it possible to send vivid pictures of life in free countries over borders, and no ideological SDI can shoot them down.

Some observers contend that we no longer need a close relationship with China, since the threat of Soviet aggression has disappeared. The other side of that coin is that the Chinese no longer need the United States to protect them against possible

Soviet aggression. Both concepts are wrong. In the era beyond peace, China and the United States need to cooperate with each other for reasons completely unrelated to the Soviet Union or Russia.

China has emerged as the world's third-strongest military and economic power. It is strong enough to play a major role in regional conflicts in Southeast Asia, the Middle East, and the Persian Gulf. It is the only country that possesses the necessary leverage to rein in North Korea's ominous nuclear weapons program. We should not underestimate China's ability to disrupt our interests around the world if our relationship becomes belligerent rather than cooperative. China's critics should remember that it did not exercise its veto in the United Nations during the Persian Gulf War. With its veto power, it could effectively bottleneck any resolution that we try to pass in the future. This does not mean that we should defer to every Chinese concern. We have leverage because China needs America's economic cooperation and respects our military might. We should use that leverage to nudge China's policies in constructive directions.

Before I went to China in 1972, one observer speculated that Mao's first question to me would be "What is the richest nation in the world planning to do for the most populous nation in the world?" During my five days of meetings with Chinese officials, they never raised economic issues. Their concerns were exclusively strategic, focusing on the growing military power of the Soviet Union. Twenty years later, on my seventh trip to China, the focus had shifted exclusively to economic issues. While the Chinese leaders may worship in a communist church, they live by capitalist scripture. They are committed to free-market economic policies—to capitalism with a Chinese face.

It is not surprising that Singapore's Lee Kwan Yew, an ethnic Chinese, saw this coming twenty-five years ago. "Mao is painting on a mosaic," he told me. "When he passes from the scene, the rains will come and wash away what he has painted, and there will still be China, always China." Politically, China has one of the most doctrinaire communist governments in the world. But economically, its people and most of its lower-level leaders are more Chinese than they are communist. The private sector, fueled by Chinese entrepreneurs and free-marketers abroad and at home, is growing far faster than the public sector. This process is irreversible.

While most Americans give China high marks for its free-market economic policies, they rightly criticize the government's continuing denial of political freedom to the Chinese people. However, we should place Chinese developments in historical perspective. After serving for six years as *The New York Times* bureau chief in China, Nicholas Kristof observed that even today's political atmosphere represents a huge improvement for most Chinese. "The government smashes those who oppose it, but it no longer tries to regulate every aspect of daily life," he wrote. "Now Chinese have regained their private lives from the Communist Party. Once again they can display personalities. Dissidents are still brutalized, but life for the average peasant who knows that politics, like explosives, are to be avoided is relatively free. It is no more than the freedom of a bird cage, but most birds would prefer to be flying around in a cage than to be skewered on a rotisserie, which is what life in China used to be like!"

Freedom is contagious. Economic freedom inevitably leads to political freedom. This happened in South Korea, Taiwan, Chile, and other countries ruled by dictatorial regimes. It will happen in China, but only if economic freedom is not suppressed by frightened political dictators or sabotaged by short-sighted U.S. policies cutting back on trade with China because of its human-rights abuses.

China is not of purely economic importance for the United States. From the late 1940s to the early 1990s, it has not hesitated to assert its interests by military means. In 1951, it entered the Korean War. In the 1950s, it put military pressure on Taiwan's offshore islands. In 1962, it clashed militarily with India.

In the 1960s and 1970s, it supported the Vietnamese and Cambodian communists in the Vietnam War. Between 1968 and 1969, Chinese and Soviet armies repeatedly clashed over the Ussuri River region. In 1979, China attacked its ideological stepchild, Vietnam, after Hanoi invaded Cambodia and persecuted ethnic Chinese in Vietnam.

Today, China and Russia exist in an uneasy "Asian détente." China's hard-liners would prefer to see the failure of Yeltsin's democratic government, because it would lessen the ideological threat of Russian democracy and weaken Russia's ability to protect its interests in East Asia. At the same time, Chinese officials fear a new resurgent, nationalistic Russia because it would inevitably clash with China over important economic regions in East Asia and force China to divert its attention from other areas.

The major concern for China's leaders lies to the east. Japan has become the economic rainmaker in Asia, investing more than $60 billion in the region. The Chinese welcome Japan's economic investments, but they are highly suspicious of the motives behind Japan's policies in Asia. China's rulers remember Japan's brutal aggression before and during World War II. That is one reason China is eager for the United States to continue its role in Asia. Even the most hard-line communist leaders in China recognize that the United States poses no threat to China and serves as an important restraining influence on its Japanese and Russian rivals.

It is ironic that many liberal scholars in the United States who strongly supported our opening to China in 1972, when Mao allowed neither political nor economic freedom, now oppose close U.S.-Chinese relations because of China's denial of political freedom and abuse of human rights. Cutting back our trade with China by revoking China's most-favored-nation status would be a tragic mistake. We cannot improve the political situation in China through a "scorched earth" economic policy. Revoking China's MFN status would hurt the free-market reformers and entrepreneurs who hold the key to China's future. Not only would it devastate the mainland's economy, it would lay waste to the surrounding region as well. No other nation in Asia supports our linking most-favored-nation status to human rights. It would do irreparable damage to Hong Kong, which serves as a conduit for over 45 percent of China's exports, and to Taiwan and Macao, which depend on trade with Hong Kong for their survival.

The threat of MFN revocation is vigorously opposed by almost all Chinese, including most dissidents, who view the high-profile grandstanding of U.S. politicians as a calculated effort to humiliate a proud nation and its people. They know that the term "most-favored nation" is a misnomer. Only 10 of the 188 nations in the world do not have that status. Several of the 178 who do have it have human-rights policies as bad as, or worse than, those of China. Ironically, many liberals who oppose extending MFN to China were among the first to endorse lifting the U.S. trade embargo against Vietnam—like China, one of the world's most repressive hard-line communist regimes.

Winston Churchill once said, "Russia fears our friendship more than our enmity." This can also be said of China's leaders today. While they know that China's economic progress depends on the continuation of free-market policies, they are aware that economic freedom is a mortal threat to a political dictatorship.

We should strongly protest China's human-rights abuses whenever and wherever we can. But punishing China's leaders for human-rights abuses by restricting and reducing our economic contacts does not serve the long-term interest of those Chinese who want more political freedom. It may make us feel better, but if we close the door to economic reform, we will lock out all prospects for peaceful political change on foreign policy in the foreseeable future. That is too high a price to pay for a sense of moral superiority.

We should also resist lecturing the Chinese about their birth control policies. Abortion is a highly inflammatory issue in the United States. I believe that no decision is more uniquely private than whether or not a woman should have an abortion. Government should not interfere with an individual's right to make that decision. I know that a great number of fair-minded people strongly disagree with my position. What we can all surely agree on is that we should not impose our views on this highly controversial issue on other nations, such as China, with massive population problems. Leaders of such nations have to choose between allowing abortion or condemning millions of people to starvation because of overpopulation.

Whatever the motives of China's critics, they are hampering the conduct of the constructive relations that we must have with the world's most populous nation, one of the world's nuclear powers, and potentially the twenty-first century's richest nation—and they are jeopardizing the best hope of the Chinese people for lives of freedom and prosperity.

The stakes are incredibly high. Nick Kristof, writing in *Foreign Affairs* last year, put the issue in perspective:

> China is becoming a fourth pole in the international system. This is particularly true when one looks at "Greater China," consisting of the People's Republic, Hong Kong, and Taiwan. According to World Bank projections, Greater China's net imports in the year 2002 will be $639 billion, compared to $521 billion for Japan. Likewise, using comparable international prices, Greater China in the year 2002 is projected to have a gross domestic product of $9.8 trillion, compared to $9.7 trillion for the United States. If those forecasts hold, in other words, Greater China would not just be another economic pole; it would be the biggest of them all.

Today, China's economic power makes U.S. lectures about morality and human rights imprudent. Within a decade, it will make them irrelevant. Within two decades, it will make them laughable. By then the Chinese may threaten to withhold most-favored-nation status from the United States unless we do more to improve living conditions in Detroit, Harlem, and South-Central Los Angeles.

China is justly criticized for promoting weapons proliferation by selling arms whenever and wherever it can, including to many pariah states. The United States' complaints about other nations' arms sales is a case of the pot calling the kettle black. We have cornered 56 percent of the world arms market, with $13 billion in sales annually, compared with $800 million for China and $1.5 billion for Russia. Although we are far more discriminating than others in choosing our clients, we are not in the best position to criticize others. The only way to stem proliferation is to reduce arms sales across the board internationally, including our own.

Unlike human-rights grandstanding, the strategy of continuing economic cooperation and relying on diplomatic pressures has had some success. China released its most famous dissident, Wei Jingsheng, after holding him in prison for almost fifteen years. Other dissidents have received lighter sentences in large part because U.S. government officials kept up the pressure for their release and lodged complaints in international conferences. In the end, democracy and human rights will be more effectively enlarged by the expansion of market forces and the influence of Chinese entrepreneurs in Hong Kong and Taiwan than by frontal assaults on the government in Beijing.

It is risky to make predictions about China. To paraphrase Lord Curzon, Great Britain's Viceroy in India one hundred years ago, China is like a great university from which the scholar never gets a degree. Most observers agree that there will be a struggle for power after Deng Xiaoping leaves the scene. Those who assume there will be a renewal of political warlordism in China are focusing too much on China's past and not enough on the new China we must deal with today. Regional leaders want more autonomy from a central system that inflicted great harm on them during the Cultural Revolution and the Great Leap Forward, but they are loyal Chinese who do not seek independence.

The greater danger is that China will be divided by a new economic wall between the rich in the coastal provinces and the poor in the interior unless more progress is made in bringing the benefits of economic prosperity to all.

Two groups are in contention to succeed Deng. Moderates favor an expansion of the rule of law, movement toward a federal system, creation of genuine private property, and rapid elimination of subsidies for agriculture, rents, and business. The more doctrinaire group favors a strong Communist Party—but one that is becoming less a revolutionary party than a ruling, technocratic party. Its leaders would prefer to see restraints on growth in the private sector and generally slower economic growth. They have a greater suspicion of the West, especially the United States. They want a continuing strong role for state corporations, even if government subsidies are necessary. Both groups claim that they support free-market reforms. They disagree on the pace and extent of those reforms.

China is permanently locked into the world market. There will be no return to the economic isolation of the 1960s and early 1970s. Even the most reactionary hard-line communists, while totally opposed to political reforms, have no choice but to support the free-market economic policies that have tripled the income of the Chinese people in the past ten years.

The good economic news from China has obscured some of the enormous problems China's new leaders will confront. The specters of corruption and unrestrained greed haunt China. This is not grease to make the economic mechanism run smoothly, as in Korea and Japan. It is money taken directly out of the system. The central authorities are trying to put the brakes on corruption, but they cannot touch the main perpetrators, the high-level party cadres and the so-called red princes. There are too many Chinese leaders who have their hands in the till for us to expect an attack on this problem now. But thoughtful Chinese leaders know that a government that tolerates corruption will inevitably become the victim of corruption.

The Chinese share with the Germans a pathological fear of

inflation. Many remember the last days of the Nationalist regime in Shanghai, when money was carted around in wheelbarrows and inflation helped destroy a dying regime. An austerity program aimed at a soft landing, launched in May of 1993 by Vice Premier Zhu, China's leading economic official, seems to have worked without causing a nosedive in GNP growth. But the tragedy of Tiananmen Square in 1989 reminds us of the danger of political unrest if inflation leads to an economic downturn.

How the post-Deng struggle will end depends mainly on what happens within China. But developments outside China, including those in Russia, can affect the result. If the Russian experiment in economic and political freedom succeeds, China's moderates will benefit. If Russia's reforms fail, this will encourage the reactionaries.

The policies of the United States will also affect the outcome of the succession struggle. If we cut back our trade with China's free-market sector in order to punish China's leaders for their human-rights abuses, we will weaken those who want to increase political freedom.

When I went to China in 1972, there was a great deal of speculation about why I had changed my hard-line position of opposing recognition of the Chinese communist government. Some suggested that I had finally seen the light and that I had recognized that the notorious "free China" lobby was wrong in demonizing the communist government of China. Others suggested that I went to China to enlist Chinese support in ending the Vietnam War. Neither of these views was right.

China and the United States were brought together in part because both were concerned about the threat to China and the rest of Asia from an aggressive Soviet Union. But I believed that even if there were no Soviet threat, it was essential to develop a new relationship with China then, when China was weak and needed us, rather than waiting until later, when China needed us less than we needed them.

The issue today is not who is for or against human rights. Those who support an open China economic policy are as profoundly concerned about human rights as those who are demanding a change in that policy. The question is what policy will be most effective in convincing the Chinese leaders to provide more political freedom and to end human-rights abuses.

For twenty-five years before 1972, we had had no contact whatever with the communist Chinese government—no trade, no diplomatic relations, no tourists, no exchange of people. China was still a completely closed society with neither economic nor political freedom. Since our opening, the Chinese have astonished the world by the progress their country has made in granting economic freedom and opening up Chinese society to the free world.

During the Cold War, the United States and China were brought together and held together by our fears. In the period beyond peace, we need new economic incentives that will help to hold us together by our hopes.

Seven centuries ago, Marco Polo described China as far ahead of any European city in the "excellence of its buildings and bridges, the number of its public hospitals, the effective maintenance of public order and the manner and refinements of its people." Between 221 and 206 B.C., the Chinese built the Great Wall and cut themselves off from the rest of the world. Four centuries ago China's development stopped, and the country fell hopelessly behind the rest of the world. Now China is again gaining international respect as one of the world's great powers.

Many who are inexperienced about China fail to understand that one of the keys to its history in this century has been the restoration of national pride and unity after generations of fractionalism and foreign exploitation. Their pride is neither communist nor noncommunist in character but simply Chinese, and it guarantees that China's leaders will not respond constructively to ultimatums.

I vividly recall calling on Deng Xiaoping in the fall of 1989, four months after the Tiananmen Square crackdown. After he had greeted me in the Great Hall of the People, I told him that there had never been a worse crisis in the relationship between our countries and that it was up to China to take steps to deal with the outrage of the civilized world. With dozens of journalists from around the world looking on, he gave a boilerplate reply about not tolerating interference in China's internal affairs.

After the cameras left, he became far more animated. By then China's battle-scarred old survivor was almost totally deaf. The conversation took on a surreal character, with the official translator shouting my comments into his left ear and his daughter screaming them into his right. But while he had great difficulty hearing, he had no difficulty seeing his responsibility as his country's paramount leader. He told me that after years of subservience to foreigners, China was now united and independent and that the Chinese people would never forgive their leaders for apologizing to another nation. In almost the next breath he introduced the subject of Fang Lizhu, the dissident who was then being sheltered at the U.S. embassy in Beijing, and made a highly constructive proposal for ending the standoff.

Deng's message was unmistakable: Our differences could be bridged by discussion behind the scenes but would be exacerbated by red-hot exchanges of public rhetoric. A few months later Fang Lizhu was released, but on China's initiative, not in response to demands by the United States.

In late 1993, Deng was widely believed to have given the Chinese government these marching orders for dealing with the new administration in Washington: "Increase trust, reduce troubles, develop cooperation, and avoid confrontation." In its first moves, the Clinton administration responded by increasing distrust, stirring up trouble, threatening noncooperation, and fomenting confrontation. A letter from President Clinton to Beijing, which listed fourteen criticisms on issues ranging from human rights to trade, set off months of diplomatic skirmishing that came close to imperiling the constructive relations between our countries. The climax came when the United States, acting on inaccurate intelligence, erroneously accused the Chinese of selling chemicals to Iran for the production of poison gas and decided to follow and later board and inspect a Chinese vessel suspected of carrying the chemicals.

Eventually, wiser heads prevailed, and Sino-U.S. relations were put back on an even keel following a summit meeting between the U.S. and Chinese Presidents in Seattle in late 1993. Still, as Don Oberdorfer wrote just before the summit, "Much of the recent rhetoric in Washington about China seems strangely disconnected from the burgeoning urban life of Beijing and the fast-growing eastern seaboard cities. Paradoxically, the United States has seemed to be more ideological in its dealings than the increasingly pragmatic communist state." In the future, particularly on foreign policy issues, we should treat China with the respect a great power deserves and not as a pariah nation.

Because of its huge natural and human resources, China will inevitably be an economic and military superpower in the next century. We will need China as a friend then. The Chinese have long memories. We must not poison the friendly relationship we risked so much to establish when we opened the door to China twenty-one years ago.

At the same time, realistic reappraisals of U.S. relations with Taiwan, and of the relations between the governments in Beijing and Taipei, are overdue. The Shanghai Communiqué negotiated by Henry Kissinger and Zhou Enlai twenty-one years ago brilliantly bridged the differences between the two governments by stating that the United States recognized that both agreed that there was one China, that each claimed to be the legitimate government of China, and that the differences should be settled peacefully. The situation has changed dramatically since then.

Mainland China is 250 times larger than Taiwan and has 55 times as many people. But in 1992 mainland China's economy was only 2.2 times larger than that of Taiwan. Tiny Taiwan is an economic giant. It has the largest foreign exchange reserve in the world, is the fourteenth-largest trading country in the world, and has the twentieth-largest GNP in the world—larger than the GNPs of three fourths of the nations in the U.N. It was the sixth-largest trading partner and the sixth-largest export market of the United States in 1992. Taiwan provides twice as big a market for American exports as mainland China.

Like a couple who have gone through a bitter divorce, China and Taiwan publicly have irreconcilable differences. The separation is permanent politically, but they are in bed together economically. China can never agree that Taiwan should have equal status as a member of the U.N. But economically the two need each other. Taiwan is rapidly becoming China's biggest foreign investor. The trade between the two, much of it thinly disguised by going through Hong Kong, is enormous.

A more prosperous Taiwan serves China's interests. A more prosperous China serves Taiwan's interests. Beijing should drop its opposition to Taiwan's membership in international economic organizations. While we should not risk jeopardizing our relations with Beijing by formally recognizing Taiwan diplomatically, we should recognize Taiwan economically by strongly supporting its efforts to become a member of such organizations. And we should begin extending to Taiwan government officials the diplomatic courtesies that the leaders of one of the world's major economic powers deserve. The best guarantee of Taiwan's security is our relationship with the People's Republic of China. The Chinese will not launch a military attack against Taiwan as long as Beijing knows such an action would jeopardize their relationship with the United States.

Similar factors affect China's relationship to Hong Kong. In 1984, when China pledged that for fifty years after Hong Kong again became part of China in 1997 it would preserve Hong Kong's capitalist way of life, some observers said this was a two-China policy—with one government and two economic systems.

Milton Friedman disagreed. He said, "One country with two systems is from a dream world. One country is one country." Economically, he has proved to be right. Despite the highly publicized disagreements between Britain's Hong Kong governor, Chris Patten, and Beijing on political issues, China and Hong Kong are one country economically and will remain so. Hong Kong is China's biggest foreign investor, and China is Hong Kong's biggest trading partner. The two economies are blended together and political differences will not pry them apart because each needs the other. Hong Kong's per capita income is $19,000, compared with Britain's $16,000. After Hong Kong again becomes part of China in 1997, their political differences will continue to appear to drive them apart, but their much stronger economic interests will inevitably draw them together. Hong Kong is one of the world's richest societies, and in the next century, China will become one. One of the reasons China will not adopt a repressive political policy in Hong Kong after 1997 is that it knows this would destroy any hope it may have to convince Taiwan to accept a similar arrangement.

VIETNAM, CUBA, AND NORTH KOREA: THE CLOSED DOOR OR THE OPEN DOOR?

The lessons of China are directly relevant to what our policies should be toward the three remaining hard-line communist states: Vietnam, Cuba, and North Korea.

In planning the American opening to China, I set one basic threshold requirement. In the 1967 article in *Foreign Affairs* in which I first publicly stressed the need for such an opening, I argued that doing so the right way would require short-run pressures "designed to persuade Peking that its interests can be served only by accepting the basic rules of international civility." For the long run, it would require "pulling China back into the world community— but as a great and progressing nation, not as the epicenter of world revolution." In other words, China had to be brought into the world community, but it could not be allowed to shoot its way in.

When I wrote that, China was still an aggressive power and a serious threat to the security of its neighbors. On taking office in January 1969, one of the first things I did was to set in motion a series of initiatives aimed at achieving an opening to China in the right way. By the time of my initial visit to Beijing in 1972, China was still repressive domestically, but except for its brief invasion of Vietnam, it was no longer a direct military threat to its neighbors.

Of the three remaining communist states, North Korea clearly remains a serious, active threat, not only to South Korea but to the peace and security of the entire Pacific Rim. It has not yet crossed the threshold that I set more than twenty-five years ago for China. Until it ceases to be a threat, we should continue to treat it as the pariah nation that its leaders still persist in making it.

Vietnam and Cuba are like North Korea in that both are still run by repressive communist regimes. Between the two there are dramatic differences. But neither presents an active threat to the peace internationally.

Vietnam's present leaders have turned the country's extraordinary energies from external aggression to internal development. Like China's leaders, they retain tight political control but are opening their economy to market forces. The result is that Vietnam is now on the verge of becoming a significant economic power. In Cuba, by contrast, Castro still gives lip service to world revolution. But his Stalinist economic policies have devastated the nation's economy, and without his former Soviet sponsors, he no longer has the resources to pose a serious external threat.

In the cases of both Cuba and Vietnam, the question before us now is how we can best serve our own national interest, the interests of the people of those two nations, and the interest of the world community: by the closed door or the open door?

Of the two, Vietnam presents the easier choice. Though repressive, its government is solidly entrenched. Clearly, neither economic nor diplomatic pressures will dislodge it. The question is how best to open it further to the winds of freedom that are sweeping the world. Again, the China analogy is instructive. Increasing economic integration with the world brings greater economic freedoms, and economic freedoms build powerful internal pressure for political freedoms.

We should start by separating the question of our political relationship with Vietnam from that of our economic relationship, letting each develop at its own pace. Even if we are totally satisfied that the Vietnamese government has done all it can to account for Americans missing in action in the Vietnam War, we should keep the political relationship in a deep freeze as long as Hanoi continues to treat as second-class citizens the millions of South Vietnamese who were our allies in the war. We should follow the administration's decision to lift the trade embargo with vigorous efforts to encourage investment in Vietnam and draw it further into the global economy, not to help the present Vietnamese regime but to strengthen the forces of change.

In the case of Cuba, much of the pressure to keep our economic embargoes in force derives from the long-standing belief, particularly among many in the Cuban exile community, that this is the best way to bring a swift end to the cruel and destructive Castro regime. It is true that the collapse of the Soviet government and the subsequent cutoff of Soviet economic subsidies have put heavy new pressures on Castro. The privation is brutal. Economic conditions on the island, bad before, have become far worse. His police state has nevertheless maintained its iron grip.

The plain fact, painful though it may be to face, is that after thirty-five years of Castro's rule, the hard line against him has failed to get rid of him. It is time to shift the central focus of our policies from hurting Cuba's government to helping its people. It is unlikely that Castro, an isolated survivor of the Soviet world, could again mount a serious subversive threat in this hemisphere, even if Cuba's economy improves. Meanwhile, the condition of his people is desperate and growing worse. They need food, they need the basic essentials of everyday life, they need the rudiments of a functioning economy, and they need freedom.

The unique nature of the relationship between the United States and Cuba gives us a special responsibility toward its people. As long as it seemed reasonable that severe economic pressures would help them overthrow the Castro dictatorship, it was appropriate to maintain those pressures. As long as Castro was part of a global network of communist aggressors, the embargo strengthened international security. But that network has vanished, and our best service to the Cuban people now would be to build pressure from within by actively stimulating Cuba's contacts with the free world. What has worked in China now has the best chance of working in Cuba.

This means we should drop the economic embargo and open the way to trade, investment, and economic interaction, while insisting that ideas and information be allowed to flow as freely as goods. Today's global economy is essentially a market economy. Where the market system penetrates, it carries along the seeds of political and economic reform. We should put the challenge squarely to Castro: If he wants his people to prosper, then let him open the door to goods and ideas. If he insists on keeping it shut, it will be clear beyond question that only his fear of freedom stands in the way of his people's escape from privation. If he opens it, then he opens it also to the winds of freedom.

The United States must learn to think of itself as an Asian-Pacific power in the same automatic, instinctual way that it thinks of itself as a part of the Atlantic Community. This is true not only because more and more of America's ablest new immigrants come from Asia but also because Asia will soon be the largest market for our goods, the greatest preoccupation of our policymakers in Washington, and the likeliest arena for the application of U.S. diplomatic and even military power. Just as we were preoccupied in 1993 with the civil war in the former Yugoslavia, we may well be preoccupied in 2003 with the threat of war over which Asian country controls oil rights in the South China Sea.

If America is to play a constructive role in Asia, the American people must be comfortable with their new role as citizens of the Pacific. We must think of Asian peoples not as threats or adversaries but as worthy competitors and partners in ensuring peace and stability in a volatile region. Japan was once called the Great Britain of Asia. Our goal should be to feel the same commonality of purpose and values with the emerging superpowers of Asia as we do with the former empires of Europe.

To do so, we will have to get over our fear of the mighty new Asia of the twenty-first century. By the year 2000, 3.5 billion of the world's 6.2 billion people will be Asians, and they will produce over half of the world's goods. To pessimists, these facts spell a West in decline, an America relegated to the margins. These analysts proceed from the fallacy that there is only so much growth and prosperity to go around, that if "they" are up, then "we" must be down. It is true that the United States will get a run for its money from China as both an economic and a military superpower by the middle of the next century. But in purely economic terms, Asia's skyrocketing growth, and with it the growth of a massive Asian middle class of consumers, will create incredible new opportunities for the West if we rise effectively to the challenge.

The pessimists are alarmed by the pace of Japanese investment in Asia, which has now reached an estimated $60 billion, because they fear it is designed to keep American and European investors out. This attitude is shortsighted, counterproductive, and wrong. In fact, Japanese investment is helping to create conditions in Asia that will be enormously beneficial to the rest of the world for decades to come.

These opportunities are there to be grasped. We will end up on the sidelines only if, by our own shortsightedness, we take ourselves out of the game. If we stay in, if we compete and cooperate as a full member of the Asian-Pacific community, everyone will score, and everyone will win.

Trade does not prevent wars, but it does require peace. As Lee Kwan Yew said to a joint session of Congress during his visit to Washington nine years ago, ambitious nations grow either by trading with their neighbors or, if they cannot trade openly, gobbling up their neighbors' territory. It is profoundly in our interest that the nations of Asia grow the peaceful way.

The ideal world beyond peace—for now, almost beyond imagining—is 188 equally rich nations trading with one another in a free, fair way, each producing what it does best and buying what it needs most. A generation from now, such an outcome may be within the world's grasp. Today, much of Asia is unimaginably richer than it was after World War II. If Asian nations that were once mired in abject poverty join the developed world in the beginning of the next century, as they are very likely to do, then the rest of the developing world—if it follows Asia's free-market example—may also pass from poverty to prosperity.

Building New Bridges to the Muslim World

During the Cold War, Americans glimpsed the Middle East and the Persian Gulf region in the harsh light cast by two distorting prisms: the conflict between the Arabs and Israel and the threat of Muslim fundamentalism, represented by such events as the seizing of American hostages in Iran in 1979. Our overwhelming interests in protecting the state of Israel and combating extremist terrorists have left the powerful impression that the Muslim world is a ragtag conglomeration of crazy, poorly shaven Arabs and fanatical medieval Persians.

Instead it is a highly diverse community of 850 million people and 190 ethnic groups living in thirty-seven countries around the world. These nations control most of the world's oil and possess many of its most powerful armies, and in the century to come they will wield extraordinary trading power as well. In the era beyond peace, our commitment to Israel must not and will not waiver. Nor should our opposition to extremist regimes in Iraq and Iran when they threaten our interests. But in fashioning a new Muslimpolitik for a new era, the United States must learn to view the Muslim world not as a unified, radical geopolitical force bent on confronting the West but rather as a diverse cultural and ethnic grouping bounded by a faith in Islam and a legacy of political turbulence.

Our failure to appreciate the diversity of the Muslim world and the genuine threats its populations face has already contributed to the tragedy in Bosnia-Herzegovina—one of the most disgraceful chapters of the post–World War II era.

The symbolic center of the Muslim world, the Persian Gulf region, is unquestionably a vital interest of the United States. It is a bridge between Europe, Asia, and Africa, sits atop 55 percent of the world's proven oil reserves, and contains two of the world's most vital chokepoints—the Suez Canal and the Strait of Hormuz. It is also the most violently unstable region in the world.

Since 1980, more than 1.4 million people in this region have lost their lives in wars and terrorist attacks. Over the last forty-five years, Israel and its Arab neighbors have fought five wars—in 1948, 1956, 1967, 1973, and 1982—that have claimed the lives of more than a hundred thousand people. In 1992, Israel and its closest neighbors, Egypt, Jordan, and Syria, spent $11 billion for defense. In that same year, the United States provided $1.8 billion for military aid and $1.2 billion for economic aid to Israel and $1.3 billion for military aid and $900 million for economic aid to Israel's Arab neighbors. Militarization of the region is not attributable to the Arab-Israeli conflict alone. Syria invaded Jordan in 1970; Iraq invaded Iran in 1980 and Kuwait in 1990; Libya invaded Chad in 1980; Syria occupied Lebanon in 1976; North and South Yemen fought a decade-long civil war before uniting. Iran has attempted to subvert democratic governments by funding terrorist groups in Lebanon, Algeria, Morocco, Tunisia, and Sudan. Muslim-versus-Muslim conflicts have cost ten times as many lives as the Arab-Israeli conflict. Those conflicts would have taken place had there been no Cold War and no Arab-Israeli conflict. Peace between Arabs and Israelis will not signal the end of conflict between Muslim nations in the area.

The West has a vital interest in maintaining access to Persian Gulf oil. Europe depends on the Gulf for over 75 percent of its oil, Japan for over 90 percent. While the United States receives only 6 percent of its oil from this region, the ripple effect of an oil cutoff from the Persian Gulf would cripple U.S. industry. Such a cutoff would be fatal to the industries of our allies in

Western Europe and Japan. As long as the West remains so dependent on Gulf oil, we must maintain the capability to defend our friends in the Persian Gulf region.

The United States also has a critical interest in the survival and security of Israel. The United States and Israel are not formal allies, but we have a moral commitment that transcends any security agreement. As I bluntly told a bipartisan meeting of congressional leaders at the beginning of the Yom Kippur war in 1973, "No American President will ever let Israel go down the tube." Israel is the haven for millions whose families endured incredible suffering in the Holocaust. It is the only democracy in the Middle East and from its birth has been besieged by countries committed to its destruction. The depth of our commitment is demonstrated by the fact that since our recognition of Israel forty-five years ago, the United States has provided $40 billion in economic and military aid to Israel, more than twice as much as was spent under the Marshall Plan. The fact that Arab governments have finally recognized the existence of Israel is testimony to their recognition that our commitment to the survival of Israel is a pillar of America's foreign policy which will never be shaken.

The dramatic handshake between Yitzhak Rabin and Yasir Arafat on September 13, 1993, in Washington could usher in a new era of peace between Israel and its Arab neighbors. This would be a historic achievement of the greatest magnitude. Whatever diplomatic agreements Israel and its neighbors reach, it will be necessary to follow up with very substantive economic aid programs to give the parties a stake in keeping the peace. These programs must not be allowed to fail for lack of financial support. In addition to the parties involved, the United States, Japan, the nations of Western Europe, and those in the Persian Gulf region have a stake in preserving peace in the Middle East and should not hesitate to make the investment needed to preserve peace.

The major threat to our vital interests in the Persian Gulf

stems from radical regimes in Iraq, Iran, Syria, Sudan, and Libya, and from the terrorist organizations that they support inside and outside the region.

Since Saddam Hussein came to power in 1979, he has made Iraq a major regional power by resorting to brute force within and outside the country. He has crushed domestic opposition in Iraq, murdered opponents in the Middle East and Europe, and expanded his power base throughout the Arab world through terrorism and intimidation. Iraq has a population of only 18 million but controls 11 percent of the world's oil reserves. Its military establishment is larger than the United Kingdom's. Even after the Persian Gulf War, Iraq's armed forces are the fifteenth-largest in the world, with more than 2,300 tanks, 310 fighter aircraft, and a million troops. Despite the efforts of the United Nations, Iraq has the most advanced nuclear weapons program in the Middle East except for Israel's.

Iraq's recent enemy, Iran, has more potential than any other nation to be the dominant regional power in the Persian Gulf. With a population of 60 million, 10 percent of the world's oil resources, and a modern technological infrastructure, Iran has more military and economic power than any other country in the Middle East except Turkey. It has an army of almost one million troops and has gone on a military buying binge in the former Soviet Union and China.

Since the end of its war with Iraq in 1988, Iran has undertaken a diabolically subtle strategy to export its brand of extremist Muslim fundamentalism without disrupting its economic relations with the West. It has funded extremist movements in Egypt, Algeria, Morocco, Tunisia, and Afghanistan, supported radical regimes in the Sudan and other countries, and embarked on an ambitious program to develop its own nuclear weapons with the aid of North Korea and China.

Iran is the major sponsor of terrorism in the Middle East, supporting Hamas in southern Lebanon, bankrolling Muslim terrorist groups based in Tehran and the October movement in

Egypt, and forming terrorist hit squads to assassinate Iranian dissidents in Western Europe. It has extended its ideological reach into Central Asia, focusing on Turkmenistan, Uzbekistan, and Tajikistan.

Because it launched the Persian Gulf War, Iraq gets more attention in the West, but Iran is by far the greater long-term threat. Iraq's threat is only military. Its secular philosophy has no appeal beyond its border. Iran's threat is both military and religious.

As Israel's Prime Minister Rabin pointed out when we met in New York in late 1993, Iran's tactics are ominously similar to those of the Soviet Union's infamous Comintern before World War II. Rather than supporting openly pro-Iranian movements in target nations it seeks to dominate, it supports nationalist opposition movements that advocate its brand of extreme Muslim fundamentalism, just as the Communist Party of the Soviet Union supported indigenous communist parties in noncommunist nations. Rabin explained that this allows an Egyptian, for example, to be an Iranian-oriented extreme Muslim fundamentalist and a loyal Egyptian at the same time, just as members of the Soviet-controlled indigenous communist parties in the West during the Cold War could be communists without being openly disloyal to their own countries.

As a result, throughout the Muslim world today there are rapidly growing fundamentalist movements whose members appear to be loyal to their own countries but whose first loyalty is to the extreme Muslim fundamentalist religion with its roots in Iran.

As Rabin emphasized, this is an insidious form of aggression. It allows the aggressor to take over its victim without risking international condemnation. Rather than going over a border, Iran in effect goes under a border and enlists citizens of the target nation who share its extreme religious faith to carry out its designs for conquest.

Iran's strategy, as the Soviets' used to be, is to expand its influence and domination over other countries by the appeal of its ideas rather than the use of raw military power. Another striking similarity between their tactics is that Iran uses terrorism to support its aggression.

The United States should adopt a policy of isolation and containment toward both Iraq and Iran. The objective should be to give both countries problems at home so that they cannot cause problems abroad.

Our strategy toward Iraq should be to completely isolate Saddam Hussein's regime from the outside and to support dissident groups on the inside. The policy now is limited to enforcing no-fly zones to protect the Kurds in the north and the Shiites in the south, maintaining economic sanctions to squeeze Saddam out of power, and enforcing U.N. inspections against Iraqi nuclear arms programs. It is not enough. We should actively support the main opposition to Saddam, the Iraqi National Congress, as it seeks to force Baghdad to open up its political system. We should also offer Jordan increased economic incentives and a major role in the Arab-Israeli peace process as encouragement to turn off the spigot of trade until Saddam Hussein falls from power.

Our strategy toward Iran should be to contain its influence inside and outside the Persian Gulf. We should keep open the possibility of directly exploiting Iran's weaknesses if it continues its campaign of terror and intimidation against Western interests. Iran has turned state-sponsored terrorism into a science. If it persists with its subversion and terrorism, we should be prepared to assist ethnic and religious factions in Iran that oppose the Tehran regime, thereby weakening its ability to threaten our interests abroad.

Iran still suffers from the devastation caused by the Iran-Iraq War, in which more than a million Iranians died. Despite its enormous oil wealth, Iran has squandered its economic opportunities through poor planning, costly statist economic projects, and financial mismanagement. As long as Iran seeks to subvert its neighbors and support terrorist groups against Western targets, we must make sure that the West does nothing to help Tehran escape its economic quandaries. We should seek agreements with the Russian government not to sell Russian military hardware and technology to the Iranians, especially in view of the fact that Iranian influence is beginning to infiltrate Muslim countries along Russia's southern border. We should increase assistance to those states, such as Egypt, that face subversion by Iranian-supported extremist groups and increase cooperation with modernist, pro-Western Muslim states, such as Turkey. Above all, we must recognize that our major long-term threat in the Gulf is Iran, not Iraq.

The best way to contain Iran's extremist threats and those of others in the region and throughout the Muslim world is to strengthen our relations with responsible leaders such as King Hassan of Morocco, President Mubarak of Egypt, King Fahd of Saudi Arabia, and President Suharto of Indonesia.

Nearly a quarter century ago, my administration, with Henry Kissinger's skillful diplomacy, was able to convince Egypt's visionary Anwar el-Sadat that he should turn away from the Soviet Union and toward the West. This proved to be one of the most significant geopolitical developments of the Cold War era. A pro-Western Egypt made the Camp David Accords, and ultimately the Rabin-Arafat agreements, possible.

When I visited Egypt in 1974, seven million people lined our routes as Sadat and I traveled the country in open cars and by train—one of the most overwhelming receptions ever accorded a state visitor. The welcome, demonstrating the Egyptian people's affection for the American people and the legacy of freedom and prosperity we represented, was offered in the traditions of hospitality, openness, and tolerance that are the true hallmarks of Muslim philosophy. It is these pro-American impulses, which hundreds of millions of Muslims share, that should be the guideposts of our policy, rather than the ravings of malcontents and tyrants. By cultivating partnerships with nations that share our interests and our political and economic ideals, the United States can help create success stories that will serve as examples to other nations and increase stability and prosperity throughout all sectors of the Islamic world while further marginalizing extremist regimes and groups.

One Muslim nation that deserves its place in a full partnership with the United States is Turkey, whose recent emergence as a major diplomatic player in the Gulf region has been a highly positive development. At the beginning of the century Turkey was often described as the sick man of Europe. During the Cold War, that image began to change as Turkey provided more troops for NATO than any other country. Now, as a result of strong leadership and the adoption of free-market policies, Turkey has the biggest economy in the Middle East. With a population of 60 million, Turkey should play a major diplomatic role commensurate with its economic and military power.

Regardless of objections from the anti-Turkish Greek lobby in the United States, we should increase our economic and military cooperation with Turkey. It can play a pivotal role as a bridge between the Muslim and Western worlds and can help check Iranian advances in the Middle East and positively influence Uzbekistan, Turkmenistan, Tajikistan, Kirgizia, and Kazakstan so they do not fall under Iranian influence.

The United States should also help moderate forces in Afghanistan who oppose extremist fundamentalism from Iran and other sources but who have been abandoned after the end of the Soviet war in Afghanistan. Afghanistan has not lost its strategic importance in terms of the fate of Central Asia. The British recognized its importance in the nineteenth century, as did the Soviets when they invaded Afghanistan in 1979. We must recognize this geopolitical reality today. If Afghanistan falls under an Iranian sphere of influence, Tehran would hold the keys to Central Asia.

With their vast oil wealth, and in view of the weakness of Saudi Arabia and the other Gulf states, the Iraqi and Iranian regimes will be in a position to threaten the Gulf indefinitely. Consequently, the United States should assume the responsibility of guaranteeing Gulf security with its military power. We should develop close relations with Saudi Arabia and other friendly Persian Gulf states. We should continue to stockpile pre-positioned materials, encourage these countries to build up their military infrastructures, be prepared to use force in any contingency that threatens our interest, and pledge further cooperation through informal agreements.

Because these regimes cannot openly embrace the United States for fear of inciting domestic violence, we should look the other way when they fail to follow our lead on other international issues. It is more important that they work with us on Gulf security issues.

Good relations with moderate Gulf states is not a substitute for a U.S. military guarantee. With a combined force of 225,000 troops, 1,300 tanks, and 567 aircraft and a total population of 18 million people, these states are military midgets in comparison with their Iraqi and Iranian neighbors. The United States must accept the fact that it is the only Western power with the military resources to project force and block Iranian and Iraqi advances in the region.

We should enhance sea- and airlift capabilities for putting U.S. troops into the Persian Gulf region. During the Persian Gulf War, it took six months to deploy the necessary soldiers and equipment. While Iraq gave us the time to prepare, the next aggressor probably will not make the same mistake. To the extent possible, we should pre-position equipment—such as tanks, heavy artillery, and light-armored vehicles—to form a limited defensive strike force that can be used in Saudi Arabia and other Gulf states to deter aggression. More important, we should invest heavily in creating a genuine rapid-deployment force so we can move heavy divisions into the region quickly and exploit new technologies.

For better or worse, only the United States can fulfill this role. We cannot afford to rely on other countries—either our Western European allies or friendly nations in the region—to protect our interests in the Persian Gulf. They may lack the military resources and possibly the political will to act decisively in a crisis.

This means that the United States faces very demanding military requirements for the foreseeable future. There is a limit to how much we can cut the defense budget if we are to maintain a strong military capable of defending our interests in such distant regions as the Persian Gulf. From 1985 to 1995, defense spending will have been cut over 50 percent in real terms. By 1998, the United States will spend less than 3.2 percent of its GNP on defense, the lowest level since the Roosevelt administration before the attack on Pearl Harbor.

As General William Odom has written, "The Persian Gulf War demonstrated to all other attentive military establishments that in the rankings of all the world's militaries, the United States not only is in first place; the next dozen or so places are not even occupied." But Odom also noted that this capability can be thrown away in a few years of mismanagement. The strength of our military capabilities should not give us a false sense of security. The requirements that we face in the Persian Gulf are extremely demanding and will stretch our capabilities to their limit. The Gulf is as far from the United States as any region in the world, and we can expect to have no forward bases. If we are to have a base-line force to defend this region, we have to pay the budgetary price.

The United States cannot afford to reduce its military budget any further. The President should use his position as Commander in Chief to build public support for maintaining a strong military, despite domestic political pressures to cut defense spending so that we can fund other programs. We are on a slippery slope toward the hollow military of the late 1970s. With the rise of regional powers in the Gulf and the decline of our defense budgets, we may not be able to repeat Operation Desert

Storm if necessary in the late 1990s. This would not be a concern if the trends in the region were toward stability, but they are not.

The Arab-Israeli peace process is another key to stemming rising instability in the Middle East. For forty-five years Arabs and Israelis battled repeatedly and talked rarely. The agreements between the PLO and Israel were a major breakthrough. But they are only the first step on the long road to a just and lasting peace.

Constructive peace talks with Arab nations and the Palestinians serve both Israel's and America's interests. Israel has won each of the five wars it has fought with its Arab neighbors, but in each war its casualties have increased. Like the Koreans and the Vietnamese, Arabs too can learn to fight. One of the most dynamic leaders I ever met was Israel's first Prime Minister, David Ben-Gurion. He observed that the "extremists" in Israel who advocate the absorption of Arab lands would deprive Israel of its mission. "If they succeed, Israel will be neither Jewish nor democratic," he said. "The Arabs will outnumber us and undemocratic, repressive measures will be needed to keep them under control." It is estimated that there will be an Arab population of 1.3 million in Israel by the year 2000; it serves Israel's interest not to continue to treat Arabs as second-class citizens.

The chances for a lasting peace in the Middle East are the best they have been since the creation of the state of Israel. Instead of an aggressive Soviet Union supporting Israel's Arab enemies, we have democratic Russia supporting the peace process. Because they were on the wrong side of the Gulf War, Israel's enemies can no longer count on financial support from the wealthy Gulf oil states. With Egypt no longer anti-Israel after the Camp David Accords, the correlation of military forces is heavily weighted in Israel's favor. Failure to seize the moment to make a lasting peace now would be a tragedy for all the people in the Middle East, particularly because such favorable factors may not last. While Israeli hard-liners oppose a settlement with the Palestinians and Arab countries, Prime Minister Rabin has courageously recognized that the time has come for Israel to bargain with its neighbors. He proved to be the right leader in the right place at the right time. It takes a strong leader to wage war, and it takes an even stronger leader to make peace.

As a hard-line leader in time of war, Rabin cannot be accused of being soft on Arafat because he made peace. After his historic handshake with Arafat on September 13, I asked him during a meeting in New York whether it had been a difficult moment for him. Rabin, who controls his deeply felt emotions as well as any leader I have ever met, almost lost his composure as he said, "It was not easy but I had no choice." He vividly remembered the terribly painful moment when eleven Israeli athletes were killed at the 1972 Olympic Games, an attack for which Arafat was responsible. But he knew too that as a result of the collapse of communism in the Soviet Union, Arafat would no longer have the support of Russia, just as he would no longer have the same level of support from Saudi Arabia and the other moderate Gulf states because he took the wrong side in the Persian Gulf War. He also knew that among the Palestinians, Arafat was being criticized for being a "moderate," and that an increasing danger existed that he might be replaced by a far more extreme Palestinian leader.

Rabin faced the classic dilemma described by Paul Johnson: "The essence of geopolitics is to be able to distinguish between different degrees of evil." Rabin knew that Arafat was evil. But the choice was not between Arafat and somebody less evil, but between Arafat and somebody more evil. Arafat needs to deal because he is weak. Israel can risk making a deal with its worst enemy because it is strong.

One of the positive fallouts from the new peace initiative between Israel and its Arab neighbors is that it reduces and may eventually eliminate a factor that has had a negative impact on U.S. relations with non-Arab Muslim nations from Morocco to Indonesia. The leaders of most of these nations often told us privately that they did not agree with the extreme anti-Israel policies of Israel's Arab neighbors. But it was politically not possible for them to do anything but go along with their fellow Muslims in opposing Israel. Arab-Israeli peace will increase the chances for improved relations between the United States and all of the Muslim nations.

Some thoughtful observers, among them Harvard professor Samuel Huntington, have warned that if the West mishandles relations with the Muslim world, a "clash of civilizations" could pit the West against Islam. Recent military conflicts support this thesis. In the former Yugoslavia, Bosnian Muslims and Christian Serbs fight over control of Bosnia-Herzegovina. In the former Soviet Union, Christian Armenians and Muslim Azerbaijanis are fighting over the Nagorno-Karabakh region. In Lebanon, Christian and Muslim militia have been slaughtering each other for years. In Central Asia, religious tensions have contributed to the fighting in Tajikistan.

The United States must not let the "clash of civilizations" become the dominant characteristic of the post–Cold War era. As Huntington observed, the real danger is not that this clash is inevitable but that by our inaction we will make it a self-fulfilling prophecy. If we continue to ignore conflicts in which Muslim nations are victims, we will invite a clash between the Western and Muslim worlds.

One such conflict that must be marked down as one of America's most unfortunate and unnecessary foreign policy failures is the carnage in the former Yugoslavia, where three years ago communist hard-liners rising from the ruins of Marshal Tito's artificial nation-state mounted a naked effort to destroy the democratic government of Croatia. From the beginning of the war there have been excesses on both sides, but the cycle of violence began as a result of Serbian aggression against other former Yugoslavian republics—aggression for which the United States and its allies have consistently and repeatedly failed to exact a price. As early as 1991, along with a number of other observers, I called upon the United Nations to lift the embargo against the victims of Serbian aggression. The United States, the United Nations, and the European Community vacillated, equivocated, orated, condemned, and ultimately did nothing to counter effectively the Serbian onslaught. The massacre of scores of shoppers and their children in Sarajevo in February 1994 would almost certainly not have occurred had the West acted sooner.

Following the massacre, the United States and its NATO allies agreed to issue an ultimatum to the Serbs to withdraw their weapons from around Sarajevo, which for the time being lifted the siege of one city without depriving the Serbs of the territorial spoils of years of aggression elsewhere in Bosnia. It is unfortunate that the United States did not take action in this protracted struggle until it was forced to do so by a public reaction to bloody images on television.

It is an awkward but unavoidable truth that had the citizens of Sarajevo been predominately Christian or Jewish, the civilized world would not have permitted the siege to reach the point it did on February 5, when a Serbian shell landed in the crowded marketplace. In such an instance, the West would have acted quickly and would have been right in doing so.

The siege of Sarajevo can have a redeeming character only if the West learns two things as a result. The first is that enlightened peoples cannot be selective about condemning aggression and genocide. When the communist Khmer Rouge massacred two million Cambodians in the late 1970s, Americans' outrage was muted compared with the anguish we justifiably suffered over the massacre of six million Jews in the Holocaust. The situation in Cambodia, it seemed, was too fraught with contradiction, especially for those Americans who had opposed our efforts to defeat the communists who carried out the massacre.

The other lesson is that because we are the last remaining superpower, no crisis is irrelevant to our interests. If the United States had been willing to lead, a number of steps short of the commitment of ground forces—for instance, revoking the arms embargo—could have been taken early in the Bosnian crisis to blunt Serbian aggression. Our failure to do so tarnished our reputation as an evenhanded player on the international stage and contributed to an image promoted by extreme Muslim fundamentalists that the West is callous to the fate of Muslim nations but protective of Christian and Jewish nations.

The nightmare scenario invoked by some, of fanatical Islam on a collision course with the West, will come true only if fundamentalist forces take over the Muslim world. But most of the Muslim world does not march to the beat of the fundamentalist drum. Fundamentalist regimes are still a minority, comprising only 10 percent of the Islamic world's total population. If the peoples of the Muslim world are able to chart their own destinies, extreme fundamentalism will not triumph. Modernist regimes range from open societies such as Turkey and Pakistan to relatively open countries such as Egypt and Indonesia. All seek to combine the best of the Muslim and Western cultures, rather than to turn back the clock to the twelfth century. They provide a compelling alternative to extreme fundamentalism for those who seek a better life.

Whittaker Chambers wrote that communism was a faith and that it was only as strong as the failure of all other faiths. Muslim fundamentalism is a strong faith. Its appeal is religious, not secular. It appeals to the soul, not the body. Secular Western values cannot compete with this faith. Neither can secular Muslim values. In the clash of civilizations, the fact that we are the strongest and richest nation in history is not enough. What will be decisive is the power of the great ideas, religious and secular, that made us a great nation. Though the West and the Muslims have profound differences in their cultural and historical development, we can learn from each other, studying the reasons for our past successes and failures.

The twentieth century has been a period of conflict between the West and the Muslim world. If we work together we can make the twenty-first century not just a time of peace in the Middle East and the Persian Gulf, but a century in which, beyond peace, two great civilizations will enrich each other and the rest of the world—not just by their arms and their wealth but by the eternal appeal of their ideals.

The Developing World:
Freedom's Last Frontier

The term "Third World" is obsolete. With the collapse of communism in the Soviet Union and Eastern Europe and with China rapidly becoming more capitalist than communist economically, only two "worlds" remain. One comprises the countries of the developed world, primarily nations in the Northern Hemisphere that are rich or becoming rich, and the other those of the developing world, primarily nations in the Southern Hemisphere that are poor and in some cases actually becoming poorer. Although the Southern Hemisphere no longer represents a strategic priority for America, it would be a profound mistake for the United States to ignore the dangers and the opportunities in the developing world, where two thirds of the world's people live.

Since the end of World War II, corrupt government officials and disastrous economic policies have stunted most of the nations in Latin America, Africa, the Mideast, and South Asia. With the end of the Cold War, two changes have dramatically improved the chances for economic and political progress.

For forty-five years, many of the nations in the developing world were pawns in the East-West struggle. The aid they received depended not upon their needs or the quality of their economic and political policies but upon which side they supported in the struggle between East and West. Now the only test is whether they have adopted economic and political policies that have a chance to advance economic progress and freedom.

Even more significant, a number of nations in the developing world have learned the secret of the West's economic progress. For the first time since the end of World War II, the nations of the developing world have a realistic chance of breaking out of the cycle of poverty and political instability that has throttled economic growth and development.

The success stories in what was formerly the Third World point the way to progress. What is the secret of East Asia's phenomenal economic progress? Economic policies that rewarded private initiatives; major investment in education; low tariff barriers and low inflation; and a stable legal framework that attracted private investment from at home and from abroad. Just as important, the nations that enjoyed economic progress rejected a major economic role for government. They recognized the fundamental truth that private rather than government enterprise produces progress.

In East Asia, the four tigers—Korea, Hong Kong, Taiwan, and Singapore—have adopted free-market economic policies that have produced explosive growth. Malaysia and Thailand are now rapidly moving in the same direction. Indonesia is starting to develop the huge potential of its human and natural resources.

India is beginning to move away from statist policies that would have doomed a nation that will be the most populous in the world in the twenty-first century to continue to be one of the poorest. The stakes are enormous. We have a profound interest in India's success in implementing free-market economic reforms. In Russia, the question is whether democratic capitalism can compete with China's communist capitalism. The jury is still out. In India, the question is whether democratic socialism can compete with China's communist capitalism. The verdict is in. The latter wins hands down. In this competition between the world's two most populous nations, India deserves support because it is trying to achieve economic progress with democracy. But it will not succeed unless it abandons socialism.

In Latin America, recent experience has shown that democracy alone is not enough. During the 1980s, twelve nations in Latin America moved from dictatorship to democracy. Yet the GNP of Latin America fell during that same period because of the failure of democratically elected leaders to abandon statist policies and adopt free-market economic policies. As a result, the 1980s became known as the lost decade.

An exciting new story is being written in the 1990s. Argentina, Brazil, Colombia, Costa Rica, Mexico, Peru, Venezuela, and even Bolivia, the poorest country in South America, have joined Chile in adopting free-market policies that are producing substantial growth in their economies and in the per capita incomes of their people. David Rockefeller, who has closely followed developments in Latin America for decades, has observed, "It is clear now that a new mood of pragmatism and enterprise is abroad in these lands."

Historically, the developing world has been an economic and political sinkhole. I vividly recall my first visit as Vice President to one such nation, Indonesia, over forty years ago. President Sukarno, dressed in an exquisitely tailored white uniform, welcomed Mrs. Nixon and me at the presidential palace. The superb cuisine and the service at the state dinner he hosted for us matched that of any Western country. But as we drove through the streets of Jakarta, then the world's most densely populated city, we saw open sewers emptying into canals. Children were swimming in the filthy water. Women were doing their laundry in it. Those who complain about the evils of industrialization and who speak nostalgically about how much better life was for people before industrialization should visit some of the nations in the developing world not yet "contaminated" by economic progress.

In many parts of the developing world, very little has changed. The combined GNP of the entire African continent south of the Sahara is less than that of Holland. Because the end of the Cold War has eroded the desire of major nations to buy friends in Africa, foreign aid has dropped. Sub-Saharan Africa is the only region in the world likely to experience an increase in absolute poverty over the next decade. Throughout the developing world, more than 192 million children suffer from malnutrition. The annual population growth rate has been 2.5 percent over recent decades, more than five times higher than the growth rate in developed countries over the last ten years. In most of these countries, per capita income has barely increased since the 1960s.

The West is not responsible for the problems of the developing world, but we have a unique responsibility and opportunity to try to help solve those problems. Without our assistance, efforts to break the cycle of poverty will fail. With our help, they have a chance to succeed. While we cannot become the world's welfare agency, we have an obligation to help these countries find solutions to their problems.

Our policies of assistance to the developing world are based not solely on altruism but also on self-interest. There are three major areas where our interests are affected by our policies toward the developing world: our economy, our security, and the ominous increase in the number of refugees clamoring to come to the United States.

Increased economic growth in the developing world will lead to increased economic prosperity in the United States. Our exports of goods and services to Canada, a vital interest of the United States and a developed country of twenty million people, were $108 billion in 1992. Our exports to Mexico, a developing nation with five times the population of Canada and also a vital interest, were $50 billion. Mexico's move up from poverty will create thousands of jobs for Mexicans and thousands more in the United States, where more than eight million jobs depend on foreign trade.

From Somalia and Bosnia we have learned that the end of superpower conflict does not mean the end of regional conflict. Instability in the developing world will continue to pose a significant threat to U.S. interests. Three of the world's five largest armies are in the developing world. All countries now seeking to become nuclear powers are in the developing world, and most of them are not friends of the United States. The nightmare of a nuclear war beginning in the developing world could become a reality.

But as the Cold War has ended, doors have been opened for diplomatic initiatives that had no chance of succeeding when the Soviet Union was opposing them. The most graphic example of this is the prospect of Mideast peace. There have been five wars between Israel and its Arab neighbors over the past forty-five years. One hundred thousand lost their lives in those wars. There have been four wars between India and Pakistan in that same forty-five year period. Over five million lost their lives in those wars. The Soviet Union played the spoiler's role in the five previous Arab-Israeli wars. Now Russia supports the peace process, giving it some chance for success.

Two of the poorest nations in the world—India and Pakistan—spent more than $11 billion a year for the purpose of waging a future war. The conflict has its roots in profound religious differences, but it has been exacerbated by the fact that the Soviet Union supported India, and China supported Pakistan. Now a window of opportunity has opened for progress on negotiations between the two. In a process similar to the Middle East negotiations, the United States, Britain, Russia, and China could help broker the peace.

Poverty in the developing world will continue to produce millions of refugees. Throughout the world, people from underdeveloped countries are moving into developed countries. On our border with Mexico, an estimated sixty thousand Mexicans cross illegally into the United States every month, putting an enormous burden on federal and state budgets that are already struggling with welfare, crime, and unemployment problems. In Europe, this economic exodus is causing increased social tensions and xenophobia in the host countries. Unless the economies of the Southern Hemisphere grow, this flood of refugees from the developing world will become a deluge.

Both the developed and developing nations must change their policies. Foreign aid is not the answer. Since the end of World War II, the United States has provided $450 billion in foreign aid to the nations of the developing world. The results have been dismal. Too often, foreign aid only reinforced the inefficiencies of statist governments, encouraged corruption, and promoted protectionism. Foreign aid was supposed to produce prosperity. Too often, it subsidized poverty.

During the Cold War, most of our foreign aid was tied directly to our security interests. Foreign aid in the period beyond peace must stand on its own: Does it serve our interests and the interests of the people of the recipient nation? The United States should continue to be generous in providing humanitarian aid where we have the capacity to do so. But foreign aid should not be used to prop up and subsidize governments that refuse to adopt political policies that promote peace, freedom, and economic policies that have a chance to succeed. Successful growth in the twenty-first century cannot be achieved by relying on the failed statist policies of the nineteenth and twentieth centuries.

We should promote free trade with these countries rather than continuing to dole out unlimited amounts of foreign aid. As *The Economist* pointed out before the summit of the industrialized democracies in Tokyo in July 1993, "If rich countries abolished all their barriers to Third World goods, the increase in developing nations' exports would be worth twice what they receive in aid." Lowering trade barriers is indispensable if the nations of the developing world are to have any chance of achieving economic growth. The United States should take the lead in implementing agreements like NAFTA and GATT because they open up our markets to developing countries as well as create markets for the capital and consumer goods and services of developed countries. A major reason for supporting free trade with the developing world is not economic but political. Some oppose free trade with Mexico and other countries because they believe U.S. industry would be put at a competitive disadvantage. Others oppose trade with nations in the developing world that are not Western-style democracies. But free trade with these countries would do more to spark political reform than any unilateral action the U.S. government could devise.

The most important lesson the developing countries can learn is to ignore the advice of those in the United States and Western Europe who still believe that only the socialist road leads to economic paradise. The last refuge of Marxists is the economic development institutions that see state-dominated rather than market-based solutions as the key to growth. They supported high tariffs against Western goods, state subsidies to struggling industries, and a mercantilist trade policy. They thought that state-led economic development would lead to economic independence. Instead it leads to an economic dead end.

Forty years ago, as Vice President, I visited all of the countries of Asia except communist China. Political leaders, journalists, teachers, and students in newly independent nations were debating what policies would produce rapid progress. Some were enamored with the Soviet model; others with the communist Chinese model; still others favored the democratic socialist model then gaining popularity in Western Europe. Now it is no contest. The communist model has been rejected by the people of the former Soviet Union and Eastern Europe. The Chinese still have a communist government, but they have used free-market economic policies to create spectacular growth. Democratic socialism has been tried and found wanting in countries as diverse as Sweden, France, and India. Free-market economic policies are the wave of the future, but they do not produce instant or uninterrupted prosperity. Nations with free-market policies go through periods of recession, slow growth, and too rapid growth. A free-market economic policy will inevitably have its successes and its failures. But the free market is the only system that can unleash the productive potential of a nation.

If a people's only interest is stability, it should not choose a free-market economy. Free markets are by nature unstable. One nineteenth-century philosopher likened capitalism to a gale of creative destruction. A command economy can produce stability, but at the cost of suppressing creativity. A free-market system encourages creativity at the cost of instability. The choice therefore is between economic progress at the cost of some instability or stability at the cost of no progress.

Supply-siders, Keynsians, monetarists, and proponents of other economic disciplines will continue to debate the merits of their various policies. The key is free debate about what does and does not work and the willingness to discard failed policies and to expand successful ones. As we advise leaders of the developing nations, we must disabuse ourselves of the notion that we have all the answers, for the simple reason that the essence of the free market is that there are no sure-fire answers. If there were, we would all be billionaires.

One of the most inspiring stories of the last fifty years has been that of countries who were mired in absolute poverty after World War II but adopted the right economic policies and triggered astonishing social and economic progress. China, Taiwan, South Korea, Singapore, Malaysia, Thailand, Chile, and others have succeeded because they stressed basic economic principles such as lower taxes, fewer government regulations, open markets, and competitive industries, and placed a high premium on education. These principles have opened up their economies and integrated them with those of the developed world. Such progress is within the reach of every nation. Within two or three decades, any country can extricate itself from poverty and join the ranks of the newly industrializing nations. By helping developing countries adopt growth-based policies, developed countries can make an enormous positive contribution to the welfare of their own people and the prosperity of all peoples.

The next generation's success stories will be written by the three towering giants of the developing world, India, Brazil, and Indonesia, all of which have turned the corner toward potential economic prosperity.

With a population of over 875 million, India is slowly shedding its reputation as a socialist economy. It has increased trade with Western Europe and the United States, reduced subsidies to state-run industries, and strengthened the rupee in the international financial markets. The literacy rate has improved by 120 percent since 1960. Per capita GNP has risen from $110 to $310 over the last twenty years. Despite the fact that India suffers from religious conflicts and civil strife, it will become a great power by the next century if it continues down the road toward free-market economics.

Brazil, with over one half the people of South America, has made a remarkable economic turnaround in the 1990s. Racked by runaway inflation, a burgeoning foreign debt, a crumbling public infrastructure, and widespread political corruption, the government of President Itamar Franco opened the door to economic reform. Brazil's GDP grew 4 percent in 1993, and industrial production rose almost 10 percent. Exports to the United States have increased 80 percent over the last 10 years. Import tariffs on products such as automobiles have dropped from 80 percent to 25 percent. Brazil still has formidable problems, but with this improved economic outlook, it has the potential to become an economic showcase for the rest of Latin America.

Indonesia is a striking example of how a developing nation can move from poverty to progress through the adoption of free-market policies. Too often overlooked by foreign policy experts, Indonesia is the fourth-most-populous nation in the world, after China, India, and the United States. It is the largest Muslim nation, with more people than all the Arab nations combined. During the past twenty-five years, the proportion of Indonesians living in absolute poverty has declined from 60 percent to 15 percent. Annual per capita income has increased from $50 to $650. Family-planning policies have reduced the annual population growth from 2.4 percent to 1.8 percent. Indonesia suffers from corruption, nepotism, and an authoritarian government. But progress toward political freedom is beginning and will continue as economic freedom is expanded.

Vietnam could become an economic success story if it

breaks with the failed political and economic policies of its past. Because its leaders are ruthless players of power politics, they will soon understand that geopolitically they cannot afford to retard their economic growth with communist policies at a time when their mortal rival, China, has achieved high growth by capitalist means. Vietnam has begun to open its economy to foreign investors, particularly from Western Europe and Japan. But most of its economic reforms are nothing more than window dressing.

Egypt has remarkable potential, particularly as many of the statist practices that impeded economic growth in the 1970s and 1980s have been repealed. Under the courageous leadership of President Hosni Mubarak, it has opened the door to free trade with Western Europe and serves as an economic conduit between Europe and the rest of the Arab world. It has doubled its exports to the United States over the last ten years. With the ominous threat of radical Muslim fundamentalists, overpopulation, and inflation, Egypt faces grave problems. But as by far the most populous and influential Muslim regime in the Mideast, it deserves maximum attention and support from the West.

Turkey has transformed itself from an economic basket case into an economic breadbasket. Beginning in the 1980s, the late Turkish Prime Minister Turgut Ozal aggressively lifted trade restrictions, liberalized policies, and integrated Turkey economically with Western Europe. These policies boosted Turkey's per capita GNP from $1,400 in 1980 to $2,000 in 1993. The new government of Tansu Ciller has pledged to keep Turkey on this same track of economic reform.

Mexico has been the economic wunderkind of the 1990s. Under the leadership of President Salinas, Mexico has increased trade with the United States, liberalized state-run industries, restored world confidence in the peso, and eliminated costly government subsidies. Since Mexico began to reduce its trade barriers in 1986, U.S. exports have climbed from $12.4 billion to $40 billion in 1992. As a result, Mexico has become Latin

America's most progressive economy and has set an example for other nations.

There have been three great wars in this century—World War I, World War II, and the Cold War. Before each there was widespread conflict. After each there was unbridled euphoria.

After World War I, many Americans hoped that the League of Nations could achieve our goal of making the world safe for democracy. But Woodrow Wilson's courageous and eloquent appeal to idealism fell victim to the tragedy of his physical breakdown and the opposition of isolationist forces in the United States. Wilson believed that under the League of Nations, countries would work together to resolve their conflicts peacefully. Twenty years later, the Axis dictatorships launched World War II.

After the defeat of Germany and Japan in World War II, America's Secretary of State, Cordell Hull, said in testimony to Congress: "There will no longer be a need for spheres of influence, for alliances, for balances of power, or any other of the separate alliances through which in the unhappy past the nations strove to safeguard their security or promote their interest." The United Nations was heralded as the body that would make all of this possible. In 1946, less than a year after the end of World War II and the founding of the United Nations, the Soviet Union launched the Cold War.

After the collapse of Soviet communism in the Cold War and the defeat of aggression in the Persian Gulf War, the conventional wisdom for a time was that we were witnessing the beginning of a new world order. Many believed that man's ability to reason would replace his instinct for aggression. The death and destruction in Bosnia is only one example of the tragic fact that the end of the Cold War between the superpowers has not meant the end of conflict between smaller powers. Immanuel Kant's dream of a "perpetual peace" has collapsed into a nightmare. In addition, with the unity of the West fractured by the end of the security threat, economics threatens to become, to paraphrase Clausewitz, a continuation of war by other means.

Great leadership will be needed to meet the challenges we face in the world in the era beyond peace. It is significant that none of the other current leaders of the Western world, although they are able men and women, have public approval ratings equal even to Boris Yeltsin's. Churchill once observed that one of Britain's nineteenth-century Prime Ministers, Lord Rosebery, "had the misfortune to live in a time of great men and small events." Historically, leaders have not been recognized as great unless they have led during times of war. We must change our thinking. Keeping peace should be recognized as an event as great as waging war. Those who meet the exciting new challenges of this historic era beyond peace will earn the mantle of greatness, because they will have had the good fortune to live in a time of great events of their own making.

What role will the United States play in this era beyond peace? In the beginning of the twentieth century we were not a military or economic superpower. While we played a significant role on the world stage, American world leadership was not an indispensable factor for maintaining peace. Today the United States is the strongest and richest nation in the world.

It is clear that there is no substitute for American leadership. What is not clear is how the United States should lead. History shows that the lessons of the past can be used to resolve the problems of the future. We face lesser dangers than we did during World War I, World War II, and the Cold War. In those three wars, the danger was tangible—we could see it, feel it, touch it. Even during the Cold War, we faced a clear and present danger. By mobilizing our economic, political, and military resources, the United States and its allies could meet and defeat those threats.

With the end of the Cold War, the threat is less but the challenge is greater. We undoubtedly have the means to maintain the military power necessary to secure the peace for which we have sacrificed so much. The cost will bc far lower because the danger has diminished as a result of the end of the Cold War. But we do not have a foreign enemy to unite us or a cause to inspire us. The profound question is whether America will unite behind a policy of enlightened world leadership—one of the greatest causes any nation could have.

We should welcome the opportunity to meet this challenge—not just for those whose freedom is threatened, but for ourselves. Only when we are engaged in an enterprise greater than ourselves can we be true to ourselves.

Are we worthy to lead? We cannot unless we project values that go beyond peace, beyond our security, beyond our wealth. Two hundred years ago we caught the imagination of the world because of the ideals of freedom for which we stood. Today the United States must once again demonstrate not just that we are the strongest and the richest nation in the world, but also that we are a good and principled country, an example for others to follow. That is our challenge beyond peace. How we meet that challenge will determine not only our future but also the future of peace, prosperity, and freedom for the rest of the world.

III

America Beyond Peace

The ultimate test of a nation's character is not how it responds to adversity in war but how it meets the challenge of peace. The end of the Cold War offers us a providential opportunity to address long-neglected domestic problems, to return to our founding principles, and to achieve a true American renewal. Our future and the future of the world depend upon whether we meet this challenge. A strong, unified, growing America can help make the next century a century of peace and freedom. A weak, fractured, stagnant America could be the catalyst for another grim century of tyranny and war.

America is the greatest, most successful social experiment ever conducted in the history of man. Nothing is more essential to the world's peace and security in the twenty-first century than the renewal and strengthening of America itself and the preservation of what it means to mankind everywhere. Unless we successfully address our serious domestic problems, they will insidiously erode our prosperity, corrode the soul of the nation, and extinguish what Lincoln called "the last best hope of man on earth."

Constant renewal has always been part of the American experience. But "renewal" and "change" are not the same. Change is good only if it happens to be improvement. Change that destroys what is good is bad. One hundred years ago, Marx's colleague, Friedrich Engels, inspired millions with the slogan "We must change the world." The changes he advocated left a terrible legacy of death, destruction, and brutal repression in its wake. As Irving Babbitt warned, "Where there is no vision, the people perish. Where there is sham vision, they perish sooner." The change we need today is the kind that restores the best we have lost, preserves the best we have, and leads us on to something better.

Restoring the best we have lost is the first essential. The domestic problems that plague the nation today result directly from the destructive changes in cultural values, social policies, and behavioral standards that have marked the course of the past three decades.

Many of our opinion leaders are satisfied to think of the United States as just "one nation" among a hundred and eighty moral, if not necessarily military or economic, equals. Most Americans disagree. We want, and the world needs, America to be something more.

From the beginning, America has been more than a place. It represents the values and ideals of a humane civilization. Our central mission is to preserve and advance those values both at home and abroad.

In my first Inaugural Address twenty-five years ago, I said, "To a crisis of the spirit we need an answer of the spirit." That was true then. It is still true today. The violence, discord, viciousness, and slovenliness that so mar the quality of life in America are products of the spirit, and they require answers of the spirit. These are behaviors, not conditions. We will get America back on the path of civilization when Americans once more respect and demand civilized behavior.

From the 1960s on, our laws and our mores have been driven by the cultural conceits that took hold during the heyday of the counterculture, including a denial of personal responsibility and the fantasy that the coercive power of government can produce spiritual uplift, cure poverty, end bigotry, legislate growth, and stamp out any number of individual and social inadequacies.

Some have called the 1960s the second-most-disastrous decade in American history, second only to the 1860s, when the nation was drenched in the blood of civil war. As Rush Limbaugh put it, "In the eyes of the 1960s activist, America could do nothing right. The United States was no longer perceived as the greatest experiment in democracy and freedom in the history of the world, but as a center of militarism, imperialism, racism, and economic oppression."

The 1960s saw an explosion of domestic violence without modern precedent. That was also the time when, in effect, the inmates took over the asylum: when the notion took hold that great universities should be run by their students, and pandering college faculties and administrations supinely acquiesced; when police departments were stripped of the right to police; when the fad for "deinstitutionalization" emptied mental hospitals of their patients, dumping them on the streets; when criminal behavior was celebrated as social protest; when welfare-rights activists succeeded in transforming the public dole into a permanent entitlement; and when the cultural avant-garde, egged on by the news and entertainment media, declared open war on the values of family, civility, and personal responsibility, and mocked the American dream.

Some are beginning to recognize this. One of America's most penetrating social thinkers, Thomas Sowell, asked recently whether anyone has noticed "how many of the adverse trends plaguing us today began in the 1960s?" In a new book, *The Dream and the Nightmare: The Sixties' Legacy to the Underclass,* *Fortune* magazine editor Myron Magnet brilliantly analyzes the multiple ills that are directly traceable to that cultural revolution. He argues that the remade system "fostered, in the underclass and the homeless, a new, intractable poverty that shocked and dismayed, that . . . went beyond the economic realm into the realm of pathology." It stripped away respect for precisely those attitudes and behaviors that have always provided the exit from poverty: thrift, hard work, deferred gratification, "and so on through the whole catalogue of antique-sounding bourgeois virtues."

The founders created a land of opportunity. For more than three centuries, opportunity was enough because the culture conditioned people to take advantage of it. But we have now created a culture in which appallingly large numbers ignore the opportunities offered by work, choosing instead those offered by the interwoven worlds of welfare and crime. Our task now is not to invent opportunity, but to enforce honest work as the route to it. We need to get America back on track before it sails off into the abyss.

To paraphrase Shakespeare, the answer is not in our laws but in ourselves. Get our culture and values back on track, and the laws will follow.

In assessing our domestic situation, we must keep a sense of proportion. Karen Elliot House, former foreign editor of *The Wall Street Journal*, has observed that we hear "ceaseless sermons of gloom and doom; decline and fall; America is overextended; America can't compete"—ideas that have been "sold like snake oil, by politicians, economists, and academic evangelists." We must not allow this dirge of pessimism to become the national anthem.

The United States is the wealthiest and most productive nation in the world. We are still the most religious nation in the advanced industrialized world. For millions of every race, creed, color, and religion, the United States represents the promised land. Immigrants from all over the world still endure great hardship and peril to become Americans. Despite our serious racial problems, the United States has made unprecedented progress toward building a society that judges individuals not by who they are but by what they do. Those who find nothing right with America should compare our record with those of other advanced industrial democracies where status is largely determined by birth or ethnicity. They should consider the plight of Turkish workers in Germany, Arabs in France, or Koreans in

Japan. Most Americans are decent, generous, hardworking people, driven by the ethic of individual responsibility, accountability for their actions, and empathy for the misfortune of others.

Yet most will agree that all is not well in America. Symptoms of our problems are depressingly familiar. Many Americans believe the political system is in gridlock, incapable of addressing serious problems because the political leadership has become inaccessible and unresponsive. Since the Great Society was launched in 1965, the federal government has spent staggering sums on new domestic programs. These programs have not delivered on their extravagant promises. This contributes to cynicism about government in all areas. Ross Perot's appeal is a symptom of this pervasive mistrust.

When President Bush left office on January 20, 1993, the national debt was over $4 trillion. The budget deficit of over $300 billion in 1993 will be added to that debt. There is little relief in sight, even by the most optimistic projections of the administration's budget plan. Low rates of savings, investment, and productivity growth menace America's global economic leadership. The vicious circle of poverty has become worse for millions, despite the billions spent to alleviate it.

There is a growing sense that the social contract essential to a free society has begun to unravel. Since the 1960s, the violent crime rate has increased more than 560 percent. Illegitimate births have increased more than 400 percent. The divorce rate has quadrupled. The percentage of children living in single-family homes has tripled. One child in eight lives on welfare, more than triple the percentage in 1960. The suicide rate among teenagers has more than doubled. Every day, 160,000 students stay home from school out of fear of violence. Drug use continues to escalate, and America's inner cities still suffer the ravages inflicted by over two million cocaine addicts.

The average American watches nearly fifty hours of television a week, a 25 percent increase since 1960, and ten hours more than the average work week. What he sees is mind-numbing, idiotic, violent, and sexually explicit. A 1991 survey revealed that adults believe television has the greatest influence on children's values—more than parents, teachers, and religious leaders combined.

What many commentators now join in calling a crisis of the spirit has affected all classes in American society. Mrs. Clinton deserves credit for her courage in articulating the absence of higher purpose in life, despite the fact that since the late 1960s many of her most liberal supporters have relentlessly assaulted traditional values in the name of liberation. Unfortunately, most of the administration's remedies would make the problems worse. Liberals remain committed economically to a further vast expansion of the welfare state; socially to an agenda of personal liberation from traditional morality and to equality not of opportunity but of result; and internationally to a weak multilateralism whose object is to make America a follower rather than a leader.

The administration's ambitious agenda to increase the size and scope of government repeats the domestic policy mistakes of the past. What the United States needs is not bigger government but a renewal of its commitment to limited but strong government; economic freedom, which is the only way to assure prosperity and individual liberty; and a moral and cultural system that strengthens the family, personal responsibility, and the instincts for civic virtue.

STRONG GOVERNMENT, BUT LIMITED GOVERNMENT

The 1992 presidential campaign dramatically demonstrated Americans' dissatisfaction with politics as usual. Three voters in four believed that the United States was on the wrong track. President Clinton and Ross Perot ran as outsiders, denouncing the status quo. Even President Bush was forced to cast himself as the candidate for change. According to polls, distrust of government is at an all-time high. Only 42 percent of Americans have at least a fair amount of confidence in the federal government. By a ratio of more than three to one, most Americans believe that it creates more problems than it solves.

Public dissatisfaction is so strong that a variety of proposals for drastic reform have won widespread support. Most liberals advocate a vast expansion of government as the remedy for the nation's ills. Many conservatives equate good government with weak government, on the theory that those who govern least govern best. There is a proposal for a one-term, six-year Presidency, another for a balanced-budget amendment. Ross Perot's answer is plebiscitary democracy, which takes power away from elected representatives and puts it directly in the hands of the people.

All are wrong.

Some proposed reforms have merit. Term limits and the line-item veto are good ideas that should be enacted into law. But the balanced-budget amendment is a bad idea. It is unduly restrictive in theory and unenforceable in practice, and would invite even more cynicism about how government operates. The one-term Presidency is an equally bad idea. Limiting the President to a six-year term would render him less effective, by making him a lame duck the first day he took office, and less accountable, by removing the public's right to render a reelection verdict.

There is nothing wrong with the American political system that a return to the founding fathers' wisdom could not cure. But the weakening of political parties, the erosion of the President's proper authority, a diffusion of authority within Congress, the emergence of an imperial judiciary, an arrogant media following their whims and answering to no one, and a vast expansion of government into areas where it does not belong—all these have fragmented the power, responsibility, focus, and accountability necessary for effective government.

We need to return to first principles on government's

proper role and the appropriate distribution of authority within government. The Constitution provides for three equal branches of government, each balancing the others. We need a limited but strong government that provides "energy in the executive." We cannot afford government dominated by an imperial judiciary and an imperial Congress dedicated primarily to involving government in subjects it does not understand and problems it cannot solve.

The most fundamental problem is widespread failure to understand the purposes of government and how it works. Our bloated and intrusive government encourages passivity, stifles initiative, and produces gridlock; for all its size, it is weak. A necessary condition for American renewal is to rediscover and act upon the great insights of the founders, which the clamor of contemporary liberals, libertarians, and populists has obscured.

The founding fathers were not utopians but were practical idealists. Recognizing that man is inherently flawed and driven by self-interest, they sought to devise a system of government that took these realities into account. Their intent was not to create a new man, to supply meaning to empty lives, to redistribute wealth, or to run the economy. Rather, their aims were limited but lofty: to create a system able to maintain the conditions of freedom against internal and external threat, to administer the nation's laws effectively, and to encourage rational deliberation and choice on the part of a self-governing people. As James Madison put it in *The Federalist,* Number 51, "If men were angels, no government would be necessary. If angels were to govern men, neither external nor internal controls on government would be necessary." Or as Immanuel Kant observed, "The best government is one that teaches us to govern ourselves."

The founders wanted government strong enough to protect their security but not so strong as to threaten their liberty, so they placed careful limits on the realm of federal government action. But they also understood that freedom could not survive without a strong Presidency. In foreign affairs, the case for a strong Presidency is overwhelming. Only the President has the capacity, vital in foreign affairs, to initiate prompt and effective action. Legislators have limited constituencies; the President represents the nation. Just as it was wrong for Congress to enact the War Powers Act in 1973, limiting the President's power to conduct foreign policy because of the unpopularity of the Vietnam War, it would be wrong to limit the President's power to conduct foreign policy in the future because of the failures of President Clinton's policies in Somalia, Haiti, and Bosnia. There is always the possibility that a President will make mistakes in acting during foreign policy crises, but it is more likely that the Congress would make an even greater mistake by not acting at all. This is particularly true now that only the United States has the power and responsibility to lead the forces of freedom in the world. The leader of the free world must be able to lead.

Today the problem is not an excessively strong Presidency, but a hobbled one. Obsessed by the danger of an imperial Presidency, many seem oblivious to the dangers of an imperial Congress. There are now more than twenty-five subcommittees in the House and Senate dealing with foreign policy. Foreign policy cannot be conducted by committee. Meanwhile, Presidents, with their limited terms, are more accountable to the electorate than an imperial Congress, to which incumbents are reelected 98 percent of the time. The President is subject to impeachment, congressional power over the purse, and other political and congressional constraints. And Presidents, particularly conservative ones, will always be restrained by an adversarial media.

Ironically, Congress has tacitly allowed the courts to appropriate legislative authority even while it has tried to appropriate executive authority. True constitutional government requires an independent judiciary, empowered to strike down legislative and executive acts that violate the Constitution. But some jurists seem to have forgotten that separation of powers depends equally on judicial restraint, which limits them to applying constitutional principles rather than creating them.

Under the guise of keeping the Constitution "current" or the doctrine of a "living and evolving Constitution," jurists too often substitute their own policy preferences for those of the people's elected representatives. This allows legislators to shift politically difficult issues away from the Congress, where they belong, to the courtroom, where they do not.

The character assassination of Robert Bork—the most highly qualified man nominated to the Supreme Court since Felix Frankfurter—illustrates the poverty of contemporary liberal thinking about the role of the judiciary under a separation-of-powers system. The founders would find it appalling that the Senate disqualified Bork because of his commitment to "original intent" as the basis for interpreting the Constitution. One of the most urgent tasks for American Presidents in the future is to educate people on the need to restore the judiciary to its proper role as guardian of the Constitution, not its amender.

Many lament the proliferation of big money and influence-peddling in Washington. This focuses on the symptom, not the cause of the problem. High-powered lobbyists go to Washington because of the vast expansion of government into every sector of society and the economy. Without significant retrenchment in the scope of government, lobbying and big money will be here to stay, simply because Washington is where the action is.

The debates about campaign finance reform and term limits, as they are being carried on among Washington's most immovably entrenched legislators, would both amuse and discourage the founders. The campaign finance reform bill favored by the administration is an incumbents-protection plan. The version favored by the Republicans is a challengers-protection plan. Similarly, opponents of congressional term limits tend to be those who are in power, usually Democrats, while proponents tend to be those who want to be in power, usually Republicans. Since it should be obvious even to the most casual observer that both sides would switch their positions on reform the instant their political fortunes were reversed, their arguments have all the moral grandeur of hogs fighting over places at the trough.

I would rather be governed by a Republican-controlled Congress than a Democratic-controlled Congress. But both parties bear a measure of the blame for the crisis of confidence that sparked the debates about campaign finance reform and term limits to begin with: the pervasive lack of trust among the American people in the competence and good faith of the federal government. Both parties are using the voters' cynicism as cover for efforts to jigger the system to fit their partisan and personal interests. Republicans and Democrats should stop posturing about campaign finance reform and develop a bipartisan program to attack the root cause of the excessive cost of campaigns: the bloated size of the federal government.

Their failure to do so thus far is the reason longtime members of Congress must be forced to step aside in favor of those who have less of a vested interest in the status quo. Term limits are an unfortunate but necessary remedy. They are unfortunate because they limit the people's power to freely choose their representatives. But they have become necessary in order to sweep away the entrenched political elite, too many of whom may have come to Washington to do good but stayed to do very well—for themselves.

Some argue that if our government can defeat Saddam Hussein so decisively, then it ought to be able to solve our domestic problems. They fundamentally misunderstand the very purpose of government. Waging war and providing for national security are among those tasks for which governments are designed. Governments are incapable of running an economy, picking winners and losers in cutting-edge industries and technologies, transforming the nature of human beings, or creating a social utopia. The fallacy of contemporary liberalism is its assumption that every problem has a government solution. It does not.

We hear too much today about how to reinvent government and not enough about how to reduce it. Vice President Gore's National Performance Review has proposed a number of initiatives aimed at consolidating redundant government agencies and instilling business skills in bureaucratic management. Although well-intentioned, these initiatives miss the forest for the trees. One American who better understands the issue is Peter Grace, whose bipartisan commission made comprehensive recommendations a decade ago for massive cuts in government spending. "While the Vice President has taken good ideas from his predecessors and introduced many of his own, he uses a butter knife on a job that requires a chain saw," Grace observes. "Taxpayers are less interested in building a better bureaucrat than in getting the bureaucracy off their backs and out of their wallets." Our aim should not be to make government more efficient in doing what it should not have tried to do in the first place.

In trying to do too much that it has no business doing, government does too little to meet its primary responsibility—to protect the lives, liberty, and property of the people, and to maintain those conditions under which a free economy can best create a new prosperity.

More than any reform plan, limiting government to its proper sphere will enhance the public's faith in government. Reinvigorating the principle of federalism by transferring power from Washington to state and local governments would permit citizens to run more of their own affairs at a manageable level. At the same time, state and local governments provide laboratories for testing new approaches to domestic problems. In Wisconsin Governor Tommy Thompson has introduced a bold state welfare reform program. If it continues to be successful in reducing welfare rolls, it could become a model for a national program.

Many liberals, some conservatives, and Ross Perot have called for more direct democracy as a cure for government gridlock and unresponsiveness. Playing to the populist gallery, Perot has advocated national "electronic town meetings" in which American citizens would decide the fate of complex issues by spontaneous impulse rather than by informed deliberation.

This fatuous idea flies in the face of both experience and the Constitution. With a few exceptions similar to the New England town meeting, systems where citizens assemble and administer the government in person have a miserable record of chaos, faction, tyranny, and mob rule. As Hobbes observed three centuries ago, direct democracy creates an "aristocracy of orators." The founders established the American system of government precisely because its deliberative institutions offered a cure for the ills of direct democracies. The purpose of delegating decisions to elected representatives is not to subvert the will of the people but to elevate and inform its judgments.

In a representative system, public opinion does matter. Presidents and congressmen who ignore it do so at their electoral peril. During his first debate with Stephen Douglas, Abraham Lincoln made an observation that is as true now as it was then: "In this and like communities, public sentiment is everything. With public sentiment, nothing can fail; without it, nothing can succeed. Consequently, he who molds public sentiment goes deeper than he who enacts statutes or pronounces decisions."

Lincoln and the founders recognized the equally great danger that public officials might merely ratify popular passions of the moment, without refinement, deliberation, or choice. This is precisely what the Constitution sought to avert by establishing a representative democracy based on elective offices and separation of powers.

Our problem today is not too little direct democracy but too many politicians who pander to the ephemeral mood swings of popular fashion.

Public opinion is a fickle mistress. What is popular is often not what is right. But what is right and unpopular can often be made popular if statesmen have the courage and foresight to lead. The contrasting political fates of Neville Chamberlain and

Winston Churchill provide a striking illustration. Chamberlain and the catastrophically mistaken policy of appeasement reached their greatest popularity just after the Munich Conference of September 1938, when Great Britain and France sacrificed democratic Czechoslovakia to Hitler in the vain hope of sparing themselves. Meanwhile, Churchill was highly unpopular for heroically urging prompt, effective action to stop Hitler before it was too late. Today most of the world celebrates Churchill as the savior of freedom in one of its darkest hours. Very few celebrate Chamberlain.

Our own history is replete with examples. If Harry Truman had followed the polls in 1947, he would have scrapped his farsighted vision for the postwar world. His popularity was low. The Republicans had overwhelming majorities in the House and Senate. Internationalism was traditionally unpopular in Republican constituencies. But he had the courage to make a powerful case for what was right. Republicans in the House and Senate provided the votes necessary for approval of the Greek-Turkish aid program, the Marshall Plan, and NATO, the cornerstones of the policy of containment that would lead to victory in the Cold War. More recently, our opening to China in 1972 and President Bush's decision to oppose Saddam Hussein's aggression against Kuwait in 1990 would not have occurred if we had followed the polls rather than leading public opinion.

Pundits frequently ridicule members of the House and Senate for failing to have the guts to vote for what is right even if they risk their seats by doing so. But expecting politicians to cast votes against their political interest is just as unreasonable as expecting reporters to turn in exposés of the business affairs of their publishers. Legislators, like journalists, are only human. A President cannot govern by asking members of Congress to sacrifice themselves. Instead he must use the powers of persuasion inherent in the nation's highest office to transform a position that is right but unpopular into one that is acclaimed. Only by persuading the American people will he be able to persuade the Congress and thus earn support for his policies.

EQUAL OPPORTUNITY, NOT EQUAL OUTCOMES

The founding fathers believed that civil rights belonged to individuals, not groups. The principle of natural rights embodied in the Declaration of Independence defined our goal as equality of opportunity, which rejects distinctions of legal status and privilege defined by race, religion, ethnicity, tribe, language, or sex. Everyone is the same in the eyes of the law. But insisting on equality of opportunity is the opposite of demanding equality of result.

Individuals differ significantly in the natural endowments of intelligence, skills, character, perseverance, and just plain luck on which success in life depends. The Constitution and its underlying philosophy affirm that individuals must be given the right to succeed on the basis of merit, which implies that not all will succeed equally.

In 1969, my administration put into effect the Philadelphia Plan, which required goals and timetables for minority hiring in connection with federal construction contracts. It was carefully crafted to crack open what were then the almost completely lily-white construction unions and to compel them to start accepting blacks into their apprentice programs and membership ranks. We deliberately distinguished between goals and quotas, even though numerical goals, over specified periods, were set in the resulting contracts. Compliance was judged not by an arbitrary look at the numbers alone but by a broad review of a contractor's effort to provide equal employment opportunity. This was the right kind of affirmative action—a specifically targeted plan, temporary in nature, designed to remedy a specific, clear denial of equal opportunity. And it worked.

In the years that followed, however, the courts, the civil rights establishment, and some federal enforcement agencies increasingly pressed the notion of affirmative action beyond equal opportunity to require equality of result, regardless of whether or not any deliberate discrimination had taken place. Broad goals became rigid quotas; in many cases the new test became one of "disparate impact"—that is, whether the ethnic composition of a company's workforce precisely mirrored the ethnic composition of the community, without regard for individual ability, interest, or anything else.

Over the past two decades, courts have sanctioned reverse discrimination and racial quotas in university admissions, hiring, and promotion. They have allowed reverse discrimination in public employment, the private sector, and government contracting. They have upheld and sometimes even demanded the creation of gerrymandered minority districts to ensure that such districts are represented by a member of a particular minority. In some cases, judges have not only authorized quotas in situations in which there was no intentional discrimination but have imposed quotas themselves.

The case of Lani Guinier is revealing. Her nomination for the top civil rights post in the Justice Department was withdrawn by President Clinton because of the storm over her advocacy of proportional representation for politically correct minorities, but what got her into trouble was more her candor than her ideas. American universities and employers routinely accept less-qualified applicants over their more-qualified competitors. In the California college system, Asian applicants with superior qualifications are often discriminated against on the grounds that Asians are overrepresented. Government employers typically give "race normal" tests, which grade minority applicants on a curve only in relation to other members of the same minority.

President Clinton's exaggerated use of the quota system to fill his cabinet was no surprise. Many liberal Democrats have not only demanded such affirmative action but have attempted to apply it to an ever-expanding category of "victims," who now make up close to two thirds of the population.

This institutionalization of preferential treatment, with the theory of group rights it represents, undermines the basic principles of our Constitution and a free society. It repudiates the idea of merit essential to a competitive and fair society. It often has the unintended consequence of encouraging rather than overcoming failure. It leads the beneficiaries to think of themselves as passive victims whose fate depends on others rather than on whether they seize the opportunities available to all Americans. It also epitomizes the corrosive entitlement mentality that increasingly pervades American society—one of the greatest threats to our fiscal health, our moral fiber, and our ability to renew our nation. It used to be said that some people thought the world owed them a living. Today, millions of Americans think Washington owes them one. Proponents of the welfare state assert that simply by virtue of living in the United States a person is entitled not only to life, liberty, and the pursuit of happiness but also to food, clothing, health care, and many other amenities of life.

Some on the right like to bash "welfare queens," suggesting that the entitlement mentality belongs exclusively to the poor. Although it is true that the Great Society programs of the 1960s fostered a lingering sense of dependency among millions of poor Americans, it is time to tear down the double standard that characterizes most debates about this issue. The poor make convenient targets. But if middle-class and even rich Americans want to find someone to blame for the burden the entitlement mentality puts on the federal budget, they should look in the mirror. Wealthy farmers say they cannot survive without price supports. Steel makers and their unions demand protection from foreign competitors. Bankers expect the federal government to cover their bad loans. Well-off retirees whose Social Security payments far exceed their contributions oppose any politician who suggests their benefits be limited. College students believe they are entitled to low-interest loans secured by taxpayers who could not afford to go to college themselves. Lawyers, doctors, and businesspeople all want their place at the federal trough.

The entitlement mentality has been created by politicians

who promise more than government can afford and professional liberals who demand that government do that which it is not competent to do. It threatens to destroy the virtues of self-reliance, individual responsibility, initiative, and enterprise that built our country and will be indispensable in any effort to renew it. All Americans should have an equal opportunity to earn the good things of life. But except for those who are unable to do so, they are not entitled to receive those good things from the earnings of others.

There is no reason why Americans should receive Social Security, medical benefits, and other government subsidies without regard to their ability to pay. Only one dollar of every five of non-means-tested entitlement goes to the poor. If our political leadership summoned the courage to cut these programs on a means-tested basis, we would achieve substantial savings and also more fairly distribute the burden of cutting costs to middle- and upper-income taxpayers. The most serious shortcoming of the Reagan and Bush administrations was their failure to cut the level of entitlement going to those who are not poor, though it is true they received no encouragement from the Democratic opposition to cut these programs. On the contrary, the current administration has continued to fight not only to preserve the present levels of entitlement but to expand the application of this corrosive principle in new and costly ways.

America was "conceived in liberty, and dedicated to the proposition that all men are created equal." It was also conceived as a society that would provide opportunity, reward effort, and encourage industry; in which people could go as far as their energy and skill would take them—but in which rights would be coupled with responsibilities.

HARDHEADED IDEALISM AND ENLIGHTENED REALISM

The founding fathers did not consider human beings irredeemably evil or innately perfectible. Instead, they had a mixed view of human nature, considering most individuals a composite of potential goodness and wickedness. Man's capacity for evil made restraints on absolute power and unbridled self-interest necessary. But his capacity for good made decent government possible. The founders believed that representative government presupposed a high degree of civic virtue, an insight that modern libertarians do not appreciate.

Knowing that the search for the perfect was the enemy of the good, they sought to establish the best practicable order to bring out man's best and restrain his worst instincts. Hamilton and Madison recognized the importance of self-interest and wished to harness it, rather than to suppress it, to serve the common good.

The grisly history of the twentieth century demonstrates tragically the evil that can be done by governments that try to change human nature. Zbigniew Brzezinski devastatingly describes the attempts of Nazi Germany and communism to achieve through coercion what each considered a utopia as the most arrogant effort in human history to attain control over the totality of the human environment, to define dogmatically man's social organization, and to condition the human personality. Though these attempts ultimately failed, they inflicted death on more than 160 million people through deliberate and "politically motivated carnage."

By contrast, the American combination of hardheaded idealism and enlightened realism has built a record of world leadership, prosperity, and essential decency that no nation, past or present, can match. It has enabled us to lead abroad and achieve a remarkable degree of prosperity and social justice at home, not on the basis of narrow and selfish interests but through the appeal of high ideals and common values.

Yet even for the United States, idealism invites danger. Utopian idealism has sometimes caused our foreign policy to swing dangerously between ideological crusades and shortsighted isolationism. As the total failure of the Great Society should warn us, the utopian impulse can lead to enormously costly and counterproductive domestic policies in pursuit of the unachievable and undesirable: a risk-free, radically egalitarian society that would ultimately extinguish man's freedom. Egalitarianism denies human nature. Compulsive risk-avoidance denies human experience. The key to success in both government and life is not risk-avoidance but risk-assessment. In determining what risks to take, we cannot be totally obsessed by what we might lose. We should always keep front and center what we might gain. We should always remember the words of St. Thomas Aquinas seven centuries ago: "If the highest aim of a captain is to preserve his ship, he would keep it in port forever."

Idealism without realism is naïve and dangerous. Realism without idealism is cynical and meaningless. The key to effective leadership at home and abroad is a realistic idealism that succumbs to neither utopianism nor despair.

THE MEDIA: FREEDOM WITHOUT CONSTRAINT

The founders profoundly believed in the importance of freedom of speech and respect for, if not agreement with, all expression of opinion. Their hope was that reasonable people would debate issues vigorously but in a spirit of openness and toleration.

Freedom of the press is essential to the vitality of representative democracy and to the protection of individual rights. It provides an indispensable arena for open debate. On good days, it can actually contribute to informing the electorate. Those of us who complain about the behavior of today's media must remember that similar complaints are as old as the republic. Washington, Adams, Jefferson, Jackson, Lincoln, Cleveland, Hoover, and Franklin Roosevelt all received media treatment as scathing as any in the present era. An adversarial media culture is a fact of life.

Nevertheless, the media bear a large share of the responsibility for the current loss of faith in American political institutions. Although far more hostile to conservatives than to liberals, their institutional bias makes for excessively harsh criticism of all politicians and public officials. There is no easy balance between legitimate inquiry and sensational interest. But competitive pressures too often push the media past the limits of responsibility, destructively and unnecessarily undermining the authority and credibility of government. One egregious example was the attempt by the media to delegitimize Ronald Reagan's victory in 1980 by attributing it, falsely and without evidence, to a deal with the Ayatollah.

Some elements of the media even continue to give credence to the ludicrous notion that Lyndon Johnson and a host of other officials engaged in a vast conspiracy in the assassination of President Kennedy. They gave serious treatment and positive reviews to the movie *JFK,* which blended historical fact with blatantly malicious fiction. If they were to be believed, it would follow that the United States has lacked any truly legitimate government since 1963. The character assassinations of Clement Haynsworth, Robert Bork, and Clarence Thomas, in which the media gleefully participated, were also disgraceful episodes that have had the effect of discouraging individuals of high merit from government service. The American press could make a major contribution to improving the American system by restoring perspective and balance to its coverage. Examining public figures with a media microscope is justifiable. Using a proctoscope goes too far.

Walter Lippmann put it best thirty-eight years ago in his classic *The Public Philosophy:* "The right to utter words whether or not they have meaning and regardless of their truth could not be a vital interest to a great state but for the presumption that they are the chaff with the utterance of true significant words. But when the chaff of silliness and deception is so voluminous that it submerges the kernels of truth, freedom of speech may produce such frivolity that it cannot be preserved against the restoration of order and decency."

Before the era of Vietnam and Watergate, the media's neglect of "kernels of truth" in favor of salaciousness and rumor-mongering was somehow more tolerable because it was at least not obscured by a veneer of sanctimoniousness. Journalists have always been an arrogant breed. Bert Andrews of *The New York Herald-Tribune,* who worked with me on the Alger Hiss case, once told me that the problem with some of his colleagues who covered the State Department was that "instead of writing about the Secretary of State, they write as if they were the Secretary of State." A bygone era's ink-stained wretches, as depicted in the classic film *The Front Page*—amiable, scandal-mongering slobs sitting around the courthouse pressroom playing cards and waiting for the next hanging—have become our era's self-certified saviors of the republic. A productive evening spent peering through a politician's bedroom window can be the key to a prestigious editorship and even someday a shot at the Chair in the Media and Public Responsibility at any number of universities. The result of the media's appointing themselves as a de facto branch of government, a sort of non-taxpayer-supported team of surrogate special prosecutors, is that they have become even more immune to criticism than ever before, even less willing to admit their errors and excesses. And that will inevitably hurt a profession whose only restraint is what it manages to impose upon itself.

The media would not have physicians certify themselves, politicians investigate themselves, or even auto mechanics license themselves, but we are taught to expect that editors, reporters, and broadcasters have a unique capacity to ensure that they themselves act responsibly. The fact that they err just as often as other human beings but atone almost never cannot be good for their professional souls; and it has been demonstrably bad for their public standing.

The 1960s and 1970s brought about a profound change in the media's perception of their role in society. Rather than pulling an oar while occasionally speaking up about the direction in which the boat is going, the prestige media now appear to observe the race from the shore, raising the occasional eyebrow at one another. Three-hour panel discussions can take place at journalism schools about whether an editor should withhold, at the government's request, publication of a story about an impending use of military power if American lives were at stake. I could name two dozen journalists from the 1950s, all of them competent pros, who would not have hesitated to come down on the side of the lives of our servicemen and women.

One reason for the change is that journalists have become even more cynical than before. Another is that they seem increasingly to have little if any conception that they share responsibility for building an atmosphere of common purpose in an increasingly fractured society. Like so much of the intellectual establishment, they seem animated by an instinctual negativity about America and its values and a sense of ambivalence about its power and stature.

If American renewal is to become a reality, the media will have to resolve to help the process along rather than to analyze and critique it so relentlessly that it dies aborning. Journalists will have to learn to look in the mirror and not be afraid their National Press Club cards will be revoked if they say, "I want America to be strong and free and fair and civil and to continue to grow and prosper."

THE MYTHS OF GOVERNMENT

Free-market capitalism has triumphed around the world, but most liberals seem to have learned nothing from the experience. They are enamored of many of the principles the victims of communism and socialism have experienced and repudiated. Still, "economic freedom" is a slippery term. During our heated private conversations in 1959, Khrushchev repeated the argument communists always made to me in my travels around the world, about why their system was better than ours. Whenever I mentioned free nations, free peoples, or free ideas, he would respond that the communists provided their people free education, free housing, and free health care. We stood for higher freedoms, I replied—freedom of the press, freedom of expression, freedom of religion, free elections, and political freedom. He rejoined that capitalism meant the freedom to be unemployed, to starve, to be homeless.

We both had a point. The freedoms he stood for were material. The freedoms I stood for were nonmaterial. In between these two concepts of freedom is the economic freedom of free markets. Khrushchev and other doctrinaire communists never accepted that principle. At this great turning point in history we must prove that democratic free-market capitalism can not only outproduce communist capitalism and provide for those in need but also provide the higher, nonmaterialist freedoms the communists denied.

This challenge requires that government finally master a delicate balancing act between opportunity and security—between growth and fairness. To grow, a democratic capitalist economy requires strong economic incentives for investment, including low taxes and minimum regulation. To be fair, it must provide some goods and services to those who cannot provide for themselves, which will inevitably take resources away from growth. Enacting too much social spending is a cruel policy, not a humane one, because it weakens the system's capacity to serve everyone. Further along this continuum is communism, which, by promising to fulfill every need, ultimately deprives an economy of the ability to fulfill any. Khrushchev was wrong when he told me housing, education, and health care were free in the Soviet Union. The price the Soviet people were paying for them was astronomical.

It is fashionable to say that communism and socialism have been discredited. But they will not be completely discredited until government overcomes its tendency to ignore the simple fact that too much social spending saps an economy's ability to produce the funds necessary to finance the social programs. Too many of the present administration's policies are rooted in the reflexive conventional wisdom of traditional liberalism: higher taxes; suffocating regulation; a vast expansion in the size, cost, and scope of government; more entitlements; managed trade; and deep cuts in military spending. We need to lay aside some of the more persistent myths that for years have confused rather than clarified public debate.

In the late 1980s, Professor Paul Kennedy of Yale popularized the thesis that excessive military spending and imperial overstretch had caused the decline of all the great powers since 1500, and would do the same to America. Mounting trade and budget deficits, combined with the growing power of allies such as Germany and Japan, gave Kennedy's argument a resonance it did not deserve. He and other critics missed the essential point that the proportion of GNP consumed by America's defense spending in 1953 was twice the share of GNP spent at the height of the Reagan military buildup.

Nor is America's decline as irrevocable or precipitous as Kennedy portrayed it. The late 1940s and 1950s represent an artificial measure of America's relative might, because World War II had devastated much of the world. Using the 1920s rather than the 1940s as a benchmark, America's share of world manufacturing and GNP has remained remarkably constant. America's share of world manufacturing actually increased during the 1980s as the Reagan recovery created 18.4 million new jobs, compared with a net gain of zero for Western Europe during the same period. Our total GNP still exceeds that of Japan, our nearest rival, by a factor of two. In industrial productivity, technological innovation, and per capita productivity we still lead the world. Our economy attracts more foreign investment than that of any other major industrial power. With a GNP close to $6 trillion, we have ample resources to play our indispensable role as a global leader. We also have the resources to build a stunning new prosperity at home, if government will become less grasping.

Liberals have vastly overstated the harmful effects of defense spending on the American economy and understated its positive impact internationally. The level of spending called for in the Bush administration's defense plan was approximately equal proportionately to what the United States spent in 1940, the year before Pearl Harbor, when we were vulnerable to aggression. This is hardly too much of a burden for the wealthiest nation of the world, especially when we consider the alternatives.

The most prevalent myth foisted on the public is that the eighties were, as some critics have gleefully labeled them, the "Decadent Decade." By trashing the 1980s, they try to justify their own agenda of a vast expansion in government's role at the expense of the private sector, a substantial redistribution of America's wealth, the socialization of America's health care system, a relentless push for equality of result, and managed rather than competitive trade. The liberal lament is familiar. President Reagan, they chant, simultaneously doubled the defense budget, reduced taxes, and cruelly cut essential social programs, so that the rich got richer, the poor got poorer, and the country amassed an enormous debt that put the U.S. economy at a significant competitive disadvantage in the world economy.

This dire portrayal is wrong. The policy implications many liberals draw from it are even more wrongheaded. Dramatically ending a prolonged period of stagflation and slow growth, which were lingering legacies of the Great Society, Reagan's tax cuts and deregulation stimulated an economic boom, seven years of uninterrupted growth during which the American economy grew by nearly a third—or by the size of the entire West German economy. Runaway inflation rates plummeted and remained low. American productivity increased significantly. America's share of the world's GNP remained constant. America's percentage of world manufacturing increased. The increased emphasis on competition and entrepreneurship rather than subsidy and regulation forced American business to take measures that would greatly increase its competitiveness for the 1990s.

While the federal budget deficit increased substantially during the Reagan years, it is crucial to keep this in perspective. On one hand, we must avoid the temptation of exaggerating the immediacy and severity of the danger. A deficit of 5 percent of GNP will not bring the apocalypse overnight. On the other hand, contrary to the claims of doctrinaire supply-siders, deficits do matter. They distort our economy over the long run by siphoning off for short-term consumption funds that could have gone toward long-term capital investment. They confer benefits on the present generation and burdens on future generations. While sustainable in the short term, and even justifiable in recession and war, deficits act like water, eroding the foundations of a strong economy.

It is wrong, however, to blame the combination of the Reagan tax cuts and defense increases for creating the deficit problem. Although defense spending doubled from $147.2 billion in 1980 to $290.2 billion in 1989, the increase in tax revenues—due in part to cuts in tax rates—exceeded the increase in defense spending. The Reagan administration's miscalculation lay not in its tax or defense policies, but in its and Congress's failure to control domestic spending, which continued to increase significantly during the 1980s and now consumes four fifths of the federal budget. The defense buildup was a bargain. It helped win the Cold War and saved both blood and treasure in the long run. Unfortunately, domestic spending has increased relentlessly over the past three decades. It is this relentless increase in domestic spending that is the curse.

The present administration has added revenues from its massive tax increases to the peace dividend from the end of the Cold War—which it has magnified through excessive cuts in defense spending—but despite its overly optimistic predictions, it still faces an out-of-control budget deficit. Even the most deft political shell game cannot hide much longer the fact that the recurring deficits are largely the result of decades of unchecked spending on domestic programs and entitlements. Each program is tied by a titanium umbilical cord to a particular interest group or lobby, which in turn is fused at the hip to the powerful members of Congress who hold the purse strings. The genetic code of government commands it to grow and to expand its authority. Like all things that take on a life of their own, it will not cheerfully commit suicide or lop off an arm or a finger. As I found when I abolished the Office of Economic Opportunity early in my administration, any President who attempts to terminate a program or department, no matter how redundant or unnecessary, is accused of insensitivity to poor people, young people, sick people, or small animals. It becomes impossible to imagine how the nation survived before the threatened program existed.

These spasms of outrage generally come from the bureaucrats, interest groups, and other organizations that receive the taxpayer dollars the federal government dispenses. All are masters at bringing political pressure to bear on the most neuralgic spot in Congress and the media. President Reagan, one of the strongest Presidents of the post–Cold War era, learned this lesson early in his first term. While in office he created the Strategic Defense Initiative, armed the Nicaraguan contras, and deployed intermediate-range nuclear missiles in Europe, all over the shrill objections of his critics. But when the giant teachers' unions got wind of his plan to abolish a relatively new megabureaucracy, the Department of Education, the sworn enemy of the Evil Empire had finally met his match and had to cry uncle.

The liberals' favorite programs are the hardest to cut. There are two for which I feel a particularly acute sense of responsibility. The first is the subsidies to public television and the national arts and humanities endowments. Their budgets increased at a healthy pace during my administration, despite my reservations, and by 1973 they were receiving a total of $129 million. After twenty years, ten of which our country spent agonizing over the deficit, their budgets have quintupled, to $640 million. If all three programs were terminated tomorrow and the unspent funds were returned to the federal treasury, Americans' quality of life would not be diminished by one iota. If enough people wanted to watch *Masterpiece Theater,* or performance art in which people do bizarre things to their bodies with vegetables, the marketplace, including the huge private foundations that support the arts, would find a way to make this possible. And yet in the current atmosphere, even if the President wanted to eliminate these programs, he could no more do so than he could fly to Mars, because they are the darlings of the liberal establishment.

Even harder to eliminate or even slow will be those programs where the tendencies of bureaucracies to grow and grow dovetail with the profound antiestablishment, antibusiness inclinations of the post-Vietnam generation of federal officials and special-interest lobbyists. The most obvious example is the way environmental programs have run amok since I created the Environmental Protection Agency and signed into law the Endangered Species Act.

I consider myself an environmentalist. No rational person can quarrel with Churchill's observation "I see little glory in an empire which can rule the waves and be unable to flush its sewers." When we established the EPA, our goal was to find a rational balance between the imperative of protecting the environment and the imperative of economic growth. Since we recognized that most well-meaning businesspeople wanted clean air and water for the sake of their children and grandchildren as urgently as did the protesters marching in the streets, we envisioned a cooperative relationship between business and the new agency, with punitive measures applied only in cases of abuse.

But as so often happens with government programs, the pendulum has swung too far. Measures designed to protect endangered species such as bears, wolves, and the bald eagle are now being used to force Idaho farmers off their land for the sake of the thumbnail-size Bruneau Hot Springs snail and to block massive developments in recession-ravaged southern California to protect the Pacific pocket mouse. Similarly, the public has been bombarded so relentlessly by apocalyptic warnings from EPA bureaucrats and private organizations about global warming and the depletion of the ozone layer that few people realize that many respected authorities believe these concerns lack any scientific foundation. Nonetheless, automobile companies have been ordered to make mind-bogglingly expensive modifications in automobile design on the basis of flimsy evidence.

Government, as bidden by radical environmentalists, has also mounted an assault on the nuclear power industry. Environmentalists' opposition to nuclear power makes no sense. It is the most abundant, cheapest, and cleanest energy source. Instead of spewing toxins and soot into the environment, nuclear power plants are self-contained and self-cleaning. Technological advances have made nuclear energy efficient, safe, and environmentally sound. In the 1960s, when nuclear energy seemed to be a threat to the big oil companies, many left-wing leaders favored it. When it became part of what they sneeringly called "the establishment," they turned against it. Government regulators became their willing accomplices in trying to hamstring an entire industry. In the 1970s and 1980s, nuclear power generating facilities were being opened at the rate of one every three months. In the 1990s, new nuclear power plants will open at the rate of one every thirty-nine months—and because of the closure of plants due to environmental and antinuclear hysteria, there will be a net gain of just one new plant by the turn of the century.

One reason for such excesses is that as new departments and offices "mature," if that is the right word, they look for new domains to conquer, new areas into which to extend their authority. Another reason is that the inherently anticapitalist impulses of the Vietnam generation are finding a new outlet in environmentalism and throughout government. Many bureaucrats come to their positions straight from graduate school and have no experience or interest in business. Employed in government agencies from city planning offices to powerful federal departments, they have been taught that the most noble calling of government is to monitor, license, inspect, regulate, and punish the private sector. A hundred and eleven years after the death of Marx, two years after the death of communism in Russia, a depressingly large number of intellectuals, journalists, and government officials, as a result of their flirtation with the left in the 1960s, are driven by the same hostility to capital that helped spark the greatest ideological excesses of our century.

We should also think twice about the impact our environmental correctness has on the developing world. Rich nations can afford stringent environmental controls. Poor nations cannot. When I first visited Bangkok in 1953, it was one of the world's most beautiful cities. The air was clean, but we could not drink the water. During my most recent visit in 1985, advances in technology had purified the water, but the air was contaminated by the smog of industrialization. All Thais would probably like cleaner air, and as their nation continues to prosper, most Thais, through their taxes, will pay for cleaner air. But few Thais would be willing to trade away their dramatically higher standard of living for it.

Nations that are on the brink of enormous economic growth should not be permitted to befoul the environment as devastatingly as the communists did in the former Soviet Union and Eastern Europe. But we should not impose such strict international controls that the growth that would benefit these nations' peoples and the rest of the world is stunted for the sake of the tender sensibilities of the purists at the Sierra Club. Some of the most extreme activists would rather keep people in the developing world squeaky-clean and close to Mother Nature than permit their nations to experience the kind of dramatic advancement through industrialization that will make them healthier and more prosperous, at the cost of some temporary damage to the environment. Such thinking can make environmentalism a cruel doctrine.

In Japan, some believe government is excessively allied with business. In the United States, it is excessively hostile to it. Government slows economic growth both by overregulating business and by sapping its strength through the increased tax bite it applies as it grows inexorably. It is adding insult to injury, therefore, to attack the budget deficit by raising taxes without cutting the size of government. To renew America and prime it for a new era of expansion and prosperity, we must keep taxes as low as possible and ruthlessly probe every dusty corner of government at all levels and do away with programs that are not needed or that serve only to dampen growth.

We should address the deficit though domestic spending cuts, not tax increases. The American people are grossly overtaxed because their government spends too much on politically alluring domestic programs. In 1992, federal, state, and local taxes claimed almost 40 percent of the GNP, a proportion larger than at any time since World War II. The administration's ill-advised tax increase will make this proportion even larger. And it does not include the enormous tax increases that would be required to finance the administration's revolutionary health care plan.

Savings and investment are central to our ability to finance industrial expansion and productivity growth. Capital gains taxes are taxes on savings. Income and payroll taxes are taxes on production. All three reduce the ability of American companies to compete in world markets.

Compared with our competitors, we Americans consume too much of what we produce and save and invest too little. Experience shows that we get more of what we invest in, and less of what we tax. Sensible tax policies would therefore shift the balance toward taxing consumption more and production less. That is why a value-added tax would be preferable to income and payroll taxes.

In the last several tax debates, liberals in Congress skillfully managed to shift the focus of public discussion away from what is taxed and toward who is taxed. They defined this as "fairness," with fairness, in turn, defined as redistributing income away from the more productive and toward the less productive. This was clever politics but disastrous economics. From the standpoint of promoting economic growth, the "who" is irrelevant; the "what" is central. The key aim of tax policy should be to raise the needed revenue with the least damage to the economy. What we have instead is a set of tax policies shaped not by the requirements of growth but by the temptations of demagoguery. When economic growth is spurred, all win; when growth is stunted, all lose.

The bottom line is that America cannot tax its way to prosperity; it cannot spend its way to prosperity; it can only grow its way to prosperity. If we want prosperity, we need to shape our policies to foster growth.

To paraphrase Mark Twain on composer Richard Wagner, capitalism works better than it sounds, while socialism sounds better than it works. Capitalism, unlike communism or other secular creeds, is not a religion. It is a morally neutral set of economic principles that makes wealth-creation likely and virtue possible, although not inevitable. Socialism and the grinding scarcity it produces are conducive neither to prosperity nor to virtue.

One of the most idealistic leaders I met on my trip to Asia forty years ago was Burma's Prime Minister U Nu, now a renowned Buddhist scholar. He proudly showed me charts listing the scores of new hospitals, schools, roads, and other public facilities he planned to build in his newly independent country. They would obviously cost billions of dollars. I asked him where he was going to get the money. He answered, with a gentle smile, "From the government." As his guest, I did not have the heart to ask the obvious follow-up question: "Where is the government going to get the money?"

Government can spend only what people produce. People produce more when they work for themselves rather than for the government. Tragically, Burma has continued to travel down the socialist road to perpetual poverty. Because it is one of Asia's last holdouts against free-market policies, the Burmese people, whom Herbert Hoover once described to me as among the happiest in Asia, suffer one of the lowest per capita incomes in the world.

Now that the collapse of communism has vindicated American policies, we would make a tragic mistake if we repudiated the values of enlightened individualism that spurred our success. We must not stumble blindly into what Margaret Thatcher derisively called the "nanny state." We should build on the many positive accomplishments of the 1980s and correct some of the decade's serious mistakes.

This means reining in domestic spending and regulation, which threatens the strength of a free economy. In order to do so, we must disabuse ourselves of the myth that much of federal domestic spending is uncontrollable. All spending, apart from interest on the debt, derives from laws that Congress enacted and that Congress can change. To argue that we cannot tamper with the spending formulas of so-called entitlement programs is to abandon any hope of bringing federal accounts into balance. Non-means-tested entitlements—payments to those who have the means to take care of their own needs—currently consume almost 40 percent of the federal budget, up from 29 percent in 1970. The figures will increase significantly during the Clinton administration, especially if his health care plan passes in anything resembling its current form. Any attempt to solve America's economic problems that does not stop the runaway growth of entitlement spending cannot succeed.

Bismarck is superficially remembered as the Iron Chancellor who laid the foundation for German aggression in World War I and World War II. Many are not aware that he was a progressive leader who made Germany the most advanced welfare state in Europe during the nineteenth century. His huge government welfare program worked as long as it was kept under control. But recently the fabled German economic miracle has fallen on hard times. The usually highly efficient and competitive German industry found itself overtaxed and overregulated because of the increased costs of the welfare programs that were once a model for the world. Draconian cuts in wages and entitlements have become necessary. The lesson is clear. Government should provide a floor for those who are unable to support themselves. But that floor must not be so high that it reaches the ceiling and snuffs out the incentive of those who must produce the income to support the floor.

We are seeing the same syndrome in other European nations and in Japan. At a time when our major competitors are slimming down their governments so that their economies can run faster, we should not be fattening up our government, which will slow down our economy.

HEALTH CARE "REFORM": MORE STEROIDS FOR BIG GOVERNMENT

The litmus test applied to every federal program should be whether it advances freedom or restricts freedom. The 1994 debate over health care will be a crucial testing ground for our faith in freedom, which, if it means anything, must mean free markets and free choice. America's health care system does need improvement, but it does not need replacement. We set the standard of health care quality for the world. When someone who can afford the best needs an operation, where does he go to get it? To Canada or to other countries that have government health care programs? No. He goes to New York Hospital, the Mayo Clinic, Dr. DeBakey's clinic in Houston, or any one of a number of America's excellent privately operated hospitals. We also lead the world in medical research and development. We make health care services available, one way or another, to virtually everyone, whether insured or not.

Even the recent rise in health care costs has to be seen in perspective. Part of that rise is due to an explosion of administrative burdens, which in turn result partly from the growing pains of a rapidly expanding health insurance system, partly from bureaucratic requirements, and partly from the litigation explosion. One recent study showed that from 1968 to 1990, the average daily number of patients in American hospitals fell from 1,378,000 to 853,000, while the average number of administrative personnel rose from 435,100 to 1,221,600.

But more fundamentally, we spend more on health care today because we use more of it, we get more from it, and we use it longer. Even so, and even without the proposed "reforms," the rate of increase in health care costs is already dramatically slowing. One reason is that inventors and innovators all across America are constantly coming up with new devices, new procedures, and new drugs that substitute for more costly older treatments.

Most people of the older generation in America grew up without health insurance. The costs of medical care were handled directly by doctors and patients. If patients could not pay for care, doctors provided it free. But one way or another, patients got care and doctors got by.

Now medical insurance is the norm, and some form of insurance coverage has become increasingly necessary. This is true in large measure because of the stunning advances in medical care. Medical technology has become infinitely more sophisticated and more effective, and this has raised its costs. But the fact that we spend more on health care now does not mean we pay more for the same service. In my own lifetime, the average life expectancy in America has increased by an astonishing 40 percent—from less than fifty-five years to more than seventy-five. We live longer and live better, in part because of the vast array of services and cures that have become available. They cost money. In view of the alternatives, most of us would consider this money well spent. Give one hundred people a choice between today's medical care at today's prices and the medical care available in 1950 at 1950 prices, and hardly a one would willingly take the 1950 option.

Today hip replacements routinely take the place of wheelchairs. Diphtheria, typhoid, tuberculosis, have been all but eliminated. Antibiotics have reduced dread diseases to common nuisances. Microsurgery makes it possible to treat once-fatal aneurysms almost on an outpatient basis. These and hundreds of other medical miracles are the direct result of America's stunning advances in medical science. Those advances in turn are the direct result of our free-market system of incentives, risk, and reward. Take away the incentives and you dry up medical research and therefore medical advances.

The Clinton plan, all 1,342 impenetrable pages of it, is less a prescription for better health care than a blueprint for the takeover by the federal government of one seventh of the nation's economy. If enacted, it would represent the ultimate revenge of the 1960s generation.

The plan epitomizes the discredited notion that taking action against a problem requires introducing a massive network of new compulsions, bureaucracies, and government controls. It calls on America to do what we have been telling Boris Yeltsin not to do. If we go down that road we will destroy not only our health care system but the underpinnings of our free society.

Under the administration's plan, doctors would be forbidden by law to accept more than the bureaucratically prescribed payment for any service, and patients would be forbidden by law to pay any more. Good doctors and bad doctors would be paid the same amount for the same procedures. Assembly-line clinics would collect the same payments as would the most caring private practitioner. Americans would be denied their basic right to buy the health care they want, even if they are willing to pay for it. This is the medical equivalent of establishing fairness in a basketball game by amputating the taller players' legs at the knees. This sort of mass-produced, compulsory universal conscription flies in the face of everything it means to live in a free society.

We have the world's best medical care because we have free markets in a free society. To throw that away in an orgy of politically correct egalitarianism would be a self-inflicted wound for which there would be no cure.

For the last four thousand years, whenever price controls have been tried, they have failed. Yet price controls are at the heart of the Clinton plan, together with compulsory conscription of every doctor and every patient into a government-controlled, government-directed, government-regulated system of medical care.

Any sensible reform of the nation's health care system must start with the patient, not with the government. The most powerful force inflating health care costs has been a system of insurance that removes the patient's own incentive to shop for value. We should increase, not diminish, the patient's role in choosing his own providers, his own level of service, his own balance between expenditures for health care and for other goods and services.

We should also seek to diminish, rather than increase, the burden health care places on employment costs. The administration's plan seeks to avoid having its costs labeled a tax increase by requiring a uniform high level of insurance coverage for all workers and requiring all employers to pay for it. This is the wrong way. It drastically increases the cost of job creation, and it drastically handicaps American goods in world markets.

The administration's plan would establish a vast new bureaucracy to run an industry whose cost exceeds $900 billion a year—three times the cost of Pentagon spending at the height of the Reagan buildup. Those who railed against waste and fraud in the Pentagon during the Cold War years apparently have no such fears when it comes to this vastly more expensive mega-monster. They should. The administration's plan would reduce the high quality of health care that most Americans now enjoy and stifle research and innovation in medicine without slowing down the soaring costs of health care for the economy as a whole. The payroll taxes the administration proposes in order to pay for the plan would cripple small business and increase unemployment in the most dynamic, entrepreneurial, and job-creating sector of our economy.

We need instead to control exploding medical costs primarily through market forces that will ensure that the quality of American medical care remains high. We should devise a system that includes greater emphasis on preventive care, sufficient public funding for health insurance for those who cannot otherwise afford it, and competition among both health care providers and insurance providers to keep down the cost of both. We also need to reform the perverse legal liability and medical-malpractice standards, which have sacrificed patient protection in favor of protecting the physician or hospital against staggeringly costly lawyer-instigated lawsuits.

Study after study has shown that government health care schemes end up costing more and delivering less. For example, the average cost of direct health care benefits, not including administrative costs, for a privately insured individual is $1,500; for a Medicaid patient, $3,300.

Bringing health care costs under control also requires behavioral changes on the public's part. Once again, we have to take more responsibility for ourselves. Dr. Roy Vagelos, the visionary chairman of Merck & Co., whose own dedication to medical research is legendary, argues that with better control of fewer than ten risk factors, we could prevent two thirds of all premature deaths. One factor he cites is inadequate prenatal care, responsible for the fact that five thousand low-birth-weight babies are born every week. Keeping just one of those babies alive can cost $1 million. Other risk factors include illegal drugs and alcohol, unused seat belts, and smoking. Cigarette smoking alone, he points out, causes more death and illness than drugs, alcohol, automobile accidents, and AIDS combined, and adds at least $65 billion a year to our nation's health care bill.

Twenty-one years ago, I proposed to Congress comprehensive health care reform that included requiring employers to provide health insurance coverage for their employees, just as the government sets requirements for minimum wages, occupational health and safety, and Social Security participation. I also proposed a vigorous program of aid and encouragement to the establishment of health maintenance organizations, together with a requirement that HMO membership be made available to those employees who chose this form of coverage. As I put it then, in HMOs "the doctors' and hospitals' incomes are determined not by how much the patient is sick, but by how much he is well. HMOs thus have the strongest possible incentive for keeping well members from becoming ill and for curing sick members as quickly as possible."

But I most emphatically did not, and would not, endorse a wholesale federal takeover of the nation's health care system. The insurance mandate on employers was far less financially burdensome then than it would be now that health care expenditures have increased more than tenfold. Employers would have been required to help pay only for their own employees, not for all the indigent in the entire community. Nor did my proposal contain anything remotely like the administration's schemes of government-created monopolies to control the insurance process, government-imposed limits on private health care spending, or a governmental body of absolute power to regulate what services can be provided. The financing and delivery reforms I proposed were portions of an overall program focused heavily on research and prevention, including health education, consumer safety, and accelerated technological advances, together with major efforts against such behavioral components of the health care burden as alcohol and drug abuse, drunk driving, and the social problems associated with the failed welfare system.

The Clinton plan, by contrast, focuses less on improving health care delivery than it does on centralizing health care control. Our program was about health. The Clinton program gives every indication of being about power.

OLD-FASHIONED LEARNING FOR A NEW ERA

For years American education has been on a downward spiral. Reading standards have declined significantly among American children of all classes and backgrounds, and recent surveys indicate that ninety million Americans cannot read adequately. Over 25 percent of Americans fail to graduate from high school. This compares with only 3 percent in Japan. In Russia, with all its problems, 95 percent of its workforce have the equivalent of a high school education. President Bush's goal of making American students first in the world in math and science by the year 2000 still looks, on present performance, like a distant dream.

If America's public schools are to do their job, they must again be civilized places of learning rather than free-fire zones. Discipline in the classroom is fundamental if learning is to be possible. Beyond that, personal, social, and intellectual discipline are all key elements of learning itself. Yet for decades, many if not most of our public schools have been progressively abandoning the trust that parents and communities have placed in them, giving up on discipline and often yielding to mob rule.

This has been an integral part of the broader collapse ushered in by the 1960s. In the schools, its destructive impact has been especially severe. The damage done by school failure is long-term, and its effects are multiplied as the students who suffer its ravages go on to raise children of their own.

The notion that our schools are failing because we spend too little on them is patent nonsense. In 1990 the United States spent an average of $5,247 per student, two and a half times what we spent in 1960 and more than is spent by any other industrial democracy. Yet SAT scores have dropped nearly 80 points in the past three decades. Study after study has shown U.S. students falling behind those of the rest of the world in such critical disciplines as math and science.

As further evidence that money is not the problem, consider that New Jersey, which spends more per student than almost any other state, ranked thirty-ninth in SAT scores. Among the top ten states in SAT scores, only Wisconsin was among the top ten in per capita expenditures, while four were among the bottom ten.

In depressingly many respects, New York City has become a paradigm of liberal failure. Nowhere is this more glaringly evident than in the city's schools, which used to be among the nation's best but are now among its worst. For decades the city has been in the grip of its municipal unions. Financial corruption and the basest sort of ward politics have permeated the administration of its school system. Janitors' pay averages nearly $60,000, more than twice the starting pay of a teacher, while union work rules prescribe that floors have to be swept only every other day and mopped only three times a year. Even a cafeteria that serves five lunch shifts a day and is used as a classroom after that has to be mopped only once a week. The ratio of administrators to pupils in the city's public schools is ten times that in private schools. No wonder less than a third of the funds spent on the city's schools ever reaches the classroom. Crumbling buildings, rampant drug-dealing, and knives and guns in the classroom have become as much a part of the system as patronage scandals and the routine promotion of functional illiterates.

In New York and elsewhere, we will not return our schools to the standards America should expect until parents and communities demand it, and until we return to the old-fashioned notions that schools are there to educate, that education is important, that civilized behavior is essential to education, and that both behavioral and educational standards must be set and enforced.

To find the best ways to reform education, the first place to look is at the schools themselves. Not all have failed. Many have succeeded, some spectacularly. We should stop doing what demonstrably fails and do instead what demonstrably succeeds. We should not blame the teachers. It has to be a labor of love for anyone to teach in one of our crime-ridden, drug-infested urban schools.

Until college, I attended public schools. Mrs. Nixon was a teacher in an excellent public high school. But today the difference between the quality of public and private schools is striking. George Will illustrates the problem graphically: "About 50 percent of urban area public school teachers with school-age children send their children to private schools. What do they know that we ought to know?" If public schools are not good enough for the children of those who teach in them, why should other children have no choice but to attend them?

The generally better results produced by private schools are to some extent due to the more selective nature of their student bodies. By definition, parents who send their children to private schools care about education, and this is communicated to the child. But time and again, where comparable conditions are created and comparable requirements set in public schools, those public schools have shown that they too can excel.

One of the most promising ways to improve public schools is to introduce competition among them, which is exactly what the school choice movement is all about. A voucher system forces schools to compete for funds by competing for students. Those schools cease to be sinecures for the educational establishment and instead become participants in a vigorous educational marketplace. Parents gain the right to shop for the best education for their children, and with that right they gain a new incentive to become active partners in the educational process. Teachers and administrators are put on notice that they too have to make passing grades.

Teachers' unions have waged all-out war against school

choice, especially those plans that allow parents, as they should, to choose private as well as public schools. In 1993, California teachers' unions, spending $18 million confiscated from teachers' paychecks and thus from taxpayers, defeated a ballot initiative on school choice with television ads that were so distorted and cynical that they made the dirtiest congressional campaign seem like High Mass at St. Patrick's Cathedral by comparison. But the unions' self-interest was blatant. School choice proposals will become policy when enough parents insist on it.

Mandatory busing, a relic of 1960s utopian thinking, is another sad example of the law of unintended consequences. It not only failed to achieve its intended result of improving American education but actually coincided with a precipitous decline in the performance of American students, especially in poor urban areas, where most of its ostensible beneficiaries reside.

Government must always be vigilant against de jure segregation—segregation by law, for which the civil rights legislation of the 1960s was a long-overdue and effective remedy. But it is both unconstitutional and bad social policy to use busing to compel integration when no de jure segregation exists. The problem in American education is not that minority students go to school together rather than to schools where they are integrated with the majority. Nor is it that they lack minority teachers. As Thomas Sowell has noted, the American educational system performed well for Irish, Germans, Italians, Jews, Japanese, Chinese, Poles, and other first- and second-generation ethnic Americans, most of whom lived in ethnic enclaves and managed to succeed regardless of the ethnic background of their teachers. American education is in crisis because of the erosion of standards of objective merit and the collapse of the social cohesion of neighborhoods; busing is at best an irrelevant remedy and at worst a factor that pulls neighborhoods farther apart.

Ultimately, the base of educational reform in America will have to be far broader than just schools themselves. Parents who leave their children's education entirely to the schools abdicate their own responsibility. The home is the key ingredient in a child's education. Habits learned there persist for a lifetime. Children from homes where knowledge is prized and reading is encouraged come to school eager to learn. Those from homes where learning is not part of life enter the schoolhouse door with two strikes against them. Couch-potato parents are likely to produce couch-potato children. As Lee Kwan Yew observed, "We should not substitute the state for the parents or the family."

A host of private nonprofit organizations are proving that the right kind of intervention in the lives of children who might otherwise be lost can make a dramatic difference. They do it without bureaucracy, without a maze of rules and prescriptions and reporting requirements. They do it by focusing on the individual child, with common sense, caring, and nurturing, and, crucially, by setting high standards and making clear that they expect the children to meet them.

Setting standards and expecting them to be met are what too much of our public education system has abandoned in its prolonged fit of patronizing and egalitarianism. Not all children can meet all standards. But those who can meet high standards should not be held back by those who cannot or will not. And those who can must be stimulated to do so.

America has some of the best universities in the world, but they must face up to their weaknesses if they are to retain that position. Under the banners of pluralism and diversity, student and faculty activists alike have demanded an admissions policy based not on academic merit but on ethnic representation; a curriculum driven not by objective intellectual standards but by the politics of race and gender; speech codes striving not to promote free intellectual debate but to impose a new sensitivity fundamentally hostile to the Western tradition. As the Hoover Institution's Dr. Martin Anderson has observed, "The percentage of professors with left liberal views has become so great that it has created a monolithic mindset." Aging 1960s radicals who now dominate the faculties of many universities have helped power the movement for political correctness, which punishes truth, penalizes merit, promotes faculty on the basis of quotas, and suffuses the campus with an atmosphere of abysmal, inflammatory ignorance. Stanford's celebrated change in its required curriculum to substitute the ravings of Frantz Fanon and other inconsequential polemicists for the likes of Plato, Aquinas, and Aristotle is all too typical. Elite universities have been abandoning objective excellence and exposure to the riches of the Western tradition in favor of hagiographic accounts of any civilization but our own.

The political consequences of this indoctrination are far less serious than the educational consequences. Young people have a way of outgrowing the fads of childhood, including political fads. But this blatant substitution of indoctrination for education cheats them of the intellectual foundation they need to prepare them for life in the twenty-first century.

Unless those responsible for our great universities—trustees, administrators, and faculty—take forceful and determined measures to restore their institutions' standards of educational integrity, they will have grossly violated their basic trust. And we as a nation will have failed our first responsibility to the next generation: to transmit to them the values, the history, and the traditions of a humane civilization, together with the knowledge and understanding to bring those values to life.

WELFARE: SICKFARE FOR AMERICA'S CITIES

The forces undermining our universities as places of learning are integral parts of the pervasive complex of cultural influences, attitudes, and behavioral patterns that is also destroying our cities.

In a remarkable speech last year to the Association for a

Better New York, Pat Moynihan asked his audience "to look back and ask yourselves what, in the last fifty years in New York City, is now better than it was."

He noted that fifty years ago "we were a city that already had a social structure, an infrastructure, the best subway system in the world, the finest housing stock, the best urban school system and, in many ways, the best-behaved citizens." Now parts of the city are "overwhelmed by the social chaos that comes in the aftermath of the inability to socialize young males." It grows worse by the year. He went on to quote from his own correspondence with a State Supreme Court Justice, Edwin Torres, who himself was raised in New York's barrio. "The slaughter of the innocent," Judge Torres wrote to him, "continues unabated: subway riders, bodega owners, cabdrivers, babies; in Laundromats, at cash machines, on elevators, in hallways." Noting that in his own courtroom he finds victims so resigned to the mayhem that they blame themselves for getting in the way of bullets, the judge wrote: "This numbness, this near-narcoleptic state, can diminish the human condition to the level of combat infantrymen who, in protracted campaigns, can eat their battlefield rations seated on the bodies of the fallen, friend and foe alike. A society that loses its sense of outrage is doomed to extinction."

To the reflexive liberal mind, urban problems are poverty problems, and the way to meet them is to throw money at them. For thirty years the United States has been doing just that. The Great Society was given a blank check. The liberals claimed it bounced because of insufficient funds. The real answer is that the check should not have been written at all. Since the War on Poverty began in 1964, government in the United States has spent $3.5 trillion on assistance programs for the poor. Adjusting for inflation, this is more than the entire cost of World War II. Since the mid-1960s, annual welfare spending has increased by more than five times. Yet the conditions it was meant to cure, as Moynihan so eloquently noted, have only gotten worse. The closely interwoven problems of crime, illegitimacy, and welfare dependency have increased astronomically.

Poverty is a symptom, not a cause, of our urban decay. The rot in our cities is a spiritual, ethical, cultural, and behavioral rot, which causes the poverty, the crime, and the degradation and abuse of public facilities.

Nothing is more directly responsible for the decay of today's cities than our corrupting, destabilizing, demoralizing, and dehumanizing welfare system. The liberal approach to welfare—spend more and demand less—means well but is tragically misguided. Its self-defeating incentives perpetuate poverty by rewarding illegitimacy, entrenching dependency, encouraging fathers to abandon their children, and thus undermining the stable family.

The worst of the violent criminal class are largely products of that system—in particular, of its positive encouragement of ignorant, unwed teenagers to produce babies that they have neither the means nor the competence to bring up. A sensible welfare system would discourage, not encourage, illegitimate births. We would not pay children to have children.

To a restless young teenager living in a crowded home, having a baby is her ticket to an apartment of her own, a cash allowance, food stamps, medical care, and an array of other social services, all with no questions asked and nothing required in return—as long as she neither works nor marries. For the single mother, welfare can provide benefits roughly equivalent to a $20,000-a-year job.

The effect of this institutionalized subsidy for illegitimacy has been disastrous, and nowhere more so than among the most fragile. Nearly thirty years ago Moynihan warned presciently about the coming social consequences of the breakdown of the black family. He was excoriated for doing so, but he was right. Writing in *The Wall Street Journal*, Charles Murray, whose 1986 book *Losing Ground* was a landmark in exposing the human damage done by the welfare system, has now issued a similarly dramatic warning about the white family.

He notes that 30 percent of all children born in the United States in 1991 were born to unwed mothers. Among blacks the figure is 68 percent; in most inner-city areas, it exceeds 80 percent. But the illegitimacy rate among whites, he points out, has also risen, to an alarming 22 percent. Of these unwed mothers, fully 82 percent are women with a high school education or less. For white women below the poverty line, nearly half of all births are now illegitimate.

Murray asks: "How much illegitimacy can a community tolerate? Nobody knows, but the historical fact is that the trendlines on black crime, dropout from the labor force, and illegitimacy all shifted sharply upward as the overall black illegitimacy rate passed 25 percent." And he adds that "the white illegitimacy rate is approaching that same problematic 25 percent region at a time when a social policy is more comprehensively wrongheaded than it was in the mid-1960s, and the cultural and sexual norms are still more degraded."

If we are serious about reclaiming our cities, the first step should be to stop rewarding illegitimate breeding by incompetent teenagers. Their offspring, growing up without the responsible adult nurturing any child needs, are the ones terrorizing the streets, dealing drugs, and turning schools into armed camps.

Part of the liberals' sensitivity revolution of recent decades has been to redefine welfare so as to eliminate its stigma for welfare recipients. But welfare should carry a stigma. Any adult who is physically and mentally capable of providing for himself or herself but chooses not to make the necessary effort to become employable or to take employment, whether or not for "chump change," should be made to feel shame. The community owes that person nothing but contempt.

The welfare system now is a giant chute down which taxpayer money is poured, with virtually nothing required of the recipients at the other end. Thanks to the poverty lobby, ever more taxpayer dollars are spent trying to attract ever more "clients" into the welfare system through programs of "outreach" and "education." As a result, more Americans now collect welfare than ever before. New York City alone carries a staggering 1.1 million people on its rolls.

The central focus of any responsible welfare system should not be to "serve" welfare "clients," but to get people off welfare and into productive jobs. The notion that welfare recipients are clients to be served is an invention of the welfare bureaucracy, which sees each new "client" as a new meal ticket for itself.

Murray proposes severe measures that would compel single young women to think twice about having babies. Their effect would be to induce those who opt for motherhood to turn for help to their families, their boyfriends, their churches, or their communities, which in turn would restore some social pressure on unwed teenagers not to have babies for fun and profit.

One way or another, this, or something close to it, is the basic direction in which we must go if we seriously intend to cure the cancer that is eating at America's cities and destroying its families. Young males should be made to discover that they cannot go on impregnating young females willy-nilly without personal consequences. Young females should be made to discover that their own irresponsibility will no longer be subsidized. The family must be restored as the basic social unit for the rearing of children. We must create powerful social pressures toward restoring to children the right to have fathers as well as mothers.

Welfare will not truly be reformed until the taxpayers who pay for it rise up and demand reform, and until they make crystal clear that by reform they mean no longer having their own pockets picked ever more insistently in order to enable ever more deadbeats to decide whether they find it more agreeable to go on welfare than to work. Irving Kristol encapsulated the principle: "The general rule has to be: If it is your own behavior that could land you on welfare, then you don't get it, or get very little of it. . . . It is crueler to entice people into the blind alley of welfare, where their humanity is dissipated and degraded, than to sternly warn them off."

CRIME AND RACE IN AMERICA

With the end of the Cold War we know freedom from the fear of war. What most Americans want more than anything else from their government today is freedom from the fear of crime. And yet we live in a culture of violence and of fear. Random acts of viciousness plague our streets and our homes. Six people are shot dead on the Long Island Rail Road by a man armed with a gun and an all-consuming racial hatred. Polly Klass, a twelve-year-old girl, is kidnapped from her bedroom and killed by a man with a rap sheet longer than the Mississippi River. Metal detectors are scanning students for weapons. There is no longer a sense of sanctuary anywhere. Millions of Americans are afraid to walk the streets or to use their parks. Since the 1960s the rate of violent crime has increased by a staggering 560 percent. In 1992 alone, fourteen million serious crimes were reported to the police. Millions more went unreported. In New York City, the number-one cause of workplace deaths is murder; two thirds of those killed at work there in 1992 were victims of homicides. To our international shame, Washington, D.C., has the highest murder rate of any capital city in the world.

Our criminal justice system has abysmally failed to deliver what should be the first freedom: freedom from fear. Young thugs openly thumb their noses at a system that operates a re-volving door, often sending those who get caught back out onto the streets at a rate that clearly carries the message that crime does pay. But the more fundamental problem is the social corro-sion that creates the criminals in the first place: the breakdown of value structures, the lack of discipline, the absence of any sense of right and wrong among many young Americans, partic-ularly in those inner-city slums that are the breeding grounds— in both senses of the term—of so much of the mindless violence.

An understandable wish to avoid appearing racist, and to avoid offending minority voters, prevents most political leaders from addressing the question of race as it affects the crime epidemic and in its many other dimensions. This cultural gag order must be lifted if the United States is to overcome the centrifugal forces of fear and envy that threaten to tear it apart. What is truly racist is to avoid addressing the problems of black America for the sake of avoiding offending people's sensibilities.

We cannot effectively address our nation's most pervasive social problems unless we face up to the fact that the urban underclass, where the breakdown of the family is worst, is primarily responsible for the plagues of violent crime and drug abuse on the streets of our great cities. Blacks are not the only members of this underclass, but they are the largest proportion of it. In 1992, half of all murder victims in the United States were black. Ninety percent were killed by other blacks. There can be no more dramatic evidence of a culture's deficiencies of values, discipline, and hope than when it turns against itself, as elements of urban America have in recent years.

The cop-out of blaming crime on poverty is morally corrupt and intellectually vacuous. When I was growing up during the Depression, there was far more poverty but far less crime. The difference was that our families and communities enforced civilized standards. We now are reaping the whirlwind stirred up by an age in which the self-appointed cultural elites sneered at the standards that helped people overcome the problems diversity can bring rather than wallow in them.

Arsonists, looters, muggers, and rioters burn, rob, and brutalize not because they are poor but because they are rotten. As Eric Hoffer has noted, "If poverty were indeed the fundamental cause of crime, history-would be about almost nothing else, for the vast majority of people in world history have lived in poverty." Today's vicious young predators show only cold-blooded contempt for their victims. They kill not for food but for a pair of fancy sneakers. They have to be shown firmly, determinedly, and relentlessly that we will not compromise in our defense of civilized standards and values. These are not negotiable.

Another harsh but uncomfortable reality is that many of these young Americans are virtually beyond hope. A collapsed bridge can be replaced, an unsafe building torn down. But human infrastructure is not subject to quick fixes, despite the routine wheedlings of the professional povertarians, who seize on any outbreak of violence as a pretext to plead for more public funds for themselves. Continuing to take seriously these pious proclamations, frequently wrapped in threats of "long hot summers" of violence if the payoffs are not made, is not an answer to the problem but an avoidance of the problem.

To renew America, we must resolve as a matter of national policy that another lost generation will not take to the streets at the beginning of the next century. But that does not mean the federal government should take the lead role. It should never be forgotten that government helped spark the crisis by fostering a climate of dependency that still hangs over our cities. It can best right its wrong by cutting the deficit, reducing the size of government, and building a strong, growing economy so everyone in urban America who is willing to work has the opportunity to do so.

The other answer can be found inside these urban communities themselves—in the homes, the churches, the community associations, the nonprofit sector, and, where a carefully circumscribed role can be fashioned, the government. Human beings gathered into sophisticated social groupings with their own values and rules long before the welfare office and the Department of Health and Human Services opened for business. If tomorrow night, in the Flatbush section of Brooklyn, New York, a man raises his hand to strike his neighbor and then lowers it again, it will not be because Congress passed a poverty program. It will be because his heart told him he should, an impulse that more likely than not was informed by a caring mother, father, or spiritual leader who took the time, free of charge, to teach him the difference between right and wrong.

To their great credit, responsible black leaders are facing up to the problem. *Washington Post* correspondent William Raspberry, from whom I received very constructive counsel when we met in the Oval Office, writes courageously, "The essence of black America's problem today is behavioral and only black Americans can do anything about it. The leadership in curbing black-on-black crime, redeeming our communities, and rescuing our children must be ours."

Racism remains a major problem in America. Most legal barriers between the races have been torn down, but powerful psychological ones remain. Many suburban whites are understandably frightened by what they see in the cities. Many members of minority groups are understandably resentful when whites are better off. Crime in the cities and the gap between rich and poor cannot be voted out of existence by Congress; each will shrink only as the economy grows. In the meantime, political, religious, and cultural leaders of all backgrounds have the responsibility to dampen the impulses of fear and envy that can fuel racism and to remind their constituencies that America can be renewed only by the common pursuit of freedom and equality that made America great.

Regrettably, some black leaders today endorse a neosegregationist line that could spark new interracial resentments and turn a new generation of black young people away from America. The extent of the new separate-but-equal movement on some campuses is so ridiculous that even a popular liberal comic-strip artist felt obliged to lampoon it in a series of drawings. Civil rights leaders who fought and died for their cause in the 1960s would wonder if it had been worth it to see separate dining-room tables and separate dormitories for whites and blacks. Any leader who is dismayed, as everyone should be, at the way ancient ethnic hatreds have brought brutal violence and suffering to the former Yugoslavia should want to do everything in his power to prevent ours from being the era in which such numbing hatreds take hold in America.

As our nation's minority populations grow, greater efforts

must be made in schools, churches, and other organizations to encourage a sense of national unity. It is fine to promote minority studies, for instance, but it is dangerously wrong to teach that studying the dominant culture is illegitimate. Scholars at our most prestigious universities argue with a straight face that European history, even though it is part of the continuum that resulted in the establishment of the United States, has nothing to say to America's black, Latino, or Asian students. And yet we need only consider a prominent black such as General Colin Powell to see that in this country—where skin color and national origin are supposed to be utterly irrelevant in determining a person's status—it is quintessentially American for a member of a minority group, even a man from a poor neighborhood in the South Bronx, not only to embrace the dominant culture but to become his era's most celebrated defender of it.

The new separate-but-equal doctrine is just as despicably racist as the old-fashioned one, the new color bar just as insidious as the old. We seldom see Serbian-Americans lobbying for Serbian studies at the expense of Plato, or Italian-Americans saying that it is wrong to consider George Washington the father of their country since he did not come from Sicily. But minority-culture lobbyists say that blacks, Latinos, and Asian-Americans should venerate their own political and historical antecedents rather than "dead white males."

It is essential that all people have the opportunity to study their own roots, which make our national tree so strong. But those who say that skin color alone entitles minority groups to an alternative set of national icons strike at the heart of what it means to be an American. In coming from other places to participate in our vast continuing experiment, our miraculous community of immigrants, Americans enter into a special kind of social contract. Being American is not about being white and Christian, or black and Muslim, or Asian and Buddhist. It is about being dedicated to a country that in principle offers virtually limitless opportunity to all, regardless of their background.

That we have failed to turn this principle into reality in every respect does not mean we should abandon it, especially if in doing so we restore divisions between races and peoples that will undermine our potential to complete the task of building a truly pluralistic, strong, prosperous nation.

Abraham Lincoln fought the Civil War with a relentless and at times even a ruthless will to victory because he knew a house divided itself could not stand. His image of a single American home is one of the most enduring political metaphors ever voiced. Today there are influential voices raised in intellectual America in favor of tearing down the single roof over us all, of sending whole communities to live, in a symbolic sense at least, somewhere else. They are the ones who say it is racist to teach Shakespeare instead of African poets to black children, and racist to force Latino children to learn standard English. Such social critics mouth a humanist line whose implications are utterly unnatural and cruel. They risk taking away from innocent schoolchildren the tools they will need to be productive Americans—to say nothing of the joy and inspiration of a heritage of great minds. They threaten to tear apart the greatest social experiment in the history of man. They should be exposed for what they are: incubators of disunity, distrust, and, ultimately, hatred.

THE CORRUPTIONS OF POPULAR CULTURE AND DRUGS

Other enemies of American renewal in the cities are those in the entertainment industry who promote violence for profit, and those who propose we raise the flag of surrender in the war against drugs.

It is encouraging that the television industry is taking preliminary steps to respond to the public's outrage at the revolting violence and sex in entertainment aimed at young people. Children whose neighborhoods are unsafe should at least have safe homes. Instead, when they watch television or listen to their stereos, the violence from the streets and schoolyards floods directly into their living rooms. Cartoon characters set things afire, rap lyrics extol the virtues of armed robbery and cop-killing, and movies make high body counts a badge of honor. They all promote violence. The vast power of our entertainment industry should be used instead to promote healing and a sense of community.

Hollywood elites claim that they are simply reflecting America and that America is sick. What they are doing is looking in the mirror. Hollywood is sick. Its values are not those of mainstream America. The depiction of violence and explicit sex sells, and Hollywood is in the business of making money. But by forgoing its responsibility to observe basic standards of decency, Hollywood has accelerated the decline of these standards in the community at large. By celebrating violence, it undermines whatever efforts families and community-based institutions are making to try to stem the tide of violence in the streets. Americans are right to be outraged at this profiteering. Unless Hollywood does even more self-censoring, it will envitably face censoring by government.

Government itself is to blame for recent signals that it is considering throwing in the towel in the fight against drugs. Late last year Surgeon General Joycelyn Elders sparked a firestorm by suggesting the possibility that drugs should be legalized. Her statement, and the administration's failure to flatly repudiate it, set back the efforts of five successive administrations over two decades to combat the sale and use of illegal drugs. An administration that includes a number of officials who have records of casual drug use cannot credibly be the one that promotes the fight against drugs—particularly because the permissiveness toward drugs of the 1960s generation has left an ugly residue on the urban underclass, a class that did not enjoy the same possibilities for extricating itself from the poison of drug dependency.

Joe Califano, Health, Education, and Welfare Secretary in the Johnson administration, observed recently, "Putting the stamp of legality on snorting cocaine and smoking crack would increase the number of addicts severalfold. Exercising their right to free speech, Madison Avenue hucksters would make it as attractive to do a few lines as to down a few beers." As a former cigarette smoker, Califano understands the cycle of addiction intimately. Legalization would not be a noble act of enlightened policy. It would be surrender.

In the long run we will not control crime until criminals stop being lionized by their peers. They will not stop being lionized by their peers until their own communities put their feet down and make civilized behavior the community standard.

Our first priority in fighting crime is to beef up the criminal justice system: police, prisons, and courts. In most cities across America, the once-familiar policeman on the beat has become almost invisible. What used to be a conspicuous and reassuring presence has become an ominous absence. Some cities are experimenting with what they now call community policing—actually returning patrolmen to the beat, where they can see and be seen, get to know the people, win the confidence of the law-abiding, and deter the predators. It works.

For decades social reformers viewed prisons primarily as places to save souls, raise up the downtrodden, and transform inmates' lives for the better. This conception, embodied in the euphemism "houses of correction," has not worked. Rehabilitation, for the most part, has been a failure. As long ago as 1975 one landmark study of more than two hundred attempts to measure the effects of rehabilitation programs concluded that these efforts had "no appreciable effect on recidivism." According to U.C.L.A. professor James Q. Wilson, "It did not seem to matter what form of treatment in the correctional system was attempted. Indeed, some forms of treatment . . . actually produced an increase in the rate of recidivism."

Some of the huge amounts spent in an unsuccessful effort to keep drugs out of the country should instead be spent to support nongovernment drug rehabilitation centers. There are some exciting examples. In 1988 I visited Daytop Village, a privately operated drug treatment center in Swan Lake, New York. It was heartwarming to see what Monsignor O'Brien and his colleagues were accomplishing in introducing young former addicts to a new drug-free life. The rate of recidivism was only ten percent. Phoenix House, another highly successful private program, puts addicts through a tough two-year boot camp. Thousands have emerged as productive citizens.

Even with a visible police presence and enough prison space to hold the criminal convicts, the system will not work unless judges let it work. Yet for thirty years the courts have been the institutions most directly responsible for undermining police protection for law-abiding citizens. The best way to change the character of the courts is to pick judges who are as dedicated to restraining the guilty as they are to protecting the innocent.

On a subway platform in New York in the summer of 1984, two muggers knocked a seventy-one-year-old man down to the floor, beat him viciously, and choked him as they rifled his pockets. The victim's screams attracted two transit police officers, who rushed to help. The muggers ran, ignoring orders to stop. When the officers fired, one mugger, a career criminal, was left crippled—and he sued the Transit Authority. The courts of the State of New York recently upheld a $4.3 million damage award to the injured mugger, ultimately to be paid, of course, by those subway riders he had not yet gotten around to mugging. The victim's claim for replacement of his shattered spectacles was rejected. If this points up the absurdity of the law's current approach to crime and criminals, it also points up the grotesque inversion of civilized values that now characterizes life in our great cities.

We cannot successfully address the fearful increase in violent crime without restoring punishment rather than rehabilitation as the central premise of our criminal justice system. In the name of compassion, liberal judges and lawyers have reduced sentences, absolved criminals of responsibility by blaming their actions on society, and granted parole even to violent criminals. They have helped undermine the system of law and order essential to a free society. Blaming society rather than the criminal is a 1960s philosophy still in vogue today.

The shocking reaction of many in the media to Vietnam protestor Katherine Power's case is an example of going overboard in expressing as much sympathy for the criminal as for the victim of the crime. There was honest disagreement about whether the United States should have been involved in Vietnam. But our understanding of those who demonstrated against the war should not lead us to excuse those who resorted to violence. In opposing war against an enemy abroad, these people waged war against innocent people at home. As syndicated columnist Charles Krauthammer put it: "This was not a flower child caught up some wild afternoon in a robbery. She was found to have in her apartment three rifles, a carbine, a pistol, a shotgun and a huge store of ammunition. She is accused of having firebombed a National Guard Armory. She took part in a bank robbery in which a hero cop, father of nine, was shot dead. This is someone very hard who has now softened out of feelings of loss, principally for herself." *Newsweek*'s reaction was typical of the response of much of the liberal media: "After all these years, it is hard to know whom to feel the most sympathy for. The nine children who lost a father or the young woman who lost her way in the tumult of the sixties." In the media, buckets of tears were shed because of the psychological trauma Power went through in coming forward after having avoided trial for twenty years under a new identity in Oregon. Very few tears were left over for the nine children who lost a father who was shot in the back trying to arrest a bank robber.

Contrary to the myths of the media, tough but fair judges and sentencing based on the principle of individual accountability are not racist but benefit poor minorities, who represent 80 percent of the victims of violent crime. The poor cannot extricate themselves from poverty unless they are secure from physical violence and unless the incentive system in their community rewards good behavior and reliably punishes criminal behavior.

Politicians often complain that the money is simply not there for more police and prisons. Yet the entire criminal justice system—police, prisons, courts, prosecutors, and public defenders, local, state, and federal—accounts for less than 4 percent of government spending. That means that shifting just 2 percent of other government spending to public safety would increase the funds available for the criminal justice system by more than 50 percent. If we have the will, we do have the resources.

If we are to have an effective offensive against crime, we should adopt and enforce strict national gun-control laws, ones much tougher than the Brady law. There are over 200 million privately owned guns in the United States. Rather than hearing the political slogans of the past—"a chicken in every pot" and "two cars in every garage"—we shall soon hear from the gun lobby that there should be two guns in every home.

With the resources, with the will, and with a determination to restore public and private respect for the values of a humane civilization, we can turn the tide against crime. But it will take all three, not just through the next election but through the next generation.

GOD AND FAMILY: REDISCOVERING THE TRUE HEART OF AMERICA

Materialists of all stripes are wrong to slight the importance of the moral-cultural system that underpins any free society. Max Weber warned against the development of a "destructive, selfish materialism—the bureaucratization of the human spirit—an 'iron cage' for the West" that would eventually erode its moral legitimacy.

Most of our most pressing problems—the woeful decline of American education, the breakdown of the family, rising crime, urban poverty and decay, the growing sense of entitlement—are at their core moral, not material, problems. We cannot even begin to solve them unless we return to the principles that made this country great. It is not enough to be both strong and rich; America must also be good. The founders envisaged not only a new nation but a new order for the ages. We must make freedom work by our exertions at home and enable freedom to win abroad by our example.

Those who call for a new "politics of meaning" are rightly distressed about the intensifying illiteracy, amorality, and rootlessness of much of American life. They are right, too, in their sense that exclusively materialist philosophies, which neglect the spiritual dimension of man, are part of the problem. But the solutions they tend to propose—more government involvement, more entitlement, less individual accountability—are themselves root causes of our ills.

A policy does not necessarily have to be a program—there is a vital distinction between a national response and a government response. America's success depends not just on government but, far more important, on private institutions and all the many centers of activity that make up our free society. In most matters that directly touch people, those organizations operate more effectively than the federal government would. We should heed Max Weber's warning: "Bureaucracy appears as a primary cause of the enslavement of modern man. Each man becomes a little cog in the machine, and aware of this, his one preoccupation is whether he can become a bigger cog. The question is what can we do to oppose this machinery in order to keep a portion of mankind free from this parceling out of the soul from the supreme mastery of the bureaucratic way of life." Einstein put it even more bluntly: "Bureaucracy is the death of any achievement."

Well-meaning government intervention has undermined the virtues of self-reliance and individual accountability. As Justice Brandeis observed, "Experience should teach us to be most on guard to protect liberty when government's purposes are benevolent." The utter failure of the Great Society is a glaring example. The more the federal government steps in and does things for people, the less they are going to do for themselves. The best spur to initiative in the private sector is to let people know that if they want something done, they had better just do it. The best role for the federal government is to create conditions conducive to doing it. Our growing reliance on government to fix every social ill has given us a shrinking conception of the concept of public service. Too often we equate it solely with being in government, even though those in private enterprise provide all the funds to pay for our public servants. The public benefits from the work of every good plumber, doctor, salesman, window washer, artist, teacher, and homemaker just as much as it does from those who are paid by the taxpayers. From now on, public service should simply mean whatever you do well.

The 1960s counterculture created a moral and spiritual vacuum that weakens the foundations of American society. The new elite of its adversary culture has disdained traditional morality—the stress on hard work, thrift, frugality, deferred gratification, the sanctity of marriage, fidelity, sexual self-control, and individual accountability. Those who still believe in these values are branded by the new elite as quaint, politically incorrect throwbacks who "just don't get it."

The sexual revolution has wreaked havoc on the American family: increasing rates of divorce, illegitimacy, and single-parent families. The glorification of recreational drug use, from which the wealthy and middle class have only recently begun to recoil, has contributed to the emergence of a permanent urban underclass. The self-indulgent notions of no-fault living, the cult of victimization, the futility of work, and the inherent injustice of American society, which the counterculture promoted, have corroded the respect for merit and personal striving, which are the human virtues surest to help individuals grow, develop moral codes, and achieve success.

Most Americans—poor, middle-class, and wealthy—are

fundamentally decent, patriotic, and enterprising. Yet the liberal elite continues to exert enormous influence on public policy, largely because Americans are too deferential to their views and because those with other views have not offered a sufficiently articulate or compelling response. Good ideas have consequences. So do bad ones. A healthy nation cannot endure indefinitely such a sharp contrast between what the elite propagates and what the American people think. Individuals need to take responsibility for their actions. But no person is an island. Parents need the support of moral-cultural institutions to instill in their children the values necessary for a decent society worth emulating. They do not have it. The entertainment industry, the artistic community, and much of the educational establishment, which so profoundly influence American culture, relentlessly assault religion, promote promiscuity, encourage illegitimacy, and bash America. They contend that children, rather than their parents, know best. They glorify violence. They degrade the idea of heroism. We need to change this moral and cultural climate to reinforce rather than undermine the traditional importance of family and religion.

We should not resort to censorship. We do not deserve to win this vital debate over values if we cannot persuade a fair-minded American people. Nor is a stifling uniformity the answer. One of this nation's great strengths is that we are a diverse nation, with many competing convictions and interests. Free and open public debate has made us stronger, not weaker. There are, however, some basic virtues that all Americans of goodwill can share: honesty, fidelity, thrift, hard work, patriotism, diligence, self-discipline, gratitude, and a belief in liberty, religious freedom, and equality of opportunity. While government cannot ensure these indispensable virtues, it can at least stop weakening them.

Edmund Burke wrote in 1791, "Men are qualified for civil liberty in exact proportion to their disposition to put moral chains upon their own appetites." Unfortunately, as Catholic

University professor Claes Ryn observed more recently, "Unlike the old virtue of character, the new virtue does not aim primarily at controlling self but at controlling others." To the extent that people cannot control themselves, government will do it for them.

Ultimately, the American people must look mainly to religion, the family, and themselves as the driving forces for spiritual renewal. Politically, conservatives must make the case for traditional values and individual accountability in a way that transcends both the mushy moral relativism of modern liberals and the inquisitorial instincts of a few religious zealots. If they do, the vitally important themes of religious renewal and family values can appeal to the vast majority of Americans rather than divide them.

Some of the keenest insights about American life were those of Alexis de Tocqueville one hundred and fifty years ago. In particular, he noted the profound and enduring influence of the religious tradition on American life, law, ideals, morals, and our image of ourselves as a free people. He considered religion even more important for democratic republics than for other types of government because it instills those habits of civic virtue, moral responsibility, deferred gratification, and concern for others on which democracy so heavily depends.

Religious beliefs also help to inoculate Americans against the "idea of the infinite perfectibility of man," to which, Tocqueville observed, democracies are especially prone.

In its most grotesque form, the utopian impulse culminated in communism and Nazism. In its milder form, it has offered the illusion of a risk-free, redistributionist, effortless abundance, which is neither practically possible nor morally desirable.

Tocqueville was right. Religious freedom has served from the beginning as the cornerstone of our economic freedom and political liberty. The American people must agree that this is true, because we remain among the most religious nations in the world. Militant secularists not only demean the faith of most

Americans but reject the moral precepts that made it possible for our society to thrive for as long as it has. The Constitution may require that we not promote religion in our public schools. But that should not mean rejection of religion in our lives.

Some argue that the basic teachings of religion, especially those that have to do with people's behavior toward one another, can easily be translated into secular terms. You do not have to believe in God, it is said, to honor your parents, to take responsibility for your actions, or to treat others as you would have them treat you. But to separate the teachings of any religion from its mysteries is to cut human beings off from the source of spiritual power that over the centuries has inspired, strengthened, and comforted millions.

Tocqueville also recognized that the separation of church and state was good for both the vitality of American religion and the health of American politics. The founders did not intend to weaken religion by separating it from civil authority. They believed that the real test of faith was whether it is strong enough to tolerate other faiths. They were right. Tocqueville also warned that "religions should be more careful to confine themselves to a proper sphere, for if they wish to extend themselves beyond spiritual matters, they run the risk of not being believed at all." This is a warning that militants on both the religious right and the religious left would do well to heed. A clergyman's mission is to change people, not to change governments. Norman Vincent Peale's enormous influence was due to the fact that he recognized this fundamental truth. It is one thing to believe devoutly in the truth of one's own religious values. It is quite another to try to impose them on others.

The profound influence of religion on American politics is vital, but it is best when indirect: on the morals, habits, and souls of individual Americans; on the political climate and the principles that should guide policy, rather than on specific policies themselves.

Government cannot reach into people's hearts. Religion

can. That is why I strongly advised Billy Graham in 1960 not to endorse me or any other candidate for office. I told him he would undermine his own ability to change people spiritually if he engaged in activities designed to change governments politically. The same period that has seen social and political crusades increasingly replace religious messages in the pulpits has seen a sharp 35 percent decline in membership of the mainline Protestant denominations associated with the National Council of Churches. In a desperate effort to be "relevant" and modern, some ministers seem to be more interested in saving the spotted owl than in saving souls. As one critic has observed, too many churches seem to have a "political agenda masked in a veneer of spirituality."

Paul Johnson has observed that businessmen and clergymen who become politicians have tended to display bad political judgment in twentieth-century democracies because they refuse to accept the hard reality that the search for the perfect is the enemy of the good. This is not an argument for moral nihilism or relativism. But the application of moral principles to complex and ambiguous circumstances requires the cautious judgment of statesmen who recognize that the art of politics is the ability to find not the perfect solution but the best solution in an imperfect world.

Those on the right and the left who believe the clergy should play an active role in politics ought to consider the dismal record of the Islamic theocracies, most recently in Iran, or the lamentable record of the mainline Protestant churches that advocated isolationism before World War II, neutralism, disarmament, and American strategic withdrawal during the Cold War, and inaction during the Gulf War.

To renew America, we need a spiritual renewal. Two years ago Henry Grunwald observed that we "may be heading into a new age of faith, when faith will again play a major part in our existence." Because they addressed spiritual values, the world's great religions—Christianity, Judaism, Islam, and Buddhism—

have inspired people for centuries. It comes down to whether the individual believes in something greater than himself. Stepan Trofimovich Verkhovensky observed in Dostoyevsky's *The Possessed*: "The one essential condition of human existence is that man should always be able to bow down before something infinitely great. If men are deprived of the infinitely great, they will not go on living and will die of despair."

We cannot achieve a spiritual renewal without nurturing the traditional family, on which the American tradition is based. That is where children learn about truth, hard work, obligation, and responsibility.

For most Americans, the family is the most cherished part of their lives. The quality of schools correlates strongly with the quality of the families from which the children come. Generally, children from stable two-parent families do significantly better than children from single-parent families. Poverty also correlates strongly with the quality of families; both its incidence and its intractability are significantly greater in single-parent families. Children of divorce have significantly more emotional, behavioral, and learning difficulties than children from stable two-parent families. It is better for a child to grow up in a healthy one-parent home than in an unhealthy two-parent home. But the evidence suggests powerfully that the best way to raise educational standards, to eradicate poverty, to increase upward mobility, and to promote civic virtue is to strengthen the healthy two-parent family.

Government can contribute to this goal by reducing the tax burdens on families and increasing the paltry size of the family deduction. It should end the bizarre and unfair welfare policies that reward unwed mothers and penalize responsible fathers. Ultimately, though, government has a limited capacity to protect family values. This is a task for religious institutions, individual citizens themselves, and the keepers of our nation's culture.

Opponents have depicted those who call for a revitalization

of traditional family values as intolerant ayatollahs. Some of the harsh, unforgiving ultraconservative rhetoric has given this charge some plausibility. But most who argue for the revival of traditional family values are neither bigoted nor intolerant. The 1992 presidential election provided one example of how, where controversial social issues are concerned, truth sits in the back of the campaign bus while political expediency takes the wheel. Few politicians have been subjected to as much harsh criticism and ridicule by the intellectual establishment as Dan Quayle was when he championed the cause of the two-parent family. Almost every leading newspaper and magazine joined in the assault. But in 1993, after President Bush and he had lost the election, the *Atlantic Monthly* published a cover story with the headline DAN QUAYLE WAS RIGHT. The article showed what every fair-minded American leader knows instinctively: that the breakdown of the family is a rot eating at the foundations of a great nation, and that its consequences are being felt most acutely in its cities, where a lost generation is being raised without functioning families and therefore without the benefit of society's best teacher of basic values of humanity and civil behavior.

Most Americans have abundant empathy for the millions of single mothers who struggle heroically to provide for their children as best they can. Many single parents were cast in that predicament by circumstances beyond their control or by honest mistakes. We cannot write them off. Nor can we write off their innocent children. Sometimes, divorce is the lesser of two evils. But many liberals wrongly lapse from justifiable empathy into the fallacy of moral equivalence. Some wrongly take a morally neutral position on the choice between traditional and nontraditional families. Much of the adversarial elite not only trashes the traditional two-parent family as a repressive institution but glorifies the alternatives, which both common sense and the overwhelming body of evidence suggest are more harmful to children and society. Charles Krauthammer offers a perceptive observation: "The deviant is declared normal. And the normal is unmasked as deviant. That of course makes us all that much more morally equal." The American people can legitimately demand a moral-cultural climate that promotes traditional family values and that brands alternatives as less desirable. Although divorce should not be prohibited nor single mothers condemned, the American legal system should make divorce and no-fault parenting more difficult than they are today. Our cultural leaders and institutions should also make crystal clear that the debate over family values is not only about right and wrong but also about the nation's future.

INDIVIDUAL MISSION, NATIONAL MISSION

The renewal of America depends on individuals striving for excellence. The founders sought to create a system that would permit individuals to define their own fulfillment with minimal interference from the state. They sought to secure each person's own individual natural rights. They believed that achieving a higher common good depended on individuals pursuing their own enlightened self-interest.

This insulated American politics from the storms of religious or ideological politics, but it also created the danger of an obsession with materialism. Foreseeing a day when secular values would triumph completely, Nietzsche warned against what he called the "last man," a creature totally obsessed with security and comfort and incapable of throwing himself into a higher cause.

We should not glorify struggle or reckless risks as ends in themselves. But we should recognize that the most important achievements in life involve at least some risk, struggle, and adversity.

For a half-century after the end of the greatest war in history, America was driven by the power of its purpose and the daring of its dreams. It was the biggest, the most free, the richest, the most blessed nation in the world. In the 1950s and 1960s, children learned in school that their nation was the greatest on earth and were taught at home that they should clean their plates because there were children starving in Asia. Today it would be considered politically incorrect and culturally insensitive for schoolteachers to say that America was greater than any other other nation, and if children are told at home to clean their plates, it is because there are people who are hungry in Newark.

The end of World War II ignited sparks of pride, ingenuity, and purpose that propelled our country forward for fifty years. The end of the Cold War, in contrast, has left Americans confused and even frightened about the future. Defeating communism was such an all-consuming mission that it was logical to expect a payoff, to assume that the world would be better when communism had been defeated and that Americans would be better off as well in their daily lives. When the giant peace dividend they had been so recklessly promised failed to materialize, it was equally logical to assume that peace was a giant rip-off. For forty-five years, the American people had been prodded and cajoled toward the promised land of a world at peace, only to find it was the political equivalent of swampland—property that could not support the foundations of the new civilization they had expected to spring up after communism had been defeated.

Americans do not know how to be second, or even first among equals. They only know how to be the best. After World War II the United States became the leader of the free world by acclamation. No other option was even conceivable. We should be just as resistant to playing a secondary role now. But if the United States is to continue to lead in the world, it will have to resolve to do so and then take those steps necessary to turn resolution into execution.

Above all, America must rediscover its commitment to the pursuit of excellence for its own sake. In the land of liberty, we have sometimes risked making an obsession out of individual freedom without requiring a concomitant sense of individual responsibility. More devastating, the absence of a national challenge has reduced our sense of common purpose. In modern America too many forces—ethnic and cultural diversity, gaps between rich and poor, distrust between old and young—pull Americans in different directions, too few impel them to pull together. Cynics who say we need another war forget how short-lived the euphoria was after the Persian Gulf War. What we need is a war on cynicism, on negativity, on purveyors of gloom about America's prospects and our role in the world.

The greatest challenge America faces in the era beyond peace is to learn the art of national unity in the absence of war or some other explicit external threat. If we fail to meet that challenge, our diversity, long a source of strength, will become a destructive force. Our individuality, long our most distinctive characteristic, will be the seed of our collapse. Our freedom, long our most cherished possession, will exist only in the history books.

In all that we confront domestically, we must remember that ours is and must remain essentially a free society. In cracking down on crime, we are not limiting freedom. We are expanding freedom from fear. In breaking down barriers between the races, in guaranteeing respect for individual rights, we also expand freedom—if we do it in ways that respect the rights of all, not just those of the currently fashionable designated minorities.

Despite our economic and social problems, there is no reason why the United States cannot do everything that is needed. This nation of immigrants from all over the world is still united in its love of freedom. Our economy is still the most powerful in the world, with the capacity to overcome its serious problems. Our universities still lead the world in science and technology, which will largely determine progress in the next century. In the past, the United States has overcome problems vastly more difficult than the ones we now face. Although only 5 percent of the world's people live in the United States, we have the resources and the vision to make the world a better place.

The United States has the resources to lead. The world needs the United States to lead. Our ideals and self-interest dictate that we should lead. But this is not enough. We should remind ourselves of Sir Robert Thompson's maxim: "National power equals applied resources plus manpower times will." When asked to meet a challenge, some people say "I can." Others say "I can't." Both may be right. It all boils down to a question of will. Does the United States have the will to lead? In the 1992 elections, 62 percent of the voters cast their ballots for presidential candidates—Bill Clinton and Ross Perot—whose campaign theme was that the country was in the throes of crisis and decline. Clinton and Perot were wrong. We are in the ascendant. We demonstrated what we can do during World War II and the Cold War. Now that we have peace, our challenge is to demonstrate that we have the will to lead beyond peace, where our enemy is not some nation abroad but is essentially within ourselves.

Our great goal should be to rekindle faith in freedom, not only abroad but at home. In the coming century, preserving freedom will require far more than "eternal vigilance," though that will be needed. A free society needs a muscular determination to make its institutions work. It requires that free people take on the responsibilities that go along with freedom. As Goethe observed, "Only he deserves his life and his freedom who conquers them anew every day." If we backslide on our responsibilities, we invite the alternatives to freedom.

Freedom has worked in America because ours was a nation founded on the idea of freedom, by people whose faith in freedom was coupled inextricably with their acceptance of the burdens of freedom. Founding a new country in a new world, each knew that he had to pull his own weight and make his own way. This idea was passed down from generation to generation, and the immigrants who came in such waves came expecting the burdens as well as the advantages of freedom. So America grew and prospered and now has set an example for the world. We nurtured and developed the free institutions that are now spreading around the world.

But we have also nurtured a cancer in our own community. The breakdown of civil order, the retreat from responsibility, the slack-jawed acceptance of the attitude that "the world owes me a living"—all are eroding and corroding the idea of liberty itself.

With the Cold War over, our first order of business here at home, more fundamental by far than jobs or health care or the fiscal deficit, is the spiritual and cultural deficit. This is at the root of what ails America.

As we prepare for the twenty-first century, eliminating that deficit, restoring our spirit, and renewing our adherence to the principles of a humane civilization that America represents are our mission.

We must never forget why America has a special meaning in the world. We are respected because we are the strongest and richest nation in the world. But even when it was weak and poor two hundred years ago, America represented a great idea, more important than military might or economic wealth—the idea of freedom in all its aspects. Millions came to our shores because America stood for free nations, free people, free markets, free elections, freedom of expression, freedom of religion. Never has it been more important for us to demonstrate to the rest of the world the power of this idea.

Sometimes profound concepts are best expressed in simple terms. Every American has automatically recited the Pledge of Allegiance to the Flag thousands of times. We sometimes forget the one simple phrase that best describes America: "one nation under God, indivisible, with liberty and justice for all."

The world particularly needs to be reminded of the American example today. Extreme nationalism, racism, and religious fanaticism are running rampant in the world. There were only 51 nations in the U.N. when it was founded at the beginning of the Cold War. Today there are 184 nations speaking over four thousand languages. If we do not find a way to keep nations together, they will fractionalize and the Cold War will be followed by scores of bloody, smaller wars. America has the responsibility and the opportunity to provide the example of how a nation with many races, religions, and nationalities can be held together by a great idea that transcends them all. We must reject the counsel of those who demagogically argue that one answer to our problems of welfare, crime, and urban decay is to close our doors to those who want to come to America and enjoy the freedom with which we are blessed. Some limitations on immigration are necessary, but the principle of America as a free nation, welcoming those who seek freedom, must never be compromised.

We must never forget how much immigrants over the past two hundred years have enriched our economy, our culture, our lives. In 1956 there was a debate in the United States as to whether we could accept the new influx of Hungarian refugees fleeing from the Soviet massacre of freedom fighters in Budapest. Before going to the Hungarian border to welcome some of the refugees, I consulted with former President Herbert Hoover. He had had more experience than anyone else in the world working with refugees during and after both World War I and World War II. Some would have expected that because of his reputation as a conservative, he would join those who opposed taking in more refugees. On the contrary, he said that his experience had been that throughout American history there was always an initial reaction against refugees, but that every group that had come in had enriched the United States politically, economically, and culturally. This was true of the Irish, the Germans, the East Europeans, the Asians, the Persians, the Latin Americans, the Africans, and the Arabs. He predicted that the same would be true of the Hungarian refugees. He proved to be right.

We should adopt a generous immigration policy and a policy of equal opportunity for all who come to America, not only because it is right to help the people involved but because they will enrich America and enable it to continue to be an example of a nation where a great idea—the idea of freedom—creates one people and overrides racial, religious, and national differences that have torn lesser countries apart.

In six years the world will celebrate an event that occurs only once every thousand years: the beginning of a new year, a new century, and a new millennium.

In one way we will remember the twentieth century as the worst in history because of the destruction of World War I and World War II. More people—71 million—have been killed in those wars than in all previous wars in the history of civilization.

At the same time, more progress has been made in the last hundred years than in all previous centuries. Economically, the world's standard of living has climbed dramatically. Global per capita income is ten times higher as we approach the end of the twentieth century than it was at the end of the nineteenth century.

As a result of new developments in agriculture and manufacturing, we now have the capability to feed, clothe, and house people at a level undreamed-of at the turn of the nineteenth century. As a result of new discoveries in medicine, we have virtually eliminated diseases such as smallpox and tuberculosis, which have ravaged entire countries, and we have found the resources to eradicate other diseases that threaten to do so in the future.

Technologically, there has been more progress in this century than in any earlier one. The automobile and the airplane have revolutionized transportation. The telephone, radio, and television have revolutionized communications. Personal computers and faxes have revolutionized the information age. The twentieth century will be remembered as a time when man invented the microchip and sent space shuttles to explore the universe.

Politically, the world has taken a U-turn in this century. Only 10 percent of the world's nations were democracies at the beginning of the century. Today over half of the world's peoples live in nations with democratic governments. The communications revolution has doomed dictatorship wherever it exists in the world. Communist and all other forms of dictatorship can survive only in closed societies. Television may have corrupted our values, but it has opened the eyes of people ruled by dictators to the free world around them.

As they consider our difficult problems at home and abroad, some young people complain about how hard it is to grow up in America today. They could not be more mistaken. There has never been a better time to be alive or a better country in which to live than America as we approach the beginning of the twenty-first century. We are most fortunate to live in these times and to have as our inspiration the building of something new in peace rather than destroying something old in war. Unlike the goals of previous superpowers or empires, America's goal is not to conquer the world by our arms or our wealth, but to lead by our example.

The Soviet communists lost the Cold War because they failed to make good on their promises. To complete the victory, we must demonstrate that freedom can produce what dictatorship promised but failed to produce. Only if our success goes beyond material progress will we prevail in the long run. Dictatorship in the short run can bring about economic progress. In the long run, people rebel against it because they need more than economic progress. Being against communism and dictatorship is not enough. Being for freedom alone is not enough. People must have enough material goods so that they can enjoy the nonmaterial qualities that distinguish free societies.

The door is now open for the victory of freedom in its broadest sense. But that door will close if those who walk through it are disappointed by what they find. People rejected communism because they knew it was politically, economically, and morally bankrupt. They were for freedom because they were convinced it would produce a better life, based on what the communications revolution told them.

Our challenge today is a positive one—a challenge to build, not to destroy, a challenge to be for, not just against, a challenge to be driven not by our fears but by our hopes.

The pessimists have been proved wrong. Winston Churchill often quoted his favorite American politician, Bourke Cochrane: "There is enough for all. The earth is a generous mother. She will provide in great abundance for all her people if they will but cultivate her soil in justice and in peace." When he said that a hundred years ago, his statement was considered too optimistic. Not today. Unlike those who lived at the beginning of the twentieth century, we now have the capability to make the coming century a century of peace, unprecedented prosperity, and freedom.

As we look back over the two hundred years of our history as a nation, no people on earth have more reason to be thankful than the American people. We should always have a true appreciation of all that has allowed us to achieve so great a measure of prosperity, security, and well-being. We are the heirs of the traditional values that have been the bedrock of America's goodness and its greatness. We should preserve and renew them, and make them once again our guides to national and individual conduct. The success we have enjoyed in the past and the success we believe we can achieve in the future should bring not a sense of lulling contentment but rather a deep and enduring realization of all that life has offered us, a full acknowledgment of our responsibilities, and an unwavering determination to show that under a free government, a great people can thrive best, materially and spiritually.

Much has been given to us, and it is only right that much will continue to be expected from us. We have duties to others and duties to ourselves and we cannot escape from either. Our relations with other nations are important, but still more important are our relations among ourselves. The conditions that allowed our material well-being and that have contributed to our can-do vigor, self-reliance, individual initiative, and uniqueness of spirit have also brought the problems inseparable from the accumulation of great prosperity and strength. The real test of America lies in our ability to eliminate the bad while advancing the good.

Our status as the world's only superpower is meaningless unless it is driven by a higher purpose. We should reach into the soul of this nation and recover the spirit and mission that first set us apart. We do not aspire to a perfect, problem-free society, but we will demand more from ourselves. We must improve ourselves at home so that our example shines more brightly abroad. Without the certainties of other eras, the era beyond peace poses great challenges and great opportunities. Freed from the demands of waging war and winning peace, we now have the high privilege of meeting the exciting new challenges beyond peace.

Author's Note

In the spring of 1993, during my second visit to post-Soviet Moscow, I met with Vice President Alexander Rutskoi, a flamboyant hero of the Soviet war in Afghanistan, in his office in the Kremlin. By then he had emerged as an outspoken opponent of Boris Yeltsin. During our meeting he complained bitterly, as generals who enter civilian government often do, about the frustrations of working with a bunch of lifelong politicians.

As I was leaving, I told him, "Mr. Vice President, as you know, our General Sherman said 'War is hell.' You may find that politics is even worse." I could not have imagined that Rutskoi would lead an armed rebellion against Yeltsin six months later, that he would be captured and jailed for it, or that he would be released in February after the Russian Parliament issued a blanket amnesty, over Yeltsin's vigorous and understandable objections, for those who had fomented rebellions against his regime, and also that of Mikhail Gorbachev in August 1991. As I read accounts of the return of Rutskoi and his tired but relieved colleagues to their homes and their grateful families, it occurred to me that he had found out that politics really could be hell—but also that, for some, there can be life after hell.

In a sense, I can say the same thing. *Beyond Peace* is my tenth book, and my ninth since resigning the Presidency twenty years ago this year. After completing my first, *Six Crises*, in 1962, I vowed that I would never write another. Since then, I have learned to make less Sherman-like promises. This volume completes a six-volume series with an emphasis on East-West

relations that I began in 1979 with *The Real War*, which warned
that the United States was risking losing the Cold War. *Real
Peace* suggested that we were missing opportunities in the early
1980s to establish a rational framework for managing our differences with Moscow. *No More Vietnams* described the lessons
to be learned from one of the Cold War's most decisive battles.
1999: Victory Without War cautioned against euphoria about
Gorbachev and his promises to reform the failed communist system rather than abandon it. *Seize the Moment,* completed as
Soviet communism finally collapsed in 1991, called on the West
to do everything it could, by supporting Yeltsin's reforms, to
ensure that democracy and free-market policies would take
communism's place.

The primary audience for the first five volumes in the series
was those who were chiefly preoccupied with foreign policy.
Beyond Peace is aimed at a broader readership. The longest section has to do not with foreign battles but with domestic ones—
over health care, education, urban decay, and other issues. For
forty-five years we fought the Cold War because we believed
that our system deserved to prevail since it offered people more
than communism. The defeat of communism requires us to keep
the promises we have made to three generations in this century
and to those who will live in the century to come. America must
prove that it really is, as Abraham Lincoln described it, the last
best hope of man on earth.

So whenever people ask me if all the travails of public life
were worth it, my answer, very briefly, is this: Politics is never
going to be heaven, and sometimes it's hell, but yes, it was worth
the trip. When I came to Washington forty-seven years ago, the
predominant issue was ensuring that the United States would
step up to the communist threat, both abroad and at home. The
ultimate satisfaction is to have lived long enough to see the West
defeat communism and begin a new, equally arduous, equally
noble campaign to ensure the victory of freedom, both abroad
and at home.

To complete what is probably my last book, I had help from an extraordinary group of friends, colleagues, and experts. From the outset of the project, Harold Evans at Random House provided incisive counsel. Kathy O'Connor, my chief of staff, ably supervised the entire project, with help from Kim Taylor, who managed the manuscript, and Elizabeth Johnston. Robert Bostock and Joseph Marx, young aides on Capitol Hill with great political promise in their own right, checked the manuscript for accuracy. Key insights were provided by Ambassador Robert F. Ellsworth, Ambassador James Lilley, Dimitri K. Simes, and Marin Strmecki. And for their invaluable editorial assistance, my special thanks to Monica Crowley of my staff; Professor Robert Kaufman of the University of Vermont; Raymond K. Price, Jr., the head of my White House speechwriting office; and John H. Taylor, director of the Richard Nixon Library & Birthplace.

—RN
Park Ridge, New Jersey
March 30, 1994

Index

ABOUT THE TYPE

This book was set in Sabon, a typeface designed by the well-known German typographer Jan Tschichold (1902–74). Sabon's design is based on the original letterforms of Claude Garamond and was created specifically to be used for three sources: foundry type for hand composition, Linotype, and Monotype. Tschichold named his typeface for the famous Frankfurt typefounder Jacques Sabon, who died in 1580.